The Geography of
Modernization in Kenya

THE SYRACUSE GEOGRAPHICAL SERIES is designed to publish distinguished work by scholars associated with the Department of Geography of Syracuse University. The initiation of the series was made possible by a generous bequest from an alumnus, Mr. Donald Lloyd, and its continuation and expansion is supported by the contributions of many other alumni, staff, and friends of the Department.

Inquiries and orders should be addressed to Syracuse University Press, Box 8, University Station, Syracuse, New York, 13210. Standard professional and library discounts are offered. Because of variations in length and illustration each number will be individually priced.

The Geography of
Modernization in Kenya

A SPATIAL ANALYSIS OF SOCIAL, ECONOMIC, AND POLITICAL CHANGE

EDWARD W. SOJA

(Ph.D., Syracuse)

Assistant Professor of Geography
Northwestern University

Syracuse Geographical Series No. 2   1968

SYRACUSE   UNIVERSITY   PRESS

SYRACUSE GEOGRAPHICAL SERIES

Editors

D. W. MEINIG

RICHARD E. DAHLBERG

No. 1   Theodore Oberlander, THE ZAGROS STREAMS:
A New Interpretation of Transverse Drainage
in an Orogenic Zone, 1965.

No. 2.   Edward W. Soja, THE GEOGRAPHY OF MODERNIZATION IN KENYA:
A Spatial Analysis of Social, Economic, and Political Change, 1968.

Published by SYRACUSE UNIVERSITY PRESS
Box 8, University Station, Syracuse   13210

Manufactured in the United States of America

PREFACE

This study was initiated by a strong feeling that the geographer's spatial perspective could contribute significantly to the rapidly expanding research cluster involved with the problems of social, economic, and political change in the developing areas. All too often, social scientists fail to recognize that the phenomena they study occur in space as well as through time and display patterns of areal variation and interaction which have important implications for their work. If one central objective can be discerned throughout this study, it is to illustrate the relevance of the spatial perspective in interdisciplinary research on modernization, not only in Kenya but throughout the developing world.

Another and closely related objective is to generate further research by geographers on the spatial dimensions of modernization. This in turn will enable geographers to benefit more widely from some of the exciting developments taking place within and among the other social sciences. Although many geographers have been concerned with the developing areas for a long period of time, only recently has geographical research been placed within the theoretical context of the modernization process itself. It is hoped that the present study can suggest not only a framework for comparative analysis but also a set of questions and avenues for more intensive research in the future on how the dynamic forces of change shape the human geography of an area.

The approach and methods used parallel these objectives by illustrating the need for greater interaction and understanding between groups of scholars interested in basically the same type of questions, but differing widely in the ways they examine them. An attempt has been made to show the mutually reinforcing results which can be reached through a com-bination of the descriptive-cartographic approach traditional to geography and some of the new quantitative techniques which are playing so important a role in contemporary geographical research.

In a sense, the problems of blending these two approaches to deal most effectively with a given set of objectives are very much like the problems facing the developing world in its transition from traditional to modern ways of life. Both involve the challenges of change, integration, and adaptive capabilities and the related desire to accommodate the best from both the old and the new systems. Just as there is a stubborn resistance to the shedding of traditional ideas and customs, even when they appear discordant with the new situation, there is also the need to assure that "something of value" is available to replace them. But most importantly, both sets of problems are today providing a stimulating arena for intellectual pursuit and innovative experimentation.

It is extremely difficult to trace the genesis of an idea, especially when it has such extensive roots. Even more difficult, however, is to express sufficient appreciation to all those who contributed in one way or another to its birth and development.

First of all, the field research for this study (four months in London and twelve months in East Africa, from September, 1963, to January, 1965) was supported under a fellowship granted by the Foreign Area Fellowship Program. Additional funds were also provided by the Program during the summer of 1965 for the writing of the doctoral dissertation from which this work has been adapted. The conclusions, opinions, and other statements in the text, however, are those of the author and not necessarily those of the Fellowship Program.

v

Some of the computer time used in the preparation of this study was supplied by the Computing Center, Syracuse University, which is supported in part by the National Science Foundation under Grant GP-1137. By far the major bulk of computations, however, was carried out at the computing facilities of the Pennsylvania State University, which also supplied the programs used. Robert Easton, a graduate student in the Department of Geography, Northwestern University, prepared the original versions of many of the maps; all of the maps have been redrafted for publication in this series by John Fonda of the Syracuse University Cartography Laboratory. Typing the final draft was admirably and efficiently accomplished by Frances M. Kavenik.

It is impossible to express my appreciation to the various officials of the Kenya government who so cooperatively enabled me to examine unpublished data in their files. Particularly helpful were representatives of the Kenya Road Authority, Kenya Postal Authority, East African Railways and Harbours Administration, East African Posts and Telecommunications Administration, the ministries of Local Government, Education, Works, Internal Affairs, and Finance and Economic Planning. Thanks must also be given to the Circulation Managers of the East African Standard and East African Newspapers publishing companies and to the very gracious and helpful district and regional administrative officials who so freely gave of their valuable time.

Much of the conceptual underpinnings for this study can be traced to the ideas and perspectives of Donald Meinig, who has also been an acute and discerning reader, critic, and counsel. Valuable suggestions resulting in considerable improvements in the text and maps were given by Professor Meinig and by Professors David Sopher, Richard Dahlberg, and John H. Thompson, all of Syracuse University. I am also particularly grateful to Professor Carl Rosberg of the University of California, Berkeley, for his detailed critique of an earlier version of the entire manuscript.

Finally, I reserve my deepest appreciation for two persons who can only be characterized by the familiar phrase, "without whose inspiration and assistance this study could not have been written." The first is Professor Peter Gould, formerly of Syracuse University and now at the Pennsylvania State University. The second is my wife, Maureen, who has patiently borne my moods and idiosyncrasies, although never quite forgiving me for taking her away from Kenya, that beautiful country where we first met and which we still love.

EDWARD W. SOJA

Evanston, Illinois
Summer, 1967

CONTENTS

FIGURES

TABLES

The Geography of
Modernization in Kenya

I

The Geography of Modernization: An Outline of Basic Premises

Among the many effects of European colonization has been the spread of a world culture based on modern science and technology and specific standards of government organization and operation. Regarding this process of diffusion, Rupert Emerson has stated that "... the future [may well] look back upon the overseas imperialism of recent centuries, less in terms of its sins of oppression, exploitation and discrimination, than as the instrument by which the spiritual, scientific and material revolution which began in Western Europe with the Renaissance was spread to the rest of the world."[1]

The essence of this diffusion process is change—psychological, social, cultural, economic, and political—and its composite impact has been labeled "modernization." In all those areas which it has affected, it has triggered off a series of processes working to reconcile the old with the new and has produced what are generally called "transitional societies," or those "in transit" between traditional and modern ways of life.

This study is a geographical analysis of modernization in Kenya, an attempt to provide a detailed description of areal variations in the extent of transition from traditional to more modern forms of social, economic, and political organization and behavior. In a broader context, it is also an examination of the spatial growth of an African nation. It seeks to understand and interpret the complex interplay of forces which has shaped the human geography of a portion of East Africa and led to the emergence of the distinct entity called Kenya.

MODERNIZATION AND NATION BUILDING

In its most pervasive form, modernization operates within the confines of a state to create a new behavioral system, mobilizing the population into interdependent positions in empathy with a central government and sufficiently united to preserve stability and technological progress. This new system is based upon the nation-state, which has been recognized almost universally as the most potent organizational form for the initiation, dissemination, and perpetuation of modern ways of life. Indeed, the belief that the nation-state is the pivotal unit of human social organization lies at the heart of the spreading world culture.[2]

In the developing areas, however, nation-states are only in their initial stages of formation. The effectively mobilized community generally considered the nation is restricted to a thin veneer of society, and wide gaps exist between the modernized elite and the masses. Modernization is occurring along with a concerted effort to mobilize the masses and assimilate them into a national society.

It is no surprise then that the term *nation building* has been found useful in describing the extensive socio-political transformations taking place in the newly independent states. Whereas in classic European nationalism, boundaries evolved in recognition of successful integration within particular areas, the new states begin with given boundaries and are now attempting to achieve some form of unity within them.

The processes involved in national political integration have been basically the same as in Europe and the rest of the world. In France or Switzerland, for example, the government never ceases in its effort to buttress national unity, intensify regional coherence, and develop further the compatibility of attitudes

---

[1] *From Empire to Nation* (1960), p. 6.

[2] Recent trends toward supranational integration and amalgamation do not negate the central position of the nation-state in world affairs. No satisfactory form of geopolitical organization has yet evolved "beyond the nation-state" which compares with it in communal identification, self-directed behavior, and control over the primary functions of a political system. Sovereignty in the contemporary world resides in the nation-state. Whether this may change in the future does not alter the fact.

1

and values which underlie national feeling. But in the new states, these processes assume the character of a major effort of construction and dissemination rather than reinforcement. There are many parallels between contemporary nation building and the early phases of European nationalism, but the former is unmatched in the heterogeneity of the parts being integrated, the rapidity deemed necessary by those involved, and the visibility of these developments in and their close interrelationships with the international political arena.

Modernization and nation building are thus viewed as related but not identical processes. One section of the state-area may experience a rapid rate of modernization, but this "regional" modernization may work directly against national political integration in the state as a whole. The relationship of Buganda to the rest of Uganda and that of the Ibo to Nigeria are examples of this regional-national conflict. Indeed, geographically uneven modernization, without the attendant growth of systematic interdependence within the entire political organized area, tends to create even greater gaps within the population than existed prior to the contact situation. It is this undirected nature of modernization that has given birth to the concept of "mobilization states" to describe those governments whose expressed intention is to control the forces of modernization and direct them toward national political integration.

THE SPATIAL DIMENSION IN MODERNIZATION

Summarizing briefly, modernization has spread throughout the world, primarily as the by-product of colonial expansion, and has triggered off a series of highly interrelated changes in non-Western traditional societies. These changes are crystallized around the drive to build cohesive national communities within the state-area, thereby creating nation-states to occupy positions of equality in the international state-system and to provide organized institutional frameworks for further modernization.

The theme of modernization and its implications for individual and group behavior has captured the attention of a growing number of scholars in many disciplines. In nearly all their works, however, modernization has been viewed either as an abstract process divorced from time and place or as a temporal development which only incidentally varies areally. But it is clear that social, economic, and political change takes place in space as well as through time and that theoretical work on the processes involved must recognize the spatial dimension in the attempt to formulate valid generalizations.

As Peter Gould has noted:

> In a sense, all social scientists are historians, and use the temporal dimension as a framework within which to examine the political, social and economic behaviour of men. But few feel comfortable trying on the geographer's spatial shoes, and, beyond an occasional location map, hesitate to examine the developments in the dimension that is his particular concern.[3]

James Coleman, for example, in discussing the discontinuities within a modernizing society which need to be bridged in order to create a unified network of political communications, stresses the powerful effects of "the extent, and particularly the evenness of the geographical incidence of modernization and social change."[4] But nowhere in the modernization literature is there a specific and systematic attempt to determine its geography—the areal differences in the level and rapidity of transition to modern ways of life—and the implications of these geographic patterns.

The present study examines the geography of modernization in Kenya—the areal differentiation caused by the varying impact of modernizing forces on its state-area, the evolution of these areal differences, their contemporary pattern, and their general relevance to the interdisciplinary investigation of modernization in the developing areas. Because of the systemic nature of the processes involved, i.e., their high level of interdependence, a holistic perspective will be maintained. Specific attention, however, will be given to the more explicitly political components: those aspects of modernization which affect

---

[3] "A Note on Research into the Diffusion of Development," *Journal of Modern African Studies* (1964), p. 123.

[4] "The Political Systems of the Developing Areas," in G. A. Almond and J. S. Coleman (eds.), *The Politics of the Developing Areas* (1960), p. 557.

political behavior and organization and are related to the search for national unity.

CONCEPTUAL FRAMEWORK

The analytical framework for this study is based upon a number of concepts and established relationships from the existing literature on modernization. They are introduced primarily to provide more operational definitions of the patterns and processes being examined. Although conceptually derived from the existing literature, the study also investigates the interrelationships developed at the intrastate level between all the component units of the state-area. In this way, it attempts to examine some commonly accepted views of modernization at the often neglected middle ground between intensive local studies and more general analyses of world-wide consistencies in the patterns and processes of modernization.

The fundamental premise of the study is that geographical patterns of modernization reflect the relative extent of social mobilization throughout the state-area and, by association, are closely linked to the development of a national network of social communications. The modernizing society is viewed as comprising an emerging spatial system, a geographical community functionally organized to promote the interrelated processes of social, economic, and political change.

Social mobilization is the general process which underlies modernization. It promotes the weakening of traditional forms of organization and behavior and provides avenues for alternative means of regrouping and restructuring of transitional society within a modern framework. The concept has been most fully developed in the works of Karl Deutsch, who defines it as follows:

> Social mobilization is a name given to an overall process of change, which happens to substantial parts of the population in countries which are moving from traditional to modern ways of life. It denotes a concept which brackets together a number of more specific processes of change, such as changes of residence, of occupation, of social setting, of face-to-face associates, of institutions, roles, and ways of acting, of experiences and expectations, and finally of personal memories, habits and needs, including the need for new patterns of group affiiliation and new images of

personal identity. Singly, and even more in their cumulative impact, these changes tend to influence and sometimes transform political behavior.[5]

Whereas social mobilization is the fundamental process behind the transition to modernity, the network of *social communications* is the grid or matrix over which modernization takes place. Social communications is a comprehensive term which includes all aspects of interpersonal contact, ranging from a weekly social meeting to the growth of markets and a money economy. Anything which broadens the information field of an individual promotes social communications.

The geography of modernization, therefore, can be viewed as the outgrowth of interaction between traditional and modern communications systems. According to Lucian Pye, "It was the pressure of communications which brought about the downfall of traditional societies. And in the future, it will be the creation of new channels of communications which will be decisive in determining the prospects of nation building."[6]

Traditional society in Kenya, for example, was characterized by small units, ethnically circumscribed and inwardly focused. Communications were almost entirely informal, personal and oral. Rarely did distinct circulatory organizations exist, for the flow of information was usually guided by social attributes, such as clan membership or position within a social hierarchy. The environment, expecially the existence of physical barriers and the friction of distance, restricted both the extent and intensity of communications so that the effective "world view" of any particular group was relatively narrow and usually confined to the group itself and its immediate neighbors.

Colonialism had the effect of creating a new and stronger pattern of circulation within larger units of organization. With the drawing of boundaries and the spread of effective administration came the genesis of transition. Traditional society was virtually forced to

---

[5] "Social Mobilization and Political Development," *American Political Science Review* (1963), p. 493. See also Deutsch's *Nationalism and Social Communication* (1953), *passim.*

[6] Introduction to *Communications and Political Development,* edited by Lucian Pye (1963), p. 3.

change, and at a more rapid pace than ever before, through increasing contact with modern cultures. The colonial boundaries outlined the geographical compartments within which the forces of social mobilization were to work, an imposed framework in which the dynamic traditional patterns of cultural and political geography were restructured and re-delimited.

Finally, considering areal society in transition as an emerging *spatial system* is useful in identifying key themes of geographical analysis. An increasing number of geographers have come to regard nodal regions as "open systems" and have begun to construct methodological frameworks for examining the growth of nodal regions based on concepts from general systems theory.[7] These frameworks focus attention on such topics as spatial *movements*; the growth of *networks*; the pattern and role of *nodes* on these networks and their arrangement into a *hierarchy*; and the development of *density surfaces* which, in a sense, put meat on the skeletal structure by expressing the areal differentiation which results from this movement, concentration, and interaction.

Although the present study is not an attempt to apply systems theory to modernization in Kenya, it does stress most of the aforementioned topics as part of its analytical framework. Thus, Chapters II and III are concerned with broad patterns of spatial movement in Kenya before and after European penetration, and chapters IV and V deal with the emergence of a network of social communications and the urban nodes which hold it together. Chapters VI through VIII involve an attempt at statistical integration of a large number of variables to produce what are basically density surfaces of modernization. And finally, Chapter IX includes an effort to bring all these themes together in an examination of the Kenya nation as a nodal region.

METHODOLOGY

The conceptual framework just described aids in identifying a set of relationships from which a series of statistical indices can be derived to measure areal variations in modernization. These relationships involve the major concomitants of the modernization process—key indicators of the progress from traditional to modern ways of life.

It is assumed, therefore, that the extent of modernization in a given subarea will be directly related to:

1. The development of a transportation network, partly in terms of the multiplication of routes but more importantly in increased traffic along these routes.

2. The expansion of communication and information media as shown by their distributional pattern and the intensity of their use.

3. Increased urbanization and the growth of an integrated urban system, including the growth of rural-urban interaction.

4. A breaking down of traditional ethnic compartmentalization.

5. The emergence of an exchange or money economy as opposed to subsistence activities.

6. The development of education, both on a per capita basis as well as in total numbers reaching particular levels of education.

7. The extent of participation in nonparochial forms of organization and activity (e.g., political parties, national elections, trade unions, and other forms of voluntary associations).

8. Geographic proximity to and interaction with the most modernized sectors of society, particularly the core area(s) acting as the major concentrator, adapter, and distributor of the forces of modernization.

9. The degree of physical, or geographic, mobility, both internally and beyond the given state-area or its subunit.

It should be noted, however, that modernization is not simply an increase in a set of indices. It involves profound changes in individual and group behavior which, indeed, may be the most important concomitants of the process.[8] These important developments have been omitted here only because of the enormous difficulty in obtaining such behavioral data,

---

[7] An outstanding recent example of this approach can be found in Peter Haggett, *Location Analysis in Human Geography* (1966). For a discussion of the need for increased use of systems theory in geographic research, see Edward A. Ackerman, "Where is a Research Frontier?" *Annals of the Association of American Geographers* (1963), pp. 429–40.

[8] For an excellent analysis of the personal dimension in modernizing societies, see Lucian Pye (ed.), *Politics, Personality, and Nation Building: Burma's Search for Identity* (1962); and Daniel Lerner, *The Passing of Traditional Society: Modernizing the Middle East* (1958), particularly "The Grocer and the Chief: A Parable," Chapter I.

especially on a geographical basis. The selection of the variables used in this study was guided by the need to devise a method to measure the extent of modernization *by district* for all of Kenya. Additional measures will no doubt suggest themselves to the reader, but those chosen were considered most amenable to quantitative analysis and the most accurate indicators of modernization from the data available for Kenya.

The relationships just described are examined first through the descriptive-cartographic techniques traditional to geography, and specific measures of these relationships are introduced and mapped. Twenty-five key variables are then chosen and subjected to a form of multi-variate analysis known as the principal components technique—a relatively new addition to the geographer's tool kit. Principal components analysis is used to provide a means of summary description for the twenty-five variables used; to examine the intercorrelations among the variables and reduce them to a smaller number of underlying "dimensions" of modernization; and to

supply a heuristic probing device into the nature of the modernization process itself.

The present study is basically an attempt to utilize available data on an intrastate level to ascertain patterns relevant to the modernization of Kenya as a whole. It also presents a picture of Kenya at a critical turning point in its history, looking back at over sixty years of colonial control and looking forward to the challenge of nation building. As an initial attempt to investigate the spatial dimension in modernization, the study may raise more questions than it answers. This is by no means undesirable. The study will have proved successful if it has suggested some questions or hypotheses and possible avenues for their investigation which have been made apparent through the spatial perspective of the geographer. It is hoped that the analysis will provide a workable conceptual framework for comparative research on the same theme, a baseline for the analysis of modernization in a future Kenya and the outlines of several contemporary problems deserving more intensive investigation.

II

The Pre-Contact Setting:
Kenya Before European Penetration

Any contemporary analysis of social change needs to consider the historical context in which the change occurred. In a sense, this chapter presents the basic cultural framework within which the processes of modernization were to interact and operate in Kenya.

THE PHYSICAL CHARACTER OF KENYA

Before examining the demographic movements which led to the peopling of Kenya by its modern inhabitants, it may be worthwhile to outline briefly the physical geography of the territory.

Kenya, which today covers an area of about 225,000 square miles—roughly the size of France—can be conveniently subdivided into four broad physical geographic regions: (1) the Coastal Plain, (2) the Arid Low Plateaus, (3) the Kenya Highlands, and (4) the Lake Victoria Borderlands (see Figure 1).[1]

The Coastal Plain in Kenya displays many characteristics typical of African coastal regions. It is relatively narrow (never much more than forty miles wide), contains few good natural harbors, and is fringed with mangroves, lagoons, and coral reefs. Rainfall is highest near Mombasa (forty-seven inches) and declines northward and southward from the island port, dipping to less than twenty-six inches near the Somali border owing to the deflection of rain-bringing northeast and southwest monsoons.

Inland from the coast are a series of dry low plateaus which stretch from the border of Tanzania in a broad arc to encompass nearly the entire northern half of Kenya. This is by far the largest physical geographic region and covers most of the 72 per cent of Kenya that cannot reliably expect an annual rainfall over twenty inches. Much of this area, in fact, has an annual rainfall probability of less than ten inches. Several small highland enclaves exist, however, such as the Taita Hills, which reach a sufficient elevation (more than 5,000 feet) to obtain a higher rainfall and support a much denser vegetation than the scrub bush prevalent in the lower areas.

The Kenya Highlands are a series of higher plateaus and volcanic surfaces generally lying between the elevations of 4,000 and 10,000 feet. Slicing through the heart of the Highlands is a portion of the eastern Rift Valley, whose escarpments and floor here attain their greatest height and heaviest rainfall within East Africa. The Rift contains a number of small lakes, including Nakuru and Naivasha, as well as several volcanic cones and plugs.

The escarpments, which rise 3,000 feet in places, dramatically hem in the central part of the Rift Valley and form the edges of the Aberdares Range in the east (in the Kikuyu Escarpment) and the Mau Hills, Kericho Highlands, and the Uasin Gishu Plateau in the west (the Mau and Elgeyo Escarpments). Fanning off from this central portion of the Highlands are several volcanic and nonvolcanic high plateaus (e.g., Laikipia, Trans-Nzoia) which extend to the foothills of the two highest peaks in Kenya, Mount Kenya (17,058 feet) northeast of the Aberdares and Mount Elgon (14,178 feet) on the border with Uganda.

Nearly all of the Kenya Highlands has a rainfall probability greater than twenty inches in four out of five years and on some of the more exposed slopes average annual rainfall exceeds eighty inches. Most of the soils are volcanic in origin and are among the most fertile in Africa. The eastern section contains the sources of Kenya's largest rivers, the Athi-

---

[1] General material on the physical geography of Kenya can be found in G. M. Hickman and W. H. G. Dickens, *The Lands and Peoples of East Africa* (1960); E. W. Russell (ed.), *The Natural Resources of East Africa* (1962); S. J. K. Baker, "The East African Environment," in R. Oliver and G. Mathew (eds.), *History of East Africa,* Vol. I (1963), pp. 1–9; and F. F. Ojany, "The Physique of Kenya: A Contribution to Landscape Analysis," *Annals of the Association of American Geographers* (1966), pp. 183–96.

FIGURE 1

PHYSICAL GEOGRAPHICAL REGIONS

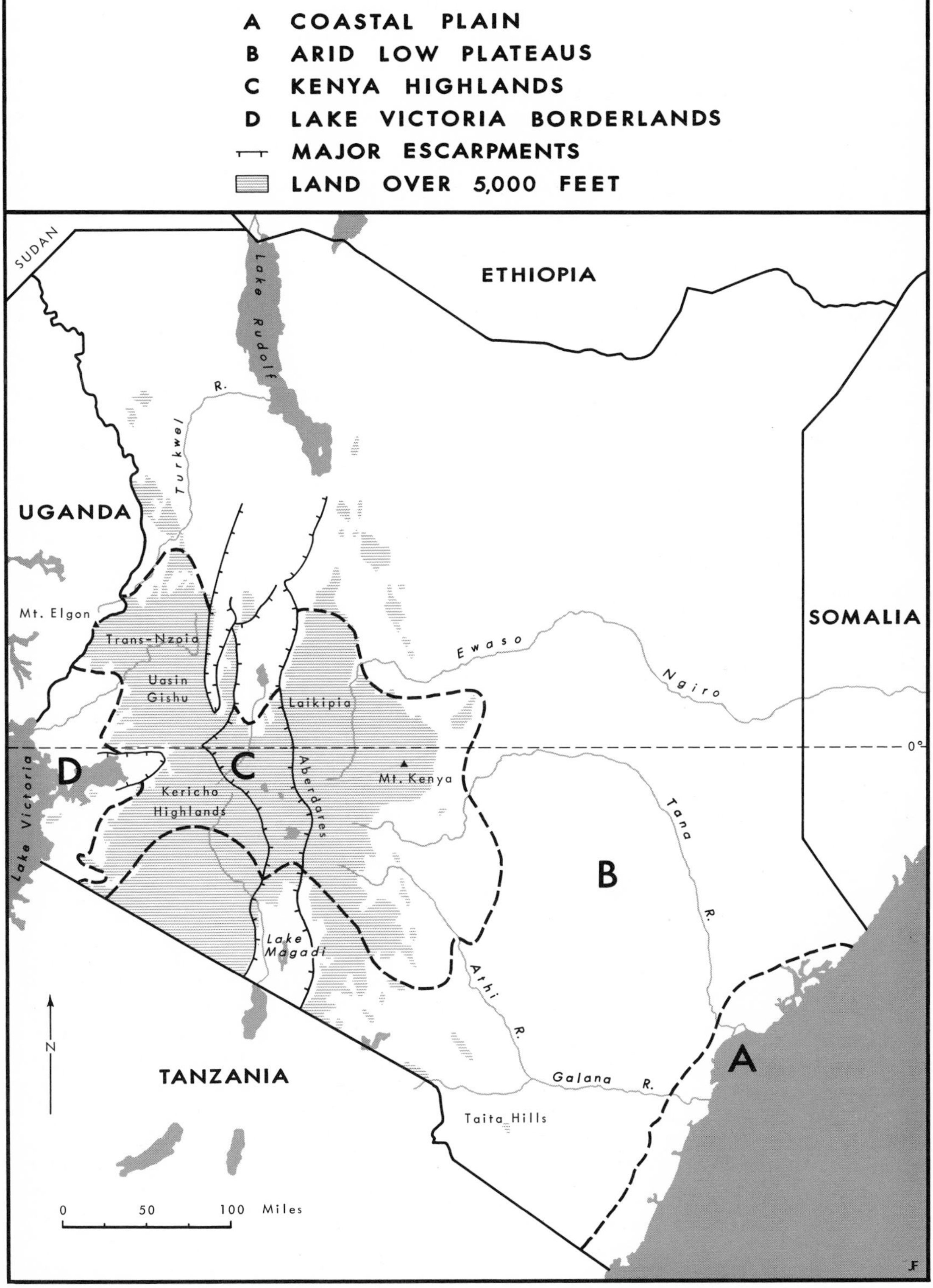

A   COASTAL PLAIN
B   ARID LOW PLATEAUS
C   KENYA HIGHLANDS
D   LAKE VICTORIA BORDERLANDS
⊤⊤   MAJOR ESCARPMENTS
▭   LAND OVER 5,000 FEET

Galana and the Tana, both of which flow through the *nyika*, or "wilderness," between the Highlands and the coast before emptying into the Indian Ocean.

The Lake Victoria, or Nyanza—Swahili for "lake"—Borderlands is an area of reliable and evenly distributed rainfall which almost everywhere exceeds thirty inches. Except for the Kano Plains, the floor of a miniature Rift Valley extending eastward from the faulted Gulf of Kavirondo, and some lowlands north of the Gulf, most of this region is composed of heavily eroded, nonvolcanic plateau surfaces and portions of the old upland massif where rainfall usually exceeds sixty inches.

In summary then, Kenya is predominantly a dry country in which nearly three-quarters of the land does not regularly receive sufficient rainfall to support nonirrigated agriculture. Only in the southwest quadrant (the Highlands and Nyanza regions), along the narrow Coastal Plain and in a few isolated highland exclaves, is there the combination of reliable rainfall and fertile soils to sustain a dense agricultural population.

THE EARLY PEOPLING OF KENYA— PATTERNS OF ETHNIC MIGRATIONS

The boundaries of modern Kenya surround a portion of East Africa artificially carved out by the colonial powers from a dynamic cultural milieu. Before the arrival of Europeans, the patterns of settlement, population density, and relative power were flexible and closely associated with environmental and cultural restrictions and the complex interplay between pastoralist and agriculturalist. Even during the last decades of the nineteenth century, several areas were in the process of receiving migrants while others were being rapidly depopulated through tribal warfare and natural disasters.

The farthest extensions of at least six major African migrations come together within the present boundaries of Kenya (Figure 2). They include:

1 and 2) Two waves of Bantu, one from the interlacustrine area north of Victoria Nyanza into the area bordering the lake on the east; and another from the south through the Taita Hills, along the coast, up the Tana River and into the area around the eastern side of the Rift Valley and Mount Kenya.

3) A southward surge of Nilo-Hamitic pastoralists from the basin of Lake Rudolf—spear-headed by the Masai—through the drier sections of the Kenya Highlands into northern Tanganyika and the more humid country west of the Rift.

4) A movement of Nilotic Luo from the upper Nile basin into the area surrounding the Kavirondo Gulf.

5 and 6) The penetration of Hamitic Galla and Somali constantly pressing southwestward from the Horn through the dry northeastern quadrant of the country.[2]

The agricultural Bantu are considered to be the first of these major migratory waves and probably entered Kenya during the last half of the first millenium A.D. For many centuries they continued to spread throughout the better watered areas, displacing or absorbing the pre-existing Caucasoid and Bushmanoid populations.[3]

In western Kenya, the Bantu settled in the lowlands around Lake Victoria and in some of the highland areas behind them. Representatives of this group include the Luhya (formerly called the Bantu Kavirondo) and the Gusii, or Kisii (with the related Kuria), who today occupy some of the most densely settled lands in Africa.[4]

The second Bantu wave spread outward from the Taita Hills, in southeastern Kenya, first moving east and then north along the coast, where contact was made with the already well-established Arab trading population. Tradition says that a secondary dispersal area existed at "Shungwaya," between the Juba River—now in Somalia—and the Tana, from which nearly all the Bantu-speaking peoples of eastern Kenya and northeastern Tanganyika trace their origin.[5] Blocked

[2] Note that Bantu, Nilotic, Nilo-Hamitic, and Hamitic are linguistic terms which have assumed ethnic connotations. In recent years, the boundaries between these groups have become blurred, particularly between the Nilotes and the Nilo-Hamites, and new linguistic terms have come into common usage (e.g., Cushitic or, more generally, Afroasiatic, for Hamitic). Furthermore, many of the ethnic stereotypes of the linguistic groups have been challenged. The terms are used here nevertheless because of their general acceptance and use in most of the relevant literature.

[3] For a discussion of the earliest occupants of East Africa, see Sonia Cole, *The Prehistory of East Africa* (1964).

[4] Bantu languages are characterized by prefixes which modify the basic meaning of the root forms. Thus, the two groups referred to here should be called the Abaluhya or Baluhya and Abagusii. For the sake of simplicity, however, only the conventional roots will be used in this study.

[5] The basic reference used here is G. W. B. Huntingford, "The Peopling of the Interior of East Africa by its Modern Inhabitants," in R. Oliver and G. Mathew (eds.), *History of East Africa,* Vol. I (1963), pp. 58–93.

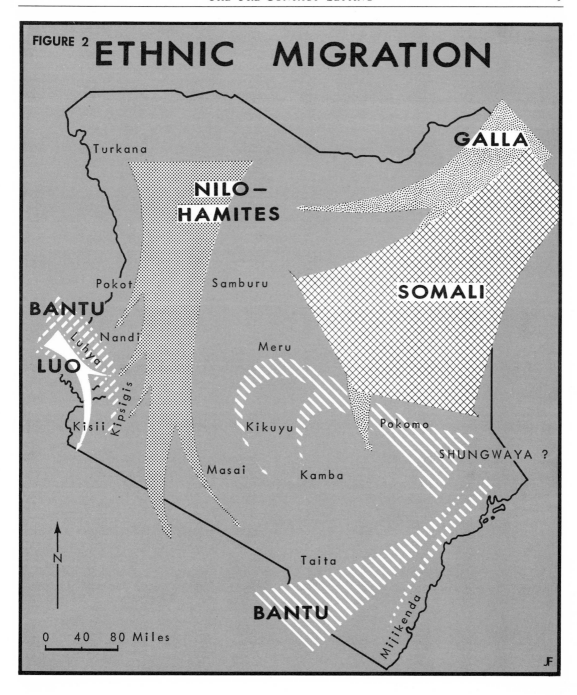

FIGURE 2 ETHNIC MIGRATION

GALLA

Turkana

NILO–
HAMITES

SOMALI

BANTU

Pokot   Samburu

Luhya   Nandi

LUO   Kisii Kipsigis

Meru

Kikuyu   Pokomo

SHUNGWAYA ?

Masai   Kamba

N

Taita

0   40   80 Miles

BANTU   Mijikenda

JF

from further northward penetration by the expanding Galla, who were already in the Tana area in the thirteenth century, the Bantu turned both southward and eastward, reoccupying the Taita-Kilimanjaro area and the coast hinterland and moving into the dry plains and more fertile highland areas between Mount Kilimanjaro and Mount Kenya. The Meru to the north and the Kikuyu-Embu to the south of Mount Kenya, the Kamba in the scattered hills and steppe country between the highlands and the coast, the Taita, the Pokomo in the Tana Valley, and the Digo, Duruma, and Giriama along the coast are the main contemporary products of this population dispersal. The mixed Bantu-Arab Swahili peoples of the coast are an additional by-product which will be discussed in a later section.

In the period between 1500 and 1850, while the Galla were still pushing westward from the Horn and the eastern Bantu migrations continued, a series of population movements from the Lake Rudolf basin resulted in the occupation of the Rift Valley and much of the highland country surrounding it. Although remaining primarily cattle keepers, some groups of these Nilo-Hamitic speaking peoples (e.g., the Nandi, Kipsigis, and Itesio, and sections of the Pokot, Sabaot, Elgeyo, Marakwet, and Tugen) turned increasingly toward agriculture in the well-watered areas of the Rift. Others, such as the Turkana, Samburu, and Masai, continued to be almost entirely dependent upon their herds and succeeded in spreading throughout the drier steppelands.

The result of the Nilo-Hamitic invasions was not only the establishment of a wall of military-oriented pastoral peoples between the eastern and western Kenya Bantu but also the further fragmentation of the Bantu areas into virtual islands of densely populated agricultural land in a sea of pastoralism. The Masai formed a wedge between the Kamba and the Taita-Kilimanjaro area while other Nilo-Hamitic groups effectively isolated the Luhya from their relatives in Uganda.

The more recent migration of the Nilotic Luo—an offshoot from a much larger series of migrations affecting all of modern Uganda—resulted in the formation of still another wedge, between the Luhya and the Kisii. The Luo themselves formed an isolated enclave of a significantly different culture amid Nilo-Hamitic and Bantu dominated western Kenya. Their most outstanding characteristic has been a remarkable ability to absorb the former Bantu inhabitants of the Kavirondo area—a process which is still continuing today, albeit probably less rapidly than before European penetration.

The last of the major migrations in Kenya, that of the Somali, was still very much in progress when the British arrived. It was not to have a great effect on the peoples outside northeastern Kenya, where the Somali steadily displaced the Galla, until the present decade.

THE FABRIC OF TRADITIONAL SOCIETY

With very minor exceptions (e.g., among some of the Luhya), no African society in Kenya achieved a level of sociopolitical organization comparable to the centralized chiefdoms and occasional strong local states of the Tanganyika Bantu. And certainly none approached the state-building activities of the interlacustrine Bantu of southern Uganda. The acephalous Kenya societies typically consisted of associations of kinship segments united primarily in response to the natural environment and the pressure of competitive groups.

Dependence upon domesticated plants and animals required an organizational structure more complex and larger in scale than that of the primitive hunting band. But, for a wide variety of reasons, including the relative lack of external contact and stimulus from more advanced societies, the traditional authority systems of Kenya lacked the functional organization of area associated with the centralized network of production and redistribution characteristic of chiefdoms and states elsewhere in Africa. A relatively elaborate hierarchical clan structure did exist among the Luo, but for nearly all the other peoples of Kenya the basic organizational pattern consisted of diffuse, egalitarian polities structured around an age-ordered, functional system of classes at one level and kinship ties (clan, lineage) at another. Territorial identification was primarily a function of kinship, with a group's "territory" being essentially the area under current occupation by a particular segment of the population.

Society was in a constant state of flux—cohesive communities were appearing and disappearing, blending and breaking off as a result of an almost ubiquitous competition for land and animals. Organized raiding and efforts to resist it, and the desire or need to expand into new grazing or agricultural land, created a fluid distribution of population and group loyalties.

Conflict and fighting took place not only between ethnically unrelated groups—particularly between pastoralist and agriculturist—but also within groups who shared a common cultural background. Although the Kikuyu, for example, are frequently considered a single unified group, they rarely fought as a unit against their traditional enemies, the Masai, and often engaged in conflicts among themselves. Indeed, segments of the Kikuyu were occasionally allied with the Masai to fight other Kikuyu.

This does not mean that there was no underlying framework of stability. Social boundaries were generally constant and identifiable, but they were also sufficiently permeable to permit peaceful absorption of outside groups when the situation arose. Clusters of related peoples developed a veneer of unity based upon sets of linkages which cut across kinship lines and, although these linkages did not always prevent internal conflict, they did provide a structure for cooperative action against outside adversaries. A key feature was a flexibility which permitted relative autonomy for small-scale communities in times of peace but also allowed for a complex system of combination and cooperation when there was stress. This fluid and kaleidoscopic nature of the traditional cultural and political geography of Kenya was to have far-reaching effects on the patterns of modernization and change growing out of British penetration.

SPATIAL PATTERNS

Competition for land and animals and the lack of a strong institutionalized territorial organization produced a situation in which there existed large areas of agricultural and grazing land—not to mention highland and desert areas—beyond the recognized domain of any ethnic group. The contact zones between ethnically related clusters of people, for example, nearly always functioned as neutral ground or buffer areas, the control of which vacillated with the relative strength of adjacent groups. For the Kikuyu, the Kenya Land Commission reports:

> All early accounts of the Kikuyu territory agree in stating that it was surrounded by a belt of forest of varying width which served to protect the tribe against its enemies. They further agree that the Kikuyu did not venture outside this belt to build or cultivate or graze their cattle beyond it until the Masai power began seriously to wane, owing to internecine warfare and the tremendous losses of their cattle by disease and until the protectorate had been declared. The land may therefore be said, broadly speaking, to have had two frontiers—the outside and the inside of the forest belt.[6]

Even beyond this forested "moat," however, there were large areas of open land, alternately dominated by one group or another, which did

---

[6] *Report of the Kenya Land Commission* (Carter Commission), Cmd. 4556 (1934), p. 16.

not become integrated within established grazing or agricultural patterns.

These factors make it impossible to draw an accurate and realistic map of Kenya representing the areal patterns of traditional authority systems and ethnic distributions unless a particular time period is chosen. Even while meeting this qualification, however, meaningful patterns cannot be portrayed with conventional, one-dimensional boundaries delimiting contiguous units, for this would fail to take into account the fluidity of ethnic frontiers and the variability with which areas were considered part of the exclusive territory of a single group.

Nevertheless, it is possible to recognize, for most of the major ethnic divisions, relatively stable core areas which could be considered the established areal domain of a given ethnic group at a particular time. This is especially true for the more settled agricultural peoples. But any attempt to portray the traditional cultural geography must include a delimitation of these changeable frontier zones as well as a warning that (a) any line drawn on the map probably misrepresents the nature and function of boundaries for the traditional societies and (b) all lines must be considered as temporal estimates fluctuating with the local situation.

Figure 3 is an attempt to represent the distribution of major ethnic groups in the southern half of Kenya during the last two decades of the nineteenth century—before the impress of British administration was felt. In a sense, this distribution provides the traditional "field" upon which the structures and processes of modernization and change were to interact. The dry northern areas of the country have been excluded for both practical and conceptual reasons, for there is little reliable information and the area is sparsely populated by nomadic pastoral peoples among whom the impact of Western influence has hardly been felt.

The most outstanding feature of Figure 3 is the previously mentioned pattern of settled and largely agricultural islands in a veritable sea of mobile pastoralists. The major territorial powers at this time were the Masai, Somali, Nandi, and Turkana. The pastoralists dominated nearly all the open plains and grasslands while the agriculturalists occupied, often not by choice, the less accessible and usually forested highland areas, the tsetse infested shores of Lake Victoria, the Tana River Val-

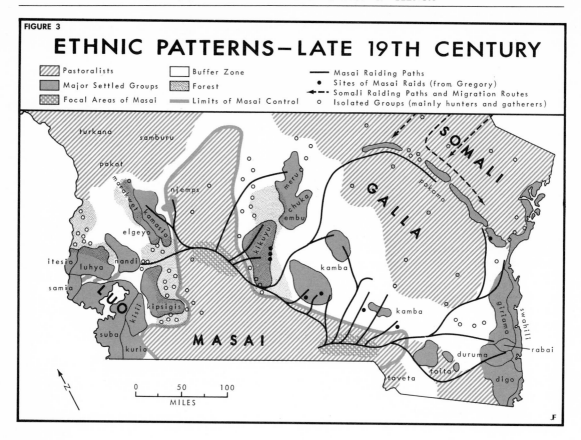

FIGURE 3

ETHNIC PATTERNS—LATE 19TH CENTURY

ley, and the coastal belt. All groups, whether pastoral or agricultural, were subject to frequent raids by their neighbors.

The Masai dominated the entire Rift Valley south of about 2° N. and the dry plains and plateaus surrounding the Rift and extending well into Tanganyika. The Masai had formerly occupied the Uasin Gishu Plateau, between the Mau-Elgeyo Escarpment and Mount Elgon, but internal fighting among the Masai resulted in a depopulating of the area after 1870.[7] It has thus been added to those other areas on the map showing zones where no single group dominated.

Although internecine warfare and a series of natural disasters (locusts, rinderpest, drought) severely weakened the Masai during the last half of the nineteenth century, their strength remained great enough to prevent any of the agricultural peoples from straying far beyond their highland sanctuaries. The Kamba, for example, were restricted to the forested ridges of their country and rarely

moved out into the drier plains between these ridges.[8] The Masai were even able to extend their raids to within sight of Mombasa harbor as late as 1889.[9]

By 1900 the Somali had become equally significant territorial powers by establishing themselves over the entire northeastern quadrant of Kenya up to and in some areas beyond the Tana River. They appeared to be pressing even farther until the *Pax Britannica* put brakes upon cattle raiding and purposefully prevented the Somali from extending their sphere of occupation. It is interesting to speculate about what might have occurred had the broad buffer of the eastern Rift Highlands been overcome and the Somali and Masai found themselves face to face in what one writer foresaw as "a fight for mastery"[10] over northern East Africa.

It would be incorrect to assume that all the agricultural peoples remained confined during

---

[7] D. A. Low, "The Northern Interior, 1840–1884," in Oliver and Mathew, op. cit., p. 306.

[8] *Kenya Land Commission: Evidence and Memoranda*, Vol. II (1934), pp. 1285–86.

[9] J. Gregory, *The Great Rift Valley* (1896), p. 363.

[10] *Ibid.*, p. 369.

this period. The Luo were relentlessly pushing southward through the lowlands fringing Lake Victoria, absorbing and displacing the pre-existing Bantu population as far as fifty miles into Tanganyika territory. The Kikuyu were also pressing southward into the Kiambu area and northward through the saddle between Mount Kenya and the Aberdares, although this movement was temporarily curtailed by the great famines and plagues of the 1880's. The Uasin Gishu became an ethnic vacuum with the reduction of the Masai threat and was slowly beginning to be inhabited by the neighboring Luhya, Nandi, Pokot, Elgeyo, and Marakwet. African society in Kenya was no different than it was for centuries prior to this time: periodically splintering, regrouping, agglomerating, and solidifying in a process aimed at achieving the rare and delicate equilibrium that passed for stability in traditional ethnic communities.

It is tempting to propose that Figure 3 also represents the frequently discussed but rarely mapped "mosaic" of traditional polities characteristic of pre-European Africa. This claim, however, would be too great a simplification. In most cases, the names on the map do not depict single autonomous groups but agglomerations of peoples having certain common cultural characteristics (e.g., language, forms of military organization, systems of land tenure). These affinities were recognized by the segments of the groups, but each segment could and did act independently.

A more accurate map of the basic autonomous units in traditional society would require much more information than is presently available. Figure 4 is offered as an example of the complexity that would be involved in such an undertaking. It is a map of the component "tribes" of the Bantu Kavirondo or, as they are now called, the Luhya.[11] Each "tribe" has a different historical tradition and is distinct in terms of its interactions with and cultural adoptions from other groups. The Nyala and Bugusu, for example, were strongly affected by the Masai and Nandi, reflecting this contact in

their physical appearance as well as in their weaponry, personal adornments, and degree of dependence upon pastoral activities.[12] The Wanga, or Hanga, on the other hand, are a much more agricultural people who claim an origin somewhere to the west of Lake Albert and a relationship to the Soga and Nyoro of Uganda. The unshaded area on the map represents the farthest extent of the Wanga chiefdom—the only example of a large, organized proto-state in Kenya on somewhat the same scale as those in Tanzania and Uganda. An accurate mosaic of traditional polities, therefore, would have to take all these basic units into consideration.

The cultural geography of traditional society in Kenya prior to the colonial period can thus be characterized as a complex and ever changing social landscape distinctly lacking any large cohesive territorial units. Clusters of peoples recognizing certain mutual affinities existed as ethnically circumscribed cells, fairly homogeneous in their core areas but highly mixed on the peripheries. Communications and contact were generally confined to within the individual units themselves except for the primarily military interchange and conflict with competitive neighbors—especially between pastoralist and agriculturalist—over land and animals. A major by-product of this unstable situation was the existence of large, apparently unused land areas which served as neutral ground, buffer zones, and reservoirs for expansion for the adjacent peoples. The distribution of these "unused" lands was to form a perceived vacuum for the British and largely to control the spatial patterns of interaction between traditional society and the modernizing influences of the West.

ARABS ON THE COAST

The East African coast, in marked contrast to the interior, has been in close contact with non-African cultures for about two thousand years. As early as A.D. 100, Arab trading ports had been established along the coast, and the "monsoon" winds were being utilized by navigators from the Mediterranean to eastern Asia.[13] Until a little over a century

---

[11] Use of the word "tribe" has been specifically avoided in this study. Many anthropologists are now rejecting the term as having little descriptive or analytical meaning, and it is also being criticized for its pejorative connotations. Here it is used only to point out that many of the traditional ethnic groups, though frequently referred to as tribes, are actually composed of virtually autonomous and, in many cases, strikingly dissimilar subdivisions.

[12] Gunter Wagner, *The Bantu of North Kavirondo*, Vol. I (1949), p. 11.

[13] The earliest surviving description of the East African coast is the *Periplus of the Erythrean Sea*, a Greek sailing guide of the late first or early second century.

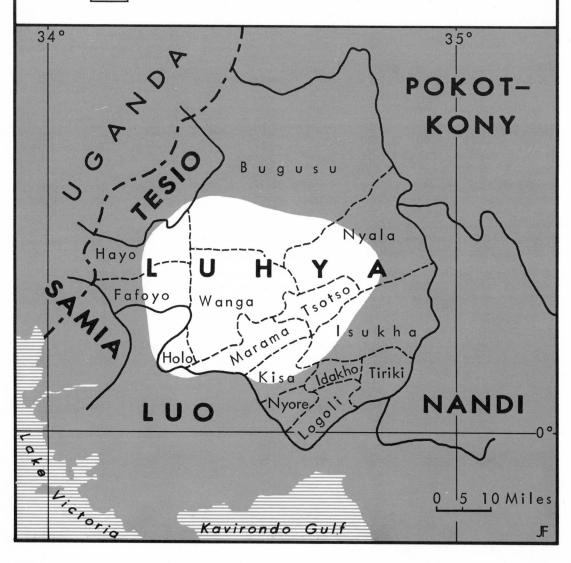

FIGURE 4

LUHYA TRIBES

-·-·- TERRITORIAL BOUNDARY

——— MAJOR "TRIBAL" BOUNDARY

- - - LUHYA "TRIBAL" BOUNDARY

☐ MAXIMUM EXTENT OF WANGA STATE

ago, this area functioned more as the western shore of the Indian Ocean than as the coast of East Africa and formed an integrated part of the Indian Ocean trading system.

The highly mixed population which came to occupy such ports as Mombasa, Malindi, Lamu, and Vanga consisted of varying blends of Arab, Persian, and Bantu, with additional elements derived from the early Caucasoid and Bushmanoid inhabitants of the interior, Indian traders, and, possibly, Southeast Asian migrants. This miscegenation gave rise to the Swahili peoples, whose syncretic language and culture came to dominate the coastal belt and later spread inland as the orientation of the coastal area turned increasingly toward the interior.

Although it is possible that further archeological investigation will discover earlier evidence of physical penetration and contact, present information indicates that the spread of coastal influences into the interior of East Africa dates mainly from the middle of the nineteenth century. Pror to this time, trade in the interior was primarily in the hands of African middlemen, such as the Nyamwezi in Tanganyika and the Kamba in Kenya, who brought ivory, slaves, and other produce to the coast in exchange for beads, cloth, and grain.

The turning point of this relationship came with the rise of the Sultanate of Zanzibar. After 1840, Arab and Swahili merchants began to take control of the trade routes and established small settlements along them. With the penetration of coastal peoples came also the spread of Islam and the Swahili language, especially along the central and southern Tanganyika routes.

The Kenya peoples most strongly affected by Swahili culture were those of the Nyika cluster of northeastern Bantu (Digo, Duruma, Giriama—today collectively called the Mijikenda), many of whom adopted Islam and the Swahili language and became absorbed into Swahili society. Eventually, the coastal Swahili came to exercise a form of hegemony over the Nyika, depending upon their support in times of stress, adjudicating over intertribal disputes and alienating some of the better lands. Trade, often combined with missionary activity, was well developed between the Swahili and the Nyika and the latter supplied large numbers of porters on the Swahili trade routes, which crossed Nyika territory and enabled them to establish contact with related Bantu peoples upcountry.[14]

The interior of Kenya, however, was affected very little by coastal contact before the turn of the century. To a limited extent, trade provided an escape for some groups who, because of famine, warfare, or social pressures, spread well beyond their traditional territory. The Kamba, for example, could be found from the coast nearly to Lake Victoria and from north of Lake Baringo well into north central Tanganyika.[15] Swahili, however, never became as firmly implanted in Kenya as in Tanganyika, nor did Islam spread very far beyond the coast. In fact, it was only in the 1880's that control of the northern trade route from Mombasa came under Arab control.[16]

[14] A. H. J. Prins, *The Coastal Tribes of the North-Eastern Bantu* (1952), pp. 37–38.
[15] Low, *op. cit.*, p. 315.
[16] *Ibid.*, p. 316.

III

Foreign Intrusions: The Spread of Europeans and Asians and the Onset of Transition

THE BEGINNINGS OF THE COLONIAL PERIOD

Whereas the caravan trade through Kenya did not act nearly as effectively as an avenue for the diffusion of coastal culture as it did further south, the route inland from Mombasa became much more important as the corridor for European penetration. During the last two decades of the nineteenth century, the closer European contracts which had helped stimulate the rapid growth of the Zanzibari domain now brought it into decline. Germany and Britain carved out spheres of influence on the mainland and, by the late 1890's, succeeded in transforming them into a series of protectorates. The Sultan was left with only his home islands of Zanzibar and Pemba, the ten-mile wide "Coastal Strip" from the Tana mouth to the Tanganyika border, and a few scattered ports to the north—and even these were under British protection. The colonial period had begun.

The old route from Mombasa to Lake Victoria rapidly became the backbone of British administration and influence. Missionary activity, efforts to suppress the slave trade, the relative wealth of the interlacustrine area, and European power politics involved in controlling the sources of the Nile all contributed to making the Kingdom of Buganda a magnet for British colonial interests. Effective penetration and control over the kingdom, however, necessitated the maintenance of a corridor of communications with the coast. Since the distance through Kenya was shorter than that of any other route and was entirely in British territory, the old northern caravan route grew in importance. With the construction of the Kenya-Uganda Railway between 1896 and 1902, the Mombasa-Buganda axis became the major artery of communications and transportation in all of East Africa, a position it still retains today, superseding the Zanzibar-

Bagamoyo-Tabora axis, which in turn had succeeded the predominantly coastal circulatory system prior to the nineteenth century (see Figure 7).

British administration in the East African Protectorate—as Kenya was then known—diffused northwestward with the extension of the railway from the coast, where treaties had been made with local leaders even before the construction of the line. Taita, Kamba, Masai, and most of the Kikuyu were acquiescent in the early spread of the British, and administrative stations were sprinkled lightly over the southern half of the protectorate. Nairobi, although initially planned as a railway town only, become the center of upcountry administration after the provincial government was transferred from Machakos (which was not on the railway).

During this period, the East African Protectorate was much more of a nuisance to the British than an asset, since it presented a vast stretch of unproductive and often troublesome territory between the coast and Buganda. The completion of the railway, however, sparked a series of developments which transformed Kenya into an important British colony and center for European settlement. The very lack of development and the existence of large apparently unpopulated areas were to play key roles in these changes.

EUROPEAN SETTLEMENT AND THE POLITICAL PARTITIONING OF KENYA

In an effort to keep the entire railway under a single administration, the Eastern Province of Uganda—consisting of the area west of the Rift Valley and east of the present boundary of Uganda—was transferred in 1902 to the East African Protectorate. Although it did not appear portentous at the time, the addition of the Eastern Province really marked the beginning of large-scale European settlement in Kenya.

The first settlement in Kenya actually took place in 1894, when a small vegetable farm was established near Machakos. Somewhat later a few more patches of land were taken up near Mombasa, at points along the railway as it was being built (e.g., Kibwezi), and especially around Nairobi. By 1902, however, the railway was complete, the Kenya Highlands were consolidated under a single authority and the obvious need to stimulate some productive economic activity in the six-hundred-mile stretch between the coast and Lake Victoria not only dominated the minds of the administrators but could now be effectively implemented.

A detailed history of European settlement in what came to be known as the "White Highlands" is not the object of this analysis.[1] There are, however, certain salient spatial patterns—some of which guided settlement and others which stemmed from it—that require additional examination in order to comprehend the evolution and contemporary patterns of economic, social, and political change.

Filling in the "Unused" Land:
Growth of the White Highlands

The potentials for European settlement in the Highlands were recognized since the early 1890's by such men as Johnston, Portal, and Lugard who, while traveling through the area, were greatly impressed by the large stretches of apparently unused land. The old caravan route skirted Kikuyuland, passed through the open grazing country of the Masai, and reached a dense population only at the edge of the highlands northeast of Lake Victoria. Throughout most of the route, the absence of a settled population was the most striking feature.

The men who gave these potentials their clearest description and greatest impetus toward realization, however, were Sir Charles Eliot, commissioner for the East African Protectorate from 1901 to 1904, and Lord Delamere, the aristocratic extrovert who became the pioneer of Kenya settlers.[2] The Crown Lands Ordinance of 1902 enabled settlers to obtain grants of 640 acres in specified areas and, encouraged in words by Eliot and through example by Delamere, the stream of settle-ment began to grow. From barely a dozen farms in 1902, the European settler population jumped to three thousand in five years.[3]

During the first phase of settlement, from 1902 to 1908, nearly all land alienation occurred around the railway towns and at other points along the line (See Figure 5). The dominance of the railway was reflected in the only definition given to the land open to white settlement during this period: that area between the stations of Kiu (alternatively, Kibwezi) in the east and Fort Ternan in the west.

The major center of early settlement was the Nairobi area, especially southern Kiambu. In 1902, when land settlement as a definite policy commenced, allotments were granted in Ngong, Kabete, Karura, Kiambu, and Ruiru, while plans were being made for futher alienation along the railway line northwest to Limuru and Escarpment stations. The first big rush of settlers soon followed, composed in large part of South African Boers escaping the discontent and depression growing out of the Boer War.

The techniques of alienation and the pattern of relationship with surrounding African peoples in the Nairobi area came to guide future development in the Highlands. In 1904, the Land Office requested that a line be drawn "to separate the uninhabited from the inhabited areas" and that this line be used to govern the parceling out of land to European settlers.[4] Thus was born the policy of considering those lands not "effectively occupied" by Africans as available for alienation.

The line was drawn in great haste and with little consideration for the nature of both traditional agriculture and nomadic grazing, of the function of the area for Kikuyu and Masai society, or of the implications of recent events on the patterns of occupance in the area. The Kikuyu had formerly occupied a large part of what came to be Kiambu District in a series of migrations toward the end of the nineteenth century. At the time of the first European alienation of land, however, these migrations had been seriously weakened by a succession of natural disasters (drought, smallpox, rinderpest, and locusts) which forced most of the Kikuyu northward into their heartland in Fort Hall District, or Murang'a. Consequently, the

[1] A more detailed discussion of this phase of Kenya's history can be found in M. F. Hill, *Permanent Way* (1949), and Elspeth Huxley, *White Man's Country* (1953).

[2] *White Man's Country* is a biography of Delamere.

[3] Hill, *op. cit.*, p. 290.

[4] Huxley, *op. cit.*, Vol. I, p. 110.

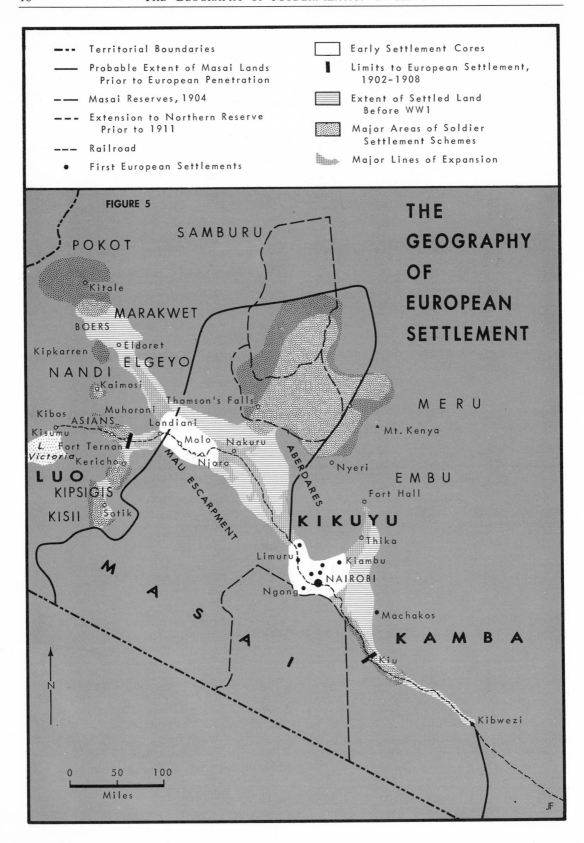

- - -   Territorial Boundaries

———   Probable Extent of Masai Lands
         Prior to European Penetration

—·—   Masai Reserves, 1904

- - -   Extension to Northern Reserve
         Prior to 1911

- - -   Railroad

●   First European Settlements

☐   Early Settlement Cores

▮   Limits to European Settlement,
        1902–1908

▨   Extent of Settled Land
        Before WW1

▨   Major Areas of Soldier
        Settlement Schemes

▨   Major Lines of Expansion

FIGURE 5

THE
GEOGRAPHY
OF
EUROPEAN
SETTLEMENT

POKOT

SAMBURU

Kitale

MARAKWET

BOERS

Kipkarren   Eldoret

NANDI   ELGEYO

Kaimosi

Thomson's Falls

MERU

Kibos   Muhoroni

ASIANS   Londiani

Kisumu   Molo   Nakuru

L.   Fort Ternan   Mt. Kenya

Victoria   Njoro

Kericho   Nyeri

LUO   EMBU

KIPSIGIS   Fort Hall

KISII   Sotik   MAU ESCARPMENT   ABERDARES

KIKUYU

Thika

M   Limuru   Kiambu

A   NAIROBI

S   Ngong

A   Machakos

I   KAMBA

Kiu

N   Kibwezi

0   50   100

Miles

JF

Kikuyu with whom the early settlers had contact appeared not to be effectively established in the area north of Nairobi.[5]

Much of the land purposely left by the Kikuyu as a forest buffer against the Masai as well as areas abandoned by those moving back to Murang'a were similarly taken over as Crown land available for alienation. The result of these operations was to establish the center of European society in Kenya directly across the line of Kikuyu cultural and demographic expansion on land which the Kikuyu claimed as traditionally their own.

In this first major conflict between African and European concepts toward the land and land ownership, the European prevailed. But it is interesting to note that the alienated lands were also considered by the colonial government to fulfill much the same function they had for traditional society—that of a buffer between the Kikuyu and the Masai. Similarly, the expansion of settlement through Thika and toward Fort Hall and along the railway to the southeast was encouraged in part to form buffers between the Kikuyu and the Kamba and the Kamba and the Masai.

The determination of "unused" or "not effectively occupied" land and the rationalization associated with setting up buffers between warring "tribes" directed the diffusion of European settlement, stimulated the establishment of Native Reserves, and eventually led to the creation of barriers against relations among ethnic groups that were to have far-reaching effects. And in some cases, the concepts of "unused" land was stretched a bit to accommodate European interests.

In addition to the Nairobi region, there was a second early core of settlement near the Mau Escarpment between the Molo and Njoro rivers, which later spread and became focused upon the town of Nakuru. This was an area largely avoided by the Masai because of mineral deficiencies in the soil and was considered by early travelers to be completely devoid of "native" population.[6] But the land between Nairobi and Nakuru, along the highest and best watered section of the Rift Valley floor, contained one of the major focal areas of the Masai. The attractiveness of this upland, the weakening of Masai power since the last decades of the nineteenth century, and the European challenge of the Masai right to *"monopolize* particular districts, and keep everybody out" as opposed to their right to *"inhabit* particular districts"[7] led to the Masai Agreement of 1904, which heralded the beginning of the Native Reserve system and eventually filled in the gap between the two early settlement cores.

Under the terms of the agreement, the Masai were split into two reserves and agreed to "remove our people, flocks and herds into definite reservations away from the railway line, and from any land that may be thrown open to European settlement. . . . [and] to vacate the entire Rift Valley." A "right to a road to include access to water" was guaranteed to retain communications between the northern, or Laikipia, and southern reserves; and another area, five miles square, was "granted" to carry out circumcision rites. This arrangement was held to be "enduring so long as the Masai as a race shall exist."[8]

The Masai agreement endured for seven years. In 1911, under a new agreement, the Laikipia—a grassland plateau between the Rift escarpment and the Mount Kenya area—was opened to European settlement; and the Masai, whose cattle had multiplied rapidly on the plateau, were moved into an expanded southern reserve which they still occupy today. By that time, a second phase of European settlement, from 1908 to World War I, had begun; and several other areas, many well beyond the railway, had been occupied by European settlers.

After 1908 large numbers of Afrikaners

[5] An excellent description of this situation and a criticism of the then prevailing view that the Kikuyu had not effectively occupied this area can be found in the evidence supplied by L. S. B. Leakey to the Kenya Land Commission in 1932 (*Evidence and Memoranda*, Vol. I, p. 658). He states that "these lands did belong effectively to the Kikuyu, but at the time the Europeans were first coming in here—after the great famine and the smallpox, which had reduced the numbers of the families very considerably—certain of that land which had formerly been occupied by the Kikuyu was once again for a short time fallow and practically unused; but I don't think, Sir, that you could argue fairly that because they temporarily ceased to use one piece of their family land that it was not theirs. I am certain that the argument will be put that certain land is not theirs because it can be shown that at some fixed year the Kikuyu were not there. On certain farms at Londiani, owing to the depression, there are no Europeans now. One might as well say that those farms do not belong to the Europeans now."

[6] Huxley, *op. cit.*, Vol. I, pp. 72–73.
[7] *Report of the Kenya Land Commission*, p. 187.
[8] *Ibid.*, Appendix 8.

"trekked" into the Uasin Gishu Plateau, at that time a no man's land not effectively occupied by any single group. They succeeded in establishing a distinct enclave in the Highlands centering around the new town of Eldoret. The frontier of settlement also expanded over the old Fort Ternan boundary and into the lowland country near Lake Victoria—below the 5,000-foot marker often used incorrectly as the boundary of the White Highlands. By the end of World War I, the entire railway line from east of Kiu almost to Kisumu, on the lake, ran through land alienated for European settlement, and branch lines were planned or under construction to serve other zones of new settlement, such as in the Thika area northwest of Nairobi.

The end of the war marked the beginning of still another phase of European settlement aimed at doubling the European population of almost ten thousand then living in Kenya. The key feature of this phase was the role played by the Ex-Soldier Settlement Schemes. Under the terms of these schemes, a demobilized British soldier could receive farms of up to 160 acres free of purchase price on a 999-year lease at the annual rent of ten cents of a rupee per acre, with larger blocks available on purchase. As a result, over 2,880,000 acres of land were added to the sphere of European settelment, which by 1925 encompassed over twelve thousand square miles.[9]

Trans-Nzoia, Laikipia, and the Mount Kenya (Nanyuki) area received the bulk of their settlers during this period as did several areas along the railway line beyond the old Kiu–Fort Ternan boundary. Despite the fact that the Crown Lands Ordinance of 1915 had further guaranteed African rights to their land, new areas were opened up for settlement on recognized "tribal" land in the Kericho-Sotik, Kaimosi and Kipkarren, and northern Trans-Nzoia areas. Rents on some of this land, however, were paid to the Local Native Councils.

The rationalization of establishing buffer zones was especially evident during this period. As the following quotations indicate, however, it accompanied settlement in nearly all parts of Kenya during every stage of growth.

The Sotik Area: . . . an area of "guerilla warfare . . . between the Kipsigis and the Kisii . . .

in the strip of Sotik farms which the government surveyed in 1906 and gave out with the idea of forming a buffer of this no man's land."[10]

The Kedong Valley: "The area alienated to Europeans—some 80,000 acres—was given out in the early days as buffer farms to discourage raiding between the Masai and Kikuyu.[11]

The area between Muhoroni and Kisumu: "Before the laying of the railway line, it is probable that a few Jaluo lived near the Nandi escarpment, but it is certain that it was chiefly a fighting ground between the Nandi and Luo and, near Kibos, between Luo themselves. . . . When the railway reached Kisumu in 1902 it is certain that it was made the boundary, and any natives between the line and the escarpment were moved back to make way for the Indian farms which were made open for alienation in 1903."[12] "It was a kind of no man's land."[13]

Kipkarren Farms: "My recommendation is that the area . . . be given over to European settlement before Masai occupation is confirmed by time."[14]

Kaimosi: "The two Europeans reported to Mr. Ainsworth that Kaimosi was excellent coffee land. Subsequently the present farms were surveyed, the idea being that they should form a buffer between the Nandi and the Kavirondo."[15]

Kiambu: "In travelling through the Kikuyu country south of the Thika [River], the main point that strikes the traveller is the sparsity of population and the large areas of good land uncultivated; it is very evident indeed that there is ample room for very extensive settlement in the country without in any way unduly encroaching on native rights or native occupation."[16]

"It has been alleged that the alienation of this land (i.e., the eastern portion of southern Kiambu) constitutes a serious blot on the administration; that the Kikuyu were thereby robbed of their best land. This, however, is only a half-truth, as much of the land so allocated was a buffer zone between the Masai and the Kikuyu."[17]

[10] W. R. McGeagh, "Short History of the Kipsigis," Memorandum Before the Kenya Land Commission, Evidence and Memoranda, Vol. III, p. 2406.

[11] R. Stephens, Memorandum Before the Kenya Land Commission, Evidence and Memoranda, Vol. II, p. 1257.

[12] H. R. Montgomery, ibid., p. 2289.

[13] Rev. Monsignor Brandsma, ibid., p. 2177.

[14] Report of Colonel Watkins in 1912, quoted in Montgomery, op. cit., p. 2290.

[15] Kaimosi Farmers Association, ibid., p. 2275.

[16] Letter, dated September 22, 1902, from Mr. John Ainsworth, Sub-Commissioner, Ukamba Province, to Mr. Jackson, Acting Commissioner, Report of the Kenya Land Commission, p. 48.

[17] C. W. Hobley, Kenya: From Chartered Company to Crown Colony (1929), p. 140.

[9] Huxley, op. cit., Vol. II, pp. 54–56.

Similar claims were made in establishing the town of Maseno, near the border of Luo and Luhya, and in the mile-wide strip along both sides of the railway between the Masai and Kamba.

In 1920, when the East African Protectorate (minus the Coastal Strip, which remained a protectorate) became Kenya Colony, the outlines of the White Highlands were already established. Two years later, the Lands Department reported that there was practically no land left for further alienation. Soon afterward, the Natives Reserves were gazetted, or formally delimited. The break with the old railway limits was now complete, but it was not long before the new settlers began clamoring for—and receiving—branch lines and roads to serve their areas. The pioneer era of settlement was over—the era of development and change had just begun.

The final touch in the formal establishment of the White Highlands came with the Report of the Kenya Land Commission in 1933–34. At that time, the total amount of alienated land in the Colony was 10,345 square miles, *less than 12 per cent of which was under cultivation.* Forty per cent consisted of grazing land, 20 per cent was occupied by African squatter-laborers, and *nearly 28 per cent was unoccupied.* Even after the report expanded the size of the Highlands to 16,700 square miles, one quarter of which was Crown Forest, the total European farming population did not exceed 5,000. In contrast, the African population of the Highlands totaled nearly 150,000 excluding those in towns.[18]

The Native Reserves comprised fifty thousand square miles, or about 22 per cent of the total area of Kenya, and contained 2,587,000 Africans—86 per cent of the Colony's population. And nearly 60 per cent of this was concentrated in two large clusters of reserves adjacent to the eastern and western borders of the Highlands, in the Kikuyu and Kavirondo (Luo, Luhya, and Kisii) areas (Figure 6).

Despite these disparities of population, the Highlands were almost always mapped as a European area, a white "reserve" on a par with the African units. The existence of large stretches of "unused land" so close to the overpopulated reserves, however, initiated the

processes of change which were eventually to culminate in the independence of African-governed Kenya in 1963, very much as the existence of large stretches of unused land had stimulated the intrusion of European settlement. Once no more than an idea, the White Highlands became the dominant element in the political, economic, and cultural development of Kenya.

Filling in an Economic Niche: The Asian Trader and Merchant

Another element to be noted in the complex picture of settlement in Kenya is the role of the Asian population. Asians (a term locally used to refer to inhabitants of the Indian subcontinent but not to Arabs) were living along the East African coast since the time of Christ, serving mainly as moneylenders to the Arab trading population. But like the Arabs, the Asians did not begin to move far into the interior until the nineteenth century, when a few merchants settled in Uganda and Machakos.

The major force behind the spread of the Asian population inland and their increase in numbers was the construction of the Kenya-Uganda Railway. Owing to the inefficiencies of local manpower, over 32,000 Indian coolies were imported as laborers and about 6,000 chose to remain in Kenya at the end of their contracts. Of these, only 2,000 remained with the railway while the others wandered off, many into remote sections of the country, as merchants and traders.[19] The railway also acted to draw the coastal Asian population into the interior as traders and financiers and to attract larger numbers of migrants from India. From less than 5,000 prior to 1900, the Asian population grew to 25,000 in 1913.[20]

Although some thought was given to large-scale Asian settlement in Kenya during the period of railway construction, the beginning of European land alienation soon resulted in the closing of the Highlands to Asian cultivators. In 1903, Sir Charles Eliot recommended racial segragation in connection with the alienation of farm land and requested that no large grants be given to Asians between Kibwezi and Fort Ternan. The only areas available to Asian cultivators, therefore, were in the lands below 5,000 feet beyond the two

---

[18] Figures are taken from the report of the Commission and from the Kenya Department of Agriculture, *Annual Report,* 1933.

[19] George Delf, *Asians in East Africa* (1963), p. 11.
[20] *Report of the East African Royal Commission, 1953–1955,* Cmd 9475 (1955), p. 38.

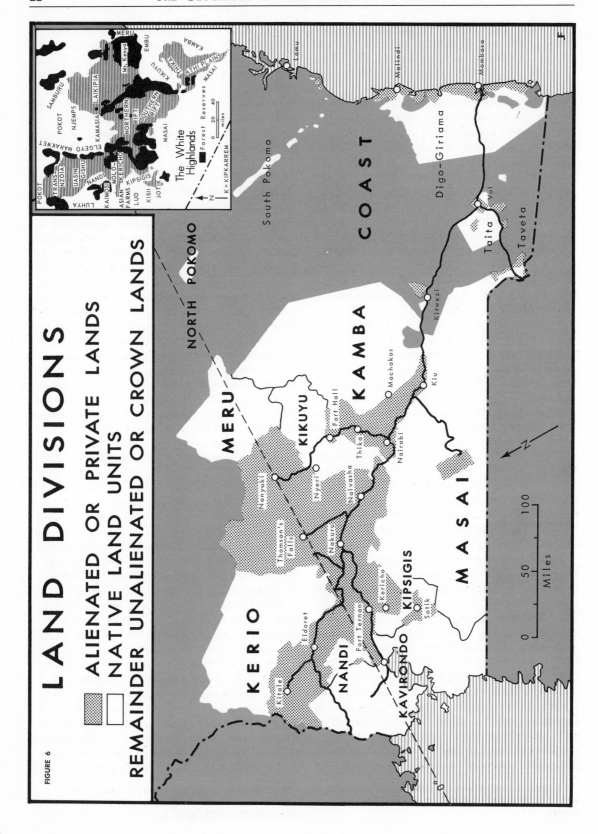

FIGURE 6

LAND DIVISIONS

ALIENATED OR PRIVATE LANDS
NATIVE LAND UNITS
REMAINDER UNALIENATED OR CROWN LANDS

boundary stations of the Highlands. Between 1905 and 1910, about sixty farm plots were taken up by Asians in the Kibos-Muhoroni area and, other than a few plots near Nairobi and along the coast, these remained the heart of Asian settlement in Kenya. In fact, the European efforts to guarantee their exclusive occupance of the Highlands were aimed primarily at preventing Asian settlement in that area.[21]

Restricted from playing a major role in agriculture, the Asians became concentrated in the towns and trading centers, filling an economic vacuum between the European farmers and administrators and the African masses. It is difficult to measure the importance of the Asian trader-merchant as a modernizing agent, but in many areas of Kenya the only contact the African had with a non-African culture was through the Indian *duka*, or shop, and in nearly all of Kenya the closest outside contact of the African was with the Asian. In the towns, the Asian held most of the lower administrative and clerical posts and virtually monopolized retail trade. The pronounced economic gap between the African and European populations in Kenya thus became rapidly filled by the Asians.

A EUROPEAN ISLAND IN AN AFRICAN SEA— THE BEGINNINGS OF TRANSITION

If the pre-European pattern of cultural geography could be characterized by islands of dense agricultural settlement in a sea of pastoralism, that which emerged with the establishment of the White Highlands was one of clusters of islands, both agricultural and pastoral, embedded in a matrix of European alienated land. The main lines of communication, transportation, and administration, focusing on the new urban centers and settled areas, provided the nexus for the transition from traditional to modern ways of life. At the same time, the spatial structure of social communications and the spatial relations between European and African areas guided this transition and helped produce the areal and societal differentiation in levels of modernization which exist today.

[21] A brief chronology of Asian settlement prior to the White Paper of 1923 on the "Indian Question" can be found in the *Evidence* to the Kenya Land Commission, Vol. III, pp. 2863–64.

The drawing of rigid administrative boundaries where there had been only zones of transition or no fixed boundaries at all created a new and in many ways stronger system of cells than had existed in traditional society. The most immediate effect was the strengthening of broad ethnic identities at the expense of other forms of affiliation. The distinctions between the Karura and the Gaki clans, for example, were largely subsumed under the general title Kikuyu, while the Tiriki, Tsotso, and Kusu began to think of themselves more strongly as a single group—the Luhya—than ever before.

This amalgamation and integration was typical of the reaction of traditional society in Kenya to outside competition—a competition which soon appeared to be virtually omnipresent, extremely powerful, and permanent. It became clear to many traditional leaders that changes were occurring and that these changes were being directed and controlled through the new administrative structure of the country. A more effective way to participate in these developments was to bring about a reorientation of traditional society around these new units.

While the fragmentation which characterized traditional society in Kenya was being reduced, however, the differences among the new groupings increased as each felt the impact of modernization to varying degrees. The broad result was, as has happened so often in colonial history, a shift in the pre-contact balance of power away from the aggressive, mobile pastoralists to the sedentary agriculturalists, who were more easily affected by the forces of change.

But even among the agricultural peoples, some became exposed to and changed by these forces to a greater extent than others. Such factors as proximity to the White Highlands, degree of land hunger and overpopulation, and the nature and adaptability of traditional political cultures acted to create wide differences among the more settled peoples in the intensity of their participation in the emerging modern social system. The roots of what is commonly called "tribalism" in Kenya today lie more in this uneven and rigidly compartmentalized impact of modernization than in any set of traditional ethnic differences.

An interesting by-product of these forces has been the growth of new ethnic subdivisions based upon the superimposed administrative units. There are "Nyeri," "Fort Hall," "Kiambu," and even "Nairobi" and "Rift Valley" Kikuyu; "Central Nyanza" and "South Nyanza" Luo; and "Machakos" and "Kitui" Kamba, each of whom attaches particular characteristics to members of each unit.[22]

The impact of this new political partitioning of Kenya was felt most strongly in the African reserves, especially those most intimately connected with the centers of European society. The more remote areas in the old Northern Province, occupied by the Turkana, Samburu, Somali, Galla, and related groups, were not organized into reserves and have remained beyond the zone of effective western contact even to the present (see Figure 6).

The growth of European settlement in the Highlands also shifted the main generators of modernizing forces away from the coast, which had for centuries undergone the greatest changes owing to extra-African influences. Kenya became one of the rare cases of an African state bordering the ocean in which the coastal population did not play a leading role in the process of modernization.

The superimposition of a Western infrastructure of communication and administration therefore produced a series of far-reaching changes in traditional society. Ethnic identity was increased as formal administrative structures were created that spanned an entire ethnic group often for the first time in its history, while at the same time the lack of interaction among these strengthened cells and the differential impact of modernization accentuated a new set of differences both among and within the major ethnic groups.[23]

---

[22] Interviewing Kikuyu brought about many interesting responses to this point. Almost unanimously, the Kiambu Kikuyu were characterized as the most economically and politically modernized and troublesome of the Kikuyu, the Fort Hall group as the most strongly traditional and resistant to change, beset by a multitude of petty politicians, and those from Nyeri as progressive, well-educated, and selectively traditional. Even greater "district" contrasts were found among the Kamba and Luo. Admittedly, these distinctions often reflect traditional tribal subdivisions, upon which the administrative structure was built, but they have now assumed new characteristics based upon the nature and extent of modernization.

[23] In many ways this is reminiscent of political change throughout the world. The growth of European nationalism similarly created greater unity within a series of strengthened cells but also increased diversity between the units

In addition, the creation of the White Highlands removed the major force which perpetuated the old cell-like system—the nearly ubiquitous pastoralist-agriculturalist conflict which acted to contain many groups within forest-fringed highland sanctuaries. The displacement of the Masai and the establishment of the Highlands created a vacuum which siphoned off hundreds of thousands of Africans from their traditional homelands to work for Europeans on the farms and in the towns. The extensive redistribution of population which followed provided the first major—and often irreversible—formal break with tradition and became one of the strongest forces behind the social mobilization of the African masses.

MODERNIZATION AND THE KIKUYU

The pull of the Highlands and the push from the reserves worked with varying intensity upon the peoples of Kenya, but a favorable combination of factors enabled the Kikuyu to dominate the history and geography of modernization even to the present. The reasons behind the pre-eminence of the Kikuyu are numerous and complex and, indeed, supply the theme for much more extensive investigation. However, the importance of just one factor—geographical position—should be emphasized; proximity to the major centers of European population, particularly Nairobi, may have been the required catalyst behind the rapid rate of mobilization and change among the Kikuyu.

The relatively straightforward impact of population pressure has frequently been considered critical to the Kikuyu move toward modernity. Parts of Kikuyuland even prior to British administration were clearly overpopulated and, as previously mentioned, the Kikuyu were in the process of migrating into the forests and grasslands surrounding their traditional homeland before the natural disasters of the late nineteenth century forced most to return.

More recently, particularly in the work of Rosberg and Nottingham, emphasis has been placed on the degree of achievement orienta-

---

themselves. The recent efforts at Western European integration can thus be compared, albeit on a different level, with the process of nation building in most of the new states of Africa and Asia, where attempts are being made to weave strands of community through a variety of ethnic units.

tion among the Kikuyu and the crosscutting linkages within their social organization which reached beyond the kinship group as explanations for the leading role the Kikuyu have played in the modernization process.[24] Of particular importance have been the dynamics of Kikuyu agricultural expansion, in which the desire for social status often forced the younger sons to break off from their kinship group to establish their own group on another piece of land. This budding-off process, stimulating and stimulated by an orientation toward achievement, reduced internal tensions among the Kikuyu by ameliorating the problem of status conflict. But this process could only be effective with an abundance of available agricultural land and a flexibility of territorial boundaries, both of which were severely curtailed with the growth of white settlement and the establishment of Native Reserves. As Rosberg and Nottingham point out, "In the absence of dramatic changes in cultural patterns, social structure, and agricultural productivity, the removal of the possibilities for acquiring extensive new land was to have critical consequences for the Kikuyu.[25]

Other reasons commonly used to explain Kikuyu pre-eminence relate to the above arguments in focusing upon the forces leading to the economic and social crises in Kikuyuland and the relative facility of Kikuyu social organization in adapting to these forces. Vigorous and early missionary activity, the reorientation of Kikuyu migrations into the European-settled area after the blockage of their traditional demographic frontiers, and the existence of a land tenure system approximating individual ownership are among the most frequently offered explanations.

There is no doubt that all these factors contributed to Kikuyu leadership, but it is suggested here that the unique geographical situation of Kikuyuland with respect to Nairobi and the major European farming areas was the necessary spark which kindled these other ingredients and thrust the Kikuyu into the modernizing vanguard.

The two early cores of settlement—around Nairobi and Nakuru—developed into major regional focuses within the Highlands, while the area between them became an important corridor of communications and transportation, initially through the railway and later, after World War II, along the first paved trunk road in the country. It was the differences in the hinterland of each focal area, however, which strongly affected the impact of European settlement upon the African population.

Northwest of Nakuru lay the Uasin Gishu and Trans-Nzoia plateaus, while to the northeast were the northern sections of the Rift Valley floor and Laikipia. Cradled between these two arms of highland settlement was the drier section of the Rift Valley floor and adjacent escarpments, sparsely occupied by Nilo-Hamitic pastoralists. Another large belt of settlement branched off to the southwest into the Kericho and Sotik areas, but the lowlands beyond Muhoroni on the railway line, closer to the dense agricultural populations of the Kavirondo reserve and including the Asian-settled areas, tended to focus more upon the lake port of Kisumu.

Radiating northward from Nairobi was a similar U-shaped pattern of settlement, one arm running through the western slopes of the Aberdares to Laikipia and the other stretching along the railway branch to Thika and, with a break, onto the western foothills of Mount Kenya and the Nanyuki area. But in contrast to the Nakuru-focused section of the Highlands, European settlement in the hinterland of Nairobi enclosed the densely populated agricultural lands of the Kikuyu on nearly all sides. The Kikuyu were the first to experience the full impact of European penetration into the Highlands and came to experience it more intensely than any other tribe.

It is important to stress that proximity was more a catalyst than a cause. But nevertheless, had the Kikuyu been located somewhere in Kenya other than on the doorstep of Nairobi, encircled by some of the most productive areas of the White Highlands, it is extremely unlikely that they could have dominated the modernization of Kenya anywhere near the extent to which they have. Conversely, had another large group of settled agriculturalists, faced with problems of land shortage and overpopulation, been located in the area of Kikuyuland, would they have become the leaders in the social, economic, and political development of Kenya?

A full explanation for the leading role played

---

[24] Carl G. Rosberg, Jr., and John Nottingham, *The Myth of Mau Mau: Nationalism in Kenya* (1966).

[25] *Ibid.*, p. 152.

by the Kikuyu still awaits more intensive comparative investigation. The stress given to the inherent characteristics of Kikuyu social and political organization and behavior, particularly their emphasis on achievement and individual initiative, needs much more thorough testing, especially in a framework that includes such closely related groups as the Meru and Embu as well as the more distantly related Kamba, Kisii, Taita, and Luhya. Similar cross-ethnic studies must be made of several other factors suggested as contributors to Kikuyu pre-eminence. It must be established that these characteristics were much more highly developed among the Kikuyu than among any of the other peoples of Kenya and are causally related to rapid social change.

Traditional differences in social and political organization and behavior have by no means been unimportant. Indeed, any comprehensive explanation of the varieties of response to modernization among the peoples of Kenya must rest largely on these differences. What is suggested, however, is that the advantages of geographical position afforded the opportunity for leadership, and it must be clearly demonstrated that other explanatory factors are not themselves consequences of locational advantages.

This argument has important implications for social science research on modernization. All too often, traditional African societies and their role in the modernization process have been examined without adequate consideration of the frequently critical intervening variable of location, particularly with respect to the pattern of early colonial contact and growth. It is usually assumed that a given society would respond in the same way had it been located elsewhere in the territory under investigation. It is hoped that this brief discussion has helped to point out the necessity to view modernization from a spatial perspective and to recognize the role of geographical position in the complex interplay of forces producing societal variations in levels of modernization throughout the developing world. In the following chapters, this theme will be returned to as the patterns of modernization in Kenya are examined in greater detail.

IV

The Development of Transportation and Communications

The previous chapters have presented a broad background to the origins and evolving spatial patterns of modernization as they reflected the uneven impact of Western contacts on the traditionally organized societies in Kenya. Chapters IV and V aim at breaking down the more general processes of change into their major component elements, to note briefly their individual patterns of evolution, and to present their contemporary development. These chapters will be followed by a statistical reintegration of these elements into summary "dimensions" of modernization and an analysis of some of the causes and consequences of variations in their areal magnitude.

THE TRANSPORTATION NETWORK

Taaffe, Morrill, and Gould have noted that: "In the economic growth of underdeveloped countries a critical factor has been the improvement of internal accessibility through the expansion of a transportation network. This expansion is from its beginning at once a continuous process of spatial diffusion and an irregular or sporadic process influenced by many specific economic, social and political forces."[1] Although their stress was on economic development, many of their conclusions and methods of analysis are applicable to other aspects of transition in the developing world.

The First Phase: Ports and Caravan Routes

The sequence of transport growth in Kenya is comparable to that in most underdeveloped countries, and, with some modifications, to the model outlined by the above mentioned authors. For more than a thousand years prior to effective European contact, no part of East Africa moved much beyond the first phase of

transport growth, characterized by a series of coastal trading centers with limited hinterlands. In Kenya, such ports as Vanga, Mombasa, Kilifi, Malindi, Lamu, and Patta dotted the coast, to a large degree independent from one another and in frequent conflict over the control of the coastal trade (see Figure 7).

With the growth of caravan trade several lines of contact were established with the interior, and new changes in traditional African societies began to take place. Some areas were strengthened by increased contact with the coast, while others were severely weakened as Arab and Swahili influences disrupted traditional social systems. Certain peoples, like the Kamba, found in the caravan trade the opportunity to spread well beyond their homelands and settle throughout wide areas of East Africa.

During the last half of the nineteenth century, a new agent—the European—entered the slowly evolving circulatory system. Coming first as explorers and missionaries and later as traders, administrators, and colonizers, the Europeans succeeded in gaining control over the development of communications and transportation and guided this development according to a set of objectives and a technology much different from that of the coastal peoples. One of the first steps in this process was the establishment of telegraph and postal connections between the coast and Western Europe.[2] This was followed by a series of developments which transformed communication patterns in the interior as well as on the coast and brought the northern half of East Africa under British influence and control.

The combination of European contact and the impact of increased caravan trade resulted in the growth of certain coastal ports at the expense of the others. In Kenya, Mombasa, Lamu, and to some extent Malindi, each

---

[1] Edward J. Taaffe, Richard L. Morrill, and Peter R. Gould, "Transport Expansion in Underdeveloped Countries," *Geographical Review* (1963), p. 503.

[2] Regular mail deliveries to Zanzibar commenced in 1872, and in 1877 telegraph connections were established.

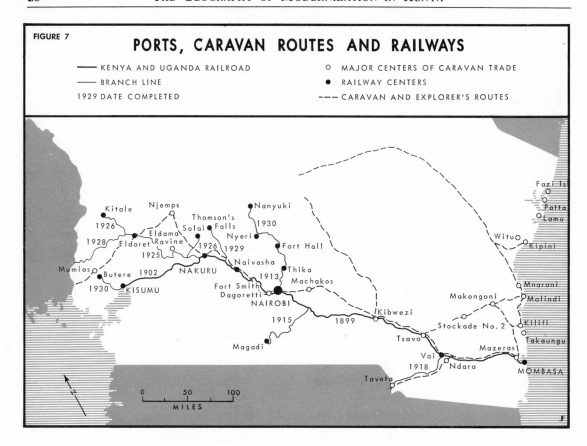

FIGURE 7

PORTS, CARAVAN ROUTES AND RAILWAYS

——— KENYA AND UGANDA RAILROAD   ○   MAJOR CENTERS OF CARAVAN TRADE
——— BRANCH LINE   ●   RAILWAY CENTERS
1929 DATE COMPLETED   – – – CARAVAN AND EXPLORER'S ROUTES

on or near the starting point of trade routes into the interior, far outstripped the other ports in size and, as evidence of their importance, the three were connected in 1895 by Kenya's first telegraph line.

The caravan trade and especially the entry of the Imperial British East Africa Company into the area between Mombasa and the lake region also created a number of important trading posts and revictualing stations in the interior, particularly at Mumias, Machakos and Eldama Ravine. Thus the characteristics of the second stage of transport growth—port concentration, lines of penetration, and the growth of small nodes along these lines—had begun to appear even before the turn of the century.

Railways and the Spread of British Administration

The construction between 1895 and 1902 of the Kenya-Uganda Railway, more than anything that preceded it, signaled the start of the second growth stage, a stage in which "the development of a penetration line sets in motion a series of spatial processes and re-adjustments as the comparative locational advantages of all centers shift."[3] Although it nearly paralleled the caravan route for most of its course, the railway produced its own nodes which superseded the old ones in importance.

Upcountry administration shifted from Machakos to Nairobi, which was established because of its location on the last stretch of level ground before the Highlands. Nakuru, similarly located with respect to the western Rift escarpment, and Naivasha replaced Eldama Ravine and the Lake Baringo area the main centers in the Highlands; and Kisumu, the terminus of the railway, soon eclipsed Mumias in importance.[4]

Although Mombasa had already begun to

---

[3] Taaffe, et al., op. cit., p. 506.

[4] Mumias stands today as a reminder of the great changes brought about by the railway. Formerly a bustling focus for trade and travel throughout the area north of Lake Victoria, with scores of shops, it is now merely a minor administrative center consisting of a handful of *dukas*, a hospital, and some schools.

dominate the coast of Kenya, the railway so solidified its position that the other coastal ports were able to retain only a small part of their former significance. Lamu was particularly affected. Although it remains today a town of nearly six thousand people, it is a distinct anachronism in modernizing Kenya, a quaint Arab port largely serving the coastal dhow traffic and "off limits" to the automobile.

The years following the completion of the Kenya-Uganda Railway saw the spread of government, the growth of European settlement, and eventually the establishment of the White Highlands and Native Reserves. The earliest "protectorate" treaties were made with the coastal peoples, but effective administration really spread with the railway—to the Ulu Kamba in 1897, the Kikuyu in 1895–98, to the Kavirondo population after the transfer of Uganda's Eastern Province in 1902, and to the Masai in 1904. Punitive expeditions were made to the Sotik area (1905), Embu (1906), Kisii (1907), Turkana (1910, 1916) and to the coastal Giriama (1914–15), whose acquiesence had probably been taken for granted with the new orientation to the Highlands. The last areas to be brought under some administrative control were the Northern Frontier District and Jubaland, though this control has always been weak and tenuous.[5]

During the years of the East African Protectorate, the interior nodes increased in size and importance as feeder lines were constructed, connecting them with major European farming areas and smaller administrative centers. Nairobi, in fact, came to dominate the entire country and functioned more like the great coastal hubs of West Africa as the primary node and center for the diffusion of modernization. For centuries the main locus for extra-African culture contact, the coast now became a neglected backwater, and the focus of modernization in Kenya shifted to the southwestern quadrant of the country. Except for this area, only Mombasa remained important as the economic outlet for Kenya, Uganda, and parts of Tanganyika.

The third phase of transport growth, distinguished by the development of feeder lines and lateral interconnections, was concentrated in the Highlands. Settlement spread beyond the railway, generally following the estab-

lishment of strong administration over nearby ethnic groups, and soon new lines were constructed to connect these areas with the main trunk (see Figure 7).

The branch to tap the soda ash deposits of Lake Magadi was completed in 1915. The Nairobi-Thika line was opened in 1913 and was extended to Fort Hall, Nyeri, and Nanyuki by 1930. Additional branches were built to Solai (1926), Thomson's Falls (1929), and Butere (1930), while the line to the Uasin Gishu, completed in 1925, was extended to Kitale in 1926 and two years later became part of the major trunk railway to Uganda.

Another line was proposed through Kericho to Sotik, but by 1931 railway construction in Kenya was completed and no new lines have been built since. Of all the branch lines built before 1931, only the Voi-Taveta link with the Northern Line of Tanganyika, built for strategic purposes during the war, was located outside the southwestern quadrant of Kenya.

The railways established the general urban pattern of Kenya, fostering the growth of important centers at key points along their route. The even spacing of these centers reflects the weak influence of local economic factors in initial urban growth, for nearly all were within 100- to 125-mile jumps from one another. Starting from Mombasa, there is Voi, Kibwezi-Makindu, Nairobi, Nakuru, Kisumu (somewhat farther because of the importance of towns such as Njoro, Molo, and Lumbwa in the early settlement core), Eldoret, and Nyeri. In the Highlands, nearly all the other major towns lie at approximately half this distance (50 miles or so) between those previously mentioned: Fort Hall, Nanyuki, Naivasha, Thomson's Falls, Eldama Ravine (just off the railway between Nakuru and Eldoret), Kitale, Bungoma, and Lumbwa.

The Road Network and the Consolidation of Control

During the early period of European colonization, roads played a very minor role in passenger transportation. The first roads to convey wheeled traffic were between Mombasa and Kibwezi (Mackinnon Road) and between Kibwezi and Kisumu (Sclaters Road), paralleling the proposed route of the railway. Except for some stretches west of Nairobi, they fell into disuse after the railway was complteed.

In 1908 (Figure 8A), there were only 510

---

[5] Jubaland was transferred to Italian Somaliland in 1923.

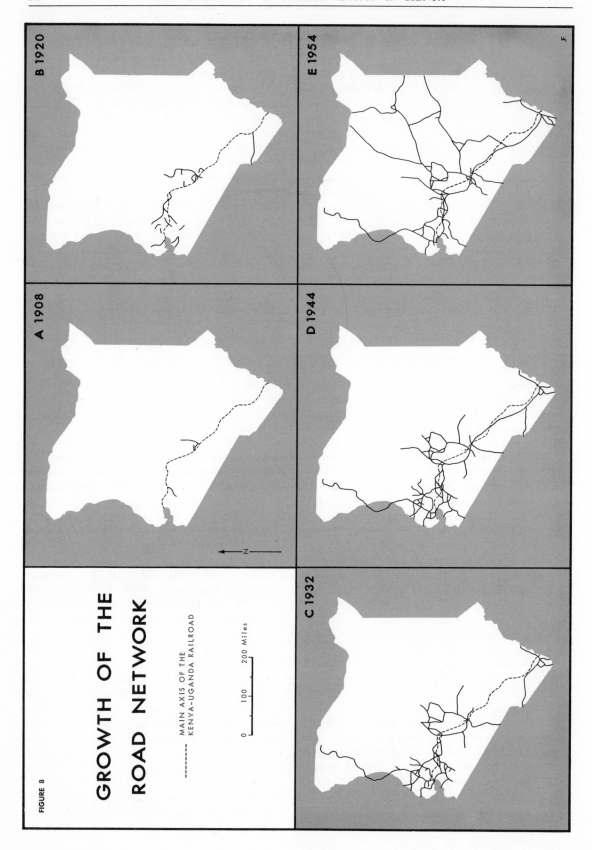

FIGURE 8

GROWTH OF THE
ROAD NETWORK

------ MAIN AXIS OF THE
       KENYA-UGANDA RAILROAD

0   100   200 Miles

A 1908

B 1920

C 1932

D 1944

E 1954

miles of motorable earth roads, the most important of which were Nairobi-Fort Hall, running through the edge of Kikuyu country, and Lumbwa-Kericho.[6] But after 1908, the road network began to play an increasing part in the relative growth and proliferation of urban centers throughout the country.

Between 1908 and World War I, nearly fifteen hundred miles of motorable roads were added, in part to provide additional administrative connections but primarily to serve the growing areas of European settlement. Several townships had already been gazetted, and the government provided them with improved road facilities. The Fort Hall road was extended to Nyeri, and the Uasin Gishu was connected to Nakuru by an all-weather road. Other shorter roads were constructed largely within the two early cores of settlement connecting new farmland with the emerging urban centers.

There was little road construction during the war years other than for military purposes: for example, the Voi-Taveta road paralleling the railway (Figure 8B). With the inception of the Ex-Soldier Settlement Schemes, however, a veritable explosion of the road network took place. By 1923, the road mileage passable to wheeled vehicles had doubled and in five more years had doubled again, to over 8,800 miles.[7]

A great many of the new roads were feeders to the railway and at first primarily in the European-settled area, but after 1923 there was a rapid increase of construction in the Native Reserves in an effort to open up the districts for labor supplies and more effective administrative control. Links were established to Narok and Kajiado in Masai country and to the areas of the Embu, Meru, Kamba (both Kitui and Machakos), Kisii, Luo, and Luhya. It is important to note that Kikuyuland was already served by good roads leading to Nairobi and the Rift Valley. By 1928, nearly 60 per cent of the road network was located in the African areas (Figure 8C).

Other forms of communication also developed rapidly. The mileage of telephone wires in exchange areas increased from 800 in 1914 to 5,750 in 1931.[8] Newspapers found their way into more African homes than ever before, and greater numbers of Africans were getting a taste of town life and education.

It was during this period of rapid communications development that African political activity first began. The European population had formerly operated with almost complete political freedom owing to its lack of contact with the masses and to the absence of large numbers of educated and mobilized Africans. The Asians in the towns and trading centers provided the only local check to the administration and were quite instrumental in preventing the settlers from establishing a South African form of government in Kenya. But with the greater opportunity for social communications stimulated by urban growth and the spread of Africans into the European farming areas, and with the physical development of the transportation and communications network, an organized African voice entered the scene.

The remainder of the interwar years saw relatively little road construction. Administrative roads were built to the Turkana and Samburu areas in the north, and some straightening out took place on the main routes south and northwest from Nairobi. Connections between the Nairobi- and Nakuru-focused settlement areas in the Mount Kenya and Laikipia districts were increased, tying the Kikuyu country even closer to the White Highlands. Similar lateral interconnections were constructed in Nyanza Province, and the outlines of a network of road transportation began to take shape (Figure 8D).

After World War II, the road network was filled in somewhat, important administrative roads were constructed to the Northern Frontier District, and road traffic rapidly began to surpass railway passenger flow in size and significance. Even earlier, the developmental role of the railway had been taken over by the road, quite fortunately for Kenya since nearly all the feeder railways constructed in other parts of East Africa after 1930 failed to fulfill the expectations of the developers.[9]

With the establishment of the Road Authority in 1951, new construction and main-

[6] Kericho is today the largest interior town in Kenya not on the railway.

[7] Data for all maps prior to 1950 are taken from the *Blue Book,* an annual statistical compendium published by the Colony and Protectorate of Kenya. The more recent maps are based on the annual Colonial Office reports on Kenya, which superseded the *Blue Book* in 1947.

[8] *Blue Book*, 1914 and 1931.

[9] See A. M. O'Connor, "New Railway Construction and the Pattern of Economic Development in East Africa," *Transactions of the Institute of British Geographers* (1965), pp. 21–30.

tenance became based on traffic density and on development actually taking place in the areas through which the roads passed. Planned improvement and intensification of the network were the major goals, while the opening up of new areas was relegated to a very minor position. Thus there were few new major arteries constructed between 1950 and 1958—except for administrative purposes, particularly in the northern and eastern sections of the country (Figure 8E).

Concurrent with the period of rapid African political development prior to independence in 1963, another great expansion in the road network took place. This construction had a dual character. For the first time, African local authorities tackled major road-building programs, primarily to serve cash crop producing areas in the former reserves.[10] At the same time, a large-scale project was initiated to improve the trunk network (Figure 9).[11]

Major local improvements took place in Kisii and Meru districts, where through traffic was not important but where expanding coffee and tea production required increased access to markets. Most were minor feeder roads and do not show up on the map of the contemporary road network, but these improvements did bring these relatively economically advanced districts into closer contact with the main centers of political activity and were one of the most important factors in moving the Kisii and Meru into the mainstream of modern African politics.

Since they were considered sufficiently isolated to assure that the quality of European-grown coffee would not be adversely affected and never supplied large numbers of laborers to the Highlands, the Kisii and Meru were the first groups in Kenya permitted to cultivate coffee. Economic development increased fairly rapidly, and Kisii and Meru Districts have consistently been leaders in African cash crop income. But their very isolation, relative economic contentment, and lack of grievances prevented the Kisii and Meru from playing major political roles before the last fifteen years.

Another aspect of postwar road development has been the intensification of certain high-priority connections, particularly those radiating in all directions from Nairobi. The construction of surfaced, or bituminized, roads has created a subsystem of primary linkages indicative of the basic framework of social communications in Kenya. These linkages reflect the major flow lines of information, ideas, and people as well as of marketable goods (Figure 10).[12]

The first surfaced trunk road was built from Nairobi to Nakuru (97 miles) and, by 1952, 345 miles of bitumen roads had been completed. In the past ten years, one major building program has been implemented and another is underway. By early 1965, there were over 1,200 miles of surfaced roads along the major trunk routes and the beginnings of a bituminized system in the Kikuyu districts. One can now travel over 300 miles from Machakos to Endebess, in Trans-Nzoia, or from Nyeri to Nairobi, Kisumu, and Kakamega on hard surface. Figure 10 also shows those roads which are expected to be bituminized or improved under the terms of the present Economic Development Plan, 1964–1970.[13]

A surfaced road not only provides greater aid and comfort to private passenger traffic but also stimulates existing bus and transport operators and opens a new field for taxis and mini-buses. It is nearly impossible to obtain accurate information on bus and taxi traffic in Kenya, but there is no doubt that it is of considerable size and importance. Along the most well-traveled route, between Nairobi and Thika, public transport of some kind can be expected at the rate of one every four or five minutes during the average working day. Anyone who has traveled on the road would be surprised to learn that it is not even more frequent.

---

[10] The Native Reserves are now known as the Non-Scheduled Areas. The former White Highlands, in turn, became the Scheduled Areas after the administrative reforms of the early 1960's.

[11] Alastair Matheson, "Kenya's Trunk Roads," *Road International* (1963), pp. 50–52.

---

[12] Owing to the lack of data and their relatively minor role in the over-all transportation pattern in Kenya, no mention has been made of coastal traffic and the air network. The former still remains important as a means of communications within the Arab trading population along the entire East African coast, but total traffic has been declining in recent years. In contrast, the role of air transport has been increasing, particularly on the route between Nairobi and Mombasa, and will most likely play a much more important part in the circulatory system of Kenya in the near future. For a map of the major air routes and aerodromes in Kenya, see the *Atlas of Kenya*, compiled by the Survey of Kenya (1962), p. 29.

[13] Government of Kenya, *Development Plan, 1964–1970*, (1964), pp. 91–92.

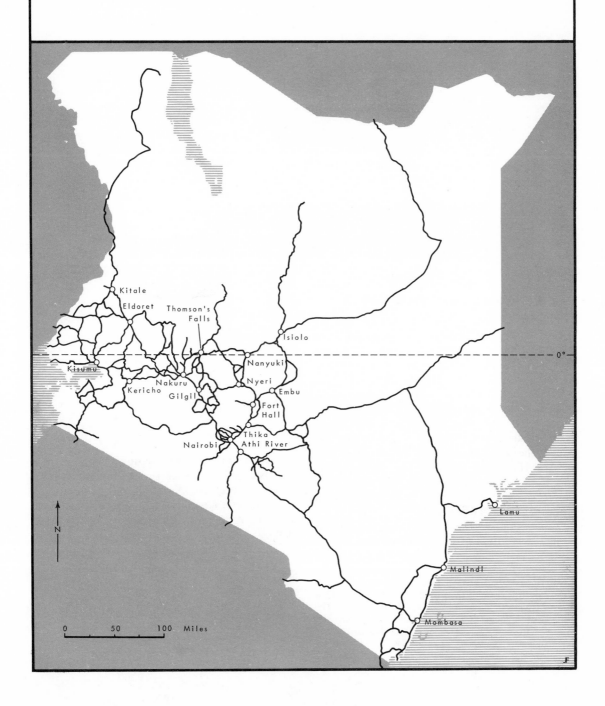

FIGURE 9

THE KENYA ROAD NETWORK, 1965

○ TOWNS OVER 5,000 POPULATION

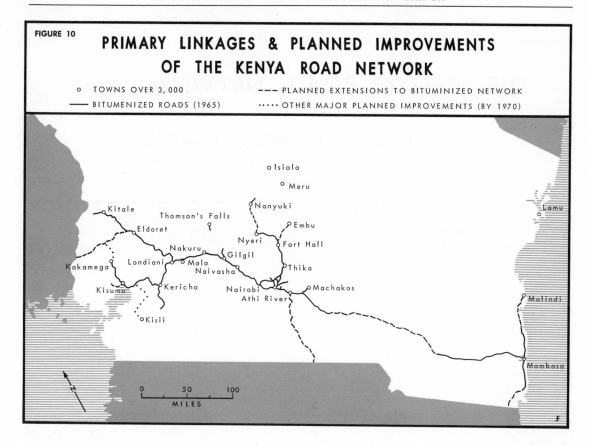

FIGURE 10

PRIMARY LINKAGES & PLANNED IMPROVEMENTS OF THE KENYA ROAD NETWORK

o   TOWNS OVER 3,000   - - - PLANNED EXTENSIONS TO BITUMINIZED NETWORK

——— BITUMENIZED ROADS (1965)   ····· OTHER MAJOR PLANNED IMPROVEMENTS (BY 1970)

Contemporary Patterns of Transport Flow

Figures 11 and 12 portray traffic flow on Kenya roads and railways at about the time of independence in 1963.[14] Figure 11 shows only those roads averaging more than 50 vehicles a day. Nairobi clearly dominates the over-all road network, with another major node at Nakuru and secondary nodes at Kitale, Eldoret, Kisumu, Kericho, Nyeri, and Mombasa. Nakuru provides the major bridge between the sub-networks in the Nyanza and Central Province regions, its characteristic role in the spatial structure of communications in Kenya. The coast again is clearly isolated from the rest of the country.

Table 1 ranks some of the major towns of Kenya according to the total number of ve-

TABLE I
AVERAGE DAILY ROAD TRAFFIC TO AND
FROM MAJOR TOWNS

Nairobi	10,950	Naivasha	2,349
Nakuru	3,573	Mombasa	2,074
Gilgil	2,859	Nyeri	1,651
Thika	2,821	Kitale	1,336
Kisumu	2,521	Kericho	1,261
Eldoret	2,455	Nanyuki	796

Source: Kenya Road Authority.

hicles entering and leaving during the average day. Nairobi has three times the traffic of its closest competitor, Nakuru, and traffic to and from Nairobi has a powerful effect on the flow pattern throughout the network. The most heavily traveled international road is that which crosses the Uganda border at Tororo.

Figure 12 displays some unexpected findings. Although Nairobi is still the most active center in terms of total traffic, the six stations along the small branch line between Kisumu and Butere (see inset) together generate and receive more passengers than the capital city. In fact, if the railway station at Kisumu Pier—serving the Lake Victoria traffic—were added

---

[14] Figure 11 is based on several maps published by the Kenya Road Authority as well as specific traffic counts from the Authority's files for the period 1961–63. Figure 12 is derived from a three-month sample (March, August, December) of stationmasters' accounts for every railway station in Kenya in 1963. The latter included origin and destination data as well. As far as is known, these maps are the most detailed yet published on road and railway passenger flow in Kenya.

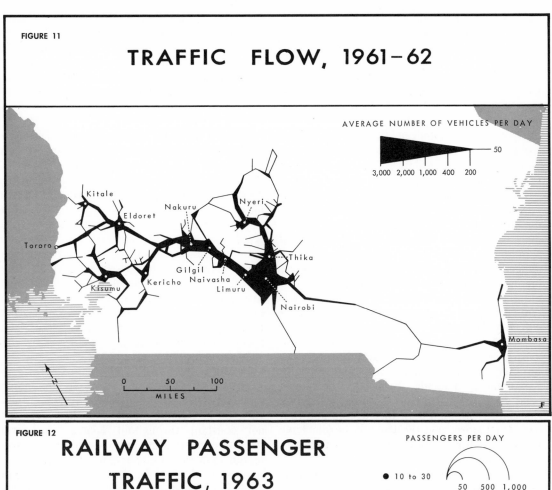

FIGURE 11

TRAFFIC FLOW, 1961–62

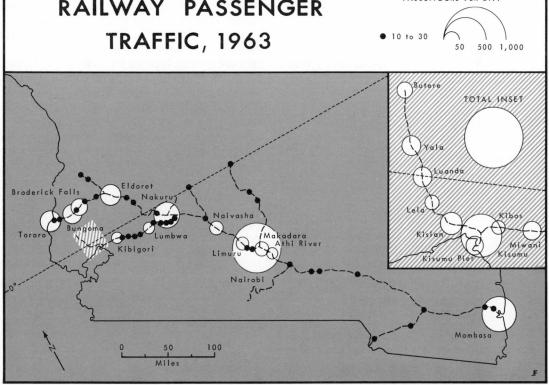

FIGURE 12

RAILWAY PASSENGER TRAFFIC, 1963

to the main Kisumu station, Kisumu itself would surpass Nairobi in total traffic.

The Butere branch was the only line built expressly to serve African commercial farmers. Although it is not nearly as important for freight traffic, the branch line is probably the most significant local sector of the Kenya railway network in passengers received and discharged per mile. Indeed, the Kisumu-Butere corridor must rank with Nairobi-Nakuru and Nairobi-Nyeri as primary lines of transport interaction in Kenya.

None of the other branch lines are important passenger carriers. This is particularly striking for the Central Province line, serving the densely populated area between Nairobi and Mount Kenya which has apparently come to depend more on roads for passenger movement. It is clear from a comparison of the two maps that the construction of good roads has tended to draw passengers away from the railway. The only other stretch with heavy railway passenger traffic is between Eldoret and Tororo, which is the last remaining gap in the bitumen network connecting Nairobi with Kampala, in Uganda. Similarly, no paved road yet exists north from Kisumu paralleling the railway, though both this stretch and that between Eldoret and the Uganda border have received high priority in the present Development Plan.

The importance of some of the small stations in western Kenya can be seen from Table 2, which shows average daily traffic over a three-month period in 1963.

TABLE 2
AVERAGE DAILY RAILWAY PASSENGER
TRAFFIC (MAJOR STATIONS)

Nairobi	506	Yala	76
Kisumu	463	Bungoma	74
Mombasa	277	Miwani	71
Nakuru	176	Luanda	70
Kisian	101	Kisumu Pier	68
Tororo (U)	100	Broderick Falls	54
(U) = Uganda			

Source: East African Railways and Harbours Administration, 1963.

COMMUNICATIONS AND MEDIA DEVELOPMENT

Postal Services

Postal service in Kenya had its origins as a branch of the Zanzibar Post Office and was initially restricted to the coast. With the construction of the railway, postal traffic at Mombasa

increased so rapidly that the combined Zanzibar and East African Protectorate services were transferred to the port in 1899. Similarly, growth in the interior resulted in the establishment of a new headquarters at Nairobi in 1909, thus completing the steplike shifts from Zanzibar to Mombasa to Nairobi which symbolized British penetration into East Africa.

Most of the early services were concentrated along the railway line but spread outward with the growth of European settlement. In 1919, there were 76 post offices and postal agencies, 30 of which were not on the railway. Of the latter, most were in Uasin Gishu, the area north of Nairobi, along the coast and in scattered administrative centers. By 1930, the number had increased to 126, but with the newly constructed branch lines, only 32 were off the railway. New facilities were established to serve other administrative centers and the expanded European settlement in Trans-Nzoia, Laikipia, and the Mount Kenya area. The postal facilities existing in 1919, 1930, and 1964 are shown in Figure 13A-C.[15]

In 1963, there were 240 postal facilities in Kenya, a ratio of one for every 36,000 people (as compared to 1:52,000 in Tanzania and 1:39,500 in Uganda). This ratio, however, was not constant throughout Kenya, the rural African areas tending to be much more poorly served than the White Highlands. Aiming for a ratio of 1:32,000, the East African Posts and Telecommunications Administration estimates that the former Nyanza Province (Luo, Luhya, Kisii, and Kipsigis) must have an additional 48 postal facilities, whereas the old European highland districts and the coast are "overserved," by 30 and 8 facilities respectively.[16]

Figure 14 shows average weekly figures for letters posted and received at all post offices and agencies in Kenya in 1963. The concentration in the southwestern quarter is again evident, as is the division there between the Nyanza and Nairobi-Kikuyu clusters of facilities and the importance of Nakuru in the corridor between them.

---

[15] Data for 1919 and 1930 were obtained from the *Blue Book* for those years. For 1963, the files of the East African Posts and Telecommunications Administration were used.

[16] *A Study of the Development of Postal Facilities in Rural Areas*, Special Report of the East African Posts and Telecommunications Administration, October 1, 1963 (mimeographed). It will be interesting to discover how well an African-controlled government redresses the inequalities of communication and transport facilities growing out of prolonged European administration and settlement.

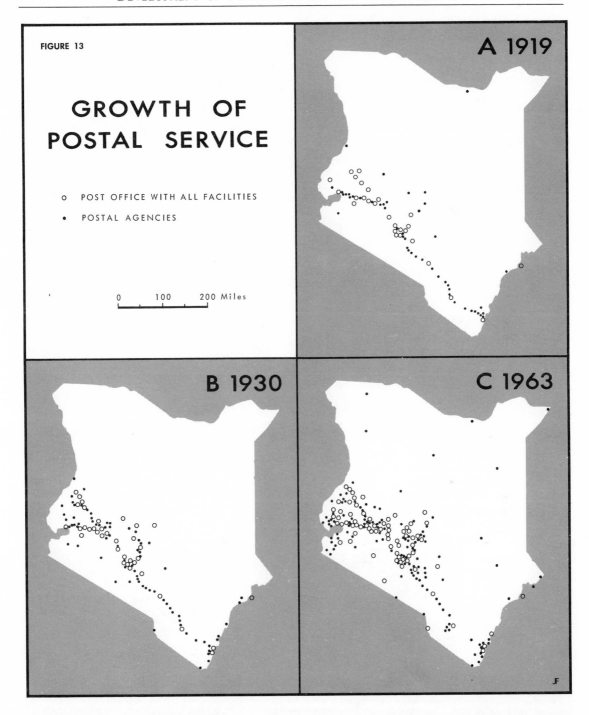

FIGURE 13

GROWTH OF
POSTAL SERVICE

o   POST OFFICE WITH ALL FACILITIES

•   POSTAL AGENCIES

0   100   200 Miles

A 1919

B 1930

C 1963

Table 3 gives the number of letters per person per week in each of the twenty-five towns with the greatest postal traffic. Of the larger towns in Kenya, Lamu, which is not included on the table, has the lowest per capita traffic, about .33 letters a week. Some of the higher per capita figures are found in Kiambu District (e.g., Kikuyu, Limuru, and Kiambu) and in the axis running northward from Kisumu along the Luo-Luhya boundary zone (e.g., Maseno and Yala). The postal facilities in these areas serve not only the small towns in which they are located but also the very dense rural population surrounding them, which was not included in determining the per capita ratios. Similarly, Nandi Hills, in an important tea-producing

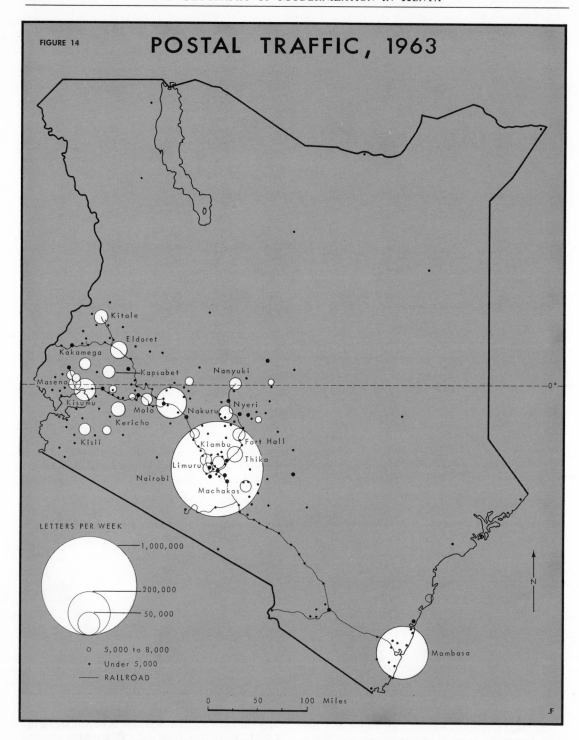

FIGURE 14

POSTAL TRAFFIC, 1963

LETTERS PER WEEK

— 1,000,000

— 200,000

— 50,000

o   5,000 to 8,000

·   Under 5,000

—   RAILROAD

0   50   100 Miles

area, and Kapsabet, the only town in Nandi District, also show large ratios. These figures reinforce many of the observations made earlier in the study on the spatial structure of the network of social communications and its areas of most intense development.

Telecommunications

The development of telecommunications in Kenya closely parallels the evolution of the postal and transport networks. The first telegraph line was constructed between Mombasa

TABLE 3

NUMBER OF LETTERS PER PERSON PER WEEK
IN 25 LARGEST POSTAL CENTERS

Name of Center	Total Postal Traffic	Ratio per Capita
Nairobi	988,595	3.7
Mombasa	296,734	1.7
Nakuru	86,839	2.3
Kisumu	51,909	2.2
Eldoret	37,766	1.9
Kitale	27,086	1.9
Nyeri	26,203	3.3
Kericho	24,746	3.2
Thika	22,480	1.6
Kapsabet	18,025	9.2
Molo	17,044	5.6
Kakamega	16,976	4.3
Machakos	16,344	3.8
Kisii	15,228	3.4
Fort Hall	15,012	2.8
Maseno	14,471	12.3
Kiambu	14,151	5.6
Nanyuki	13,962	1.3
Limuru	11,485	31.9
Thomson's Falls	10,758	2.0
Naivasha	10,480	2.2
Kikuyu	10,190	33.9
Nandi Hills	9,966	10.0
Yala	9,631	25.3
Sotik	9,477	7.9

Source: East African Posts and Telecommunications Administration, 1963.

and Lamu by the Imperial British East Africa Company in 1895. In the following year, it was decided that a telegraph line was necessary along the proposed route of the railway.

The building of the telegraph lines then preceded the railway, first to Kikuyu and in 1899 to Kisumu. A small connection was built in 1903 between Londiani Station and Eldama Ravine, and in the following years telegraph connections were extended along all the railway branches and to nearly all the administrative centers.

With the growth of a telephone network, however, the telegraph began to play a much smaller role than it did during the "railway era" before 1930. Today, only in the most remote sections of northern Kenya is the telegraph important. But even here its role has decreased rapidly since 1960, when radio-telephone service enabled isolated centers to be connected with any telephone exchange and thus superseded the telegraph as the major means of interdistrict communications.

The present distribution of telegraph facili-

ties consists of all those centers labeled "Post Office with all facilities" on Figure 13C, all the postal agencies on the railway, plus the following: Lokitaung, Lodwar, Maralal, Marsabit, Moyale, Mandera, Wajir, and Garissa in the northern districts; Kabarnet (Baringo), Timau (Nanyuki); and Witu, Vipingo, Kwale, Ukunda, and Gazi along the coast.

The earliest telephone installations, at Nairobi, Mombasa, and Kisumu, were initially for administrative purposes only, but were made available to public subscribers in 1908. The major exchanges in 1914, 1931, and 1945 are shown in Figure 15A-C. Major expansion took place during and after World War II when posts and telecommunications, lagging some fifteen or twenty years behind the transport network, began to develop significantly in the African areas.[17] Notice also the degree to which the growth of telecommunications took place as a diffusion from the two early settlement cores.

Figure 16 shows telephone traffic (trunk calls only) in 1963 from a nine-hour sample during the peak hours of flow, 9:00 A.M. to 12 noon week days. The pattern is similar to that for postal traffic except for the slightly weaker position of Nairobi and Mombasa and the higher proportions in some of the other major towns, notably Nakuru, Kisumu, and Nyeri, since only calls within Kenya are included.[18]

Another striking feature is the greater traffic in the eastern half of the southwestern quadrant as compared with the western sector, indicative perhaps of a generally greater intensity of circulation around Nairobi, particularly in the Kikuyu areas to the north.

TABLE 4

TOTAL TELEPHONE TRAFFIC
(NINE-HOUR SAMPLE CENSUS, 1963)

Nairobi	4882	Ruiru	412
Nakuru	1682	Naivasha	391
Mombasa	1265	Nanyuki	368
Kisumu	828	Kitale	367
Eldoret	579	Kericho	358
Nyeri	578	Molo	303

Source: East African Posts and Telecommunications Administration, 1963.

[17] Much of the expansion was due to the role of East Africa as the main transit center between northern and southern Africa during the war and to the requirements of the 1941 campaign in Ethiopia and Somalia.

[18] The postal figures included all items received and posted, whether internal or external.

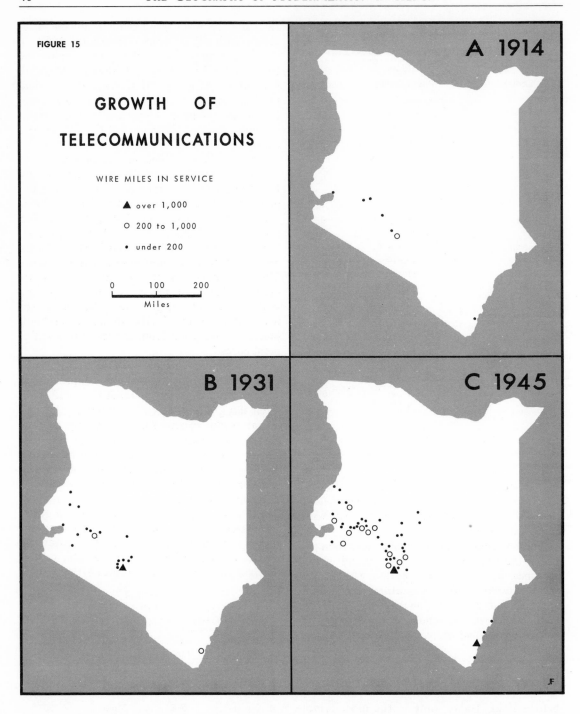

FIGURE 15

GROWTH OF
TELECOMMUNICATIONS

WIRE MILES IN SERVICE

▲ over 1,000

○ 200 to 1,000

• under 200

0   100   200
Miles

A 1914

B 1931

C 1945

The towns with the greatest telephone traffic are listed in Table 4. Most are in or adjacent to the former White Highlands, but in recent years the number of telephone receivers in the European farming areas has been decreasing as more and more settlers leave the country, while the opposite has been occurring in the major centers of African population.

Newspaper Circulation

Kenya's oldest established paper is the *East African Standard*, which began publishing in

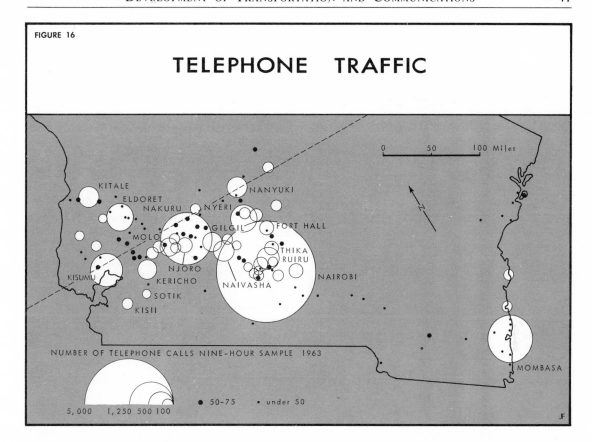

FIGURE 16

TELEPHONE TRAFFIC

NUMBER OF TELEPHONE CALLS NINE-HOUR SAMPLE 1963

5,000   1,250 500 100   ● 50-75   • under 50

1905.[19] It reigned supreme as the major European newspaper for over fifty years, during which time it served as the voice of Kenya's settlers. With the turning tide of African political development, it moved increasingly toward a more sympathetic treatment of African affairs and today is a staunch supporter of the government.

In addition to the *Standard* (daily circulation, 28,000; Friday edition, 44,000),[20] the same organization also published *Baraza* (weekly, 37,300), the first newspaper published in Swahili, founded in 1939.

In recent years, the need for a popular newspaper more closely oriented to the African has been largely filled by the East African Newspapers group. Since its foundation in 1959, by the Aga Khan, East African Newspapers has become the largest and probably most influential publishing group serving all of East Africa. Its main publications in Kenya include the *Daily Nation* (17,000), *Taifa Leo* ("the nation today," 21,300)—which is the only Swahili daily—and the weekly *Sunday Nation* (31,000) and *Taifa Kenya* (32,000).

Table 5 lists the major English, Asian, Swahili, and vernacular publications still in print in 1964, with their founding date and approximate circulation. Many important newspapers, including the KANU-controlled Kikuyu language *Wiyathi* (weekly, 10,000 in 1960), the Luo *Ramogi* (weekly, 4,000 in 1962), the English and Swahili monthly *Jicho* (5,000 in 1962), and the Asian weekly *Colonial Times* (5,000 in 1962) have ceased publication in recent years. Also omitted is the large number of Swahili and vernacular newspapers and newssheets spawned by and in turn stimulating the rapid rate of social mobilization of the African

---

[19] The paper was started in Mombasa by an Indian, A. M. Jeevanjee, in 1901 as the *African Standard*. It was purchased by a European two years later and renamed the *East African Standard* in 1905. See George Bennett, "Settlers and Politics in Kenya," in V. Harlow and E. M. Chilver (eds.), *History of East Africa*, Vol. II (1965), p. 267.

[20] Audit Bureau of Circulation figures for 1963. In 1964, the respective figures were 29,248 and 40,673 (*East African Standard*, October 21, 1964). All circulation figures in the text will be for 1963 unless otherwise stated.

TABLE 5

MAJOR NEWSPAPERS IN KENYA, 1964

(Weekly except Where Noted)

English	Established	Average Circulation per Issue
East African Standard (Friday)	1906	44,000
Sunday Nation	1960	31,000
*East African Standard	1906	28,000
*Daily Nation	1960	17,000
Sunday Post	1961	16,000
Kenya Weekly News	1931	6,300
Reporter (F)	1961	6,000
*Mombasa Times (ceased publication in 1966)	1916	4,800
Swahili		
Baraza	1939	33,000
Taifa Kenya	1958	32,000
*Taifa Leo	1960	23,000
Sauti Mwafrika	1962	15,000
Nyota Afrika (M)	1963	9,600
Mfanyi Kazi (also in English)	1962	3,000
Lengo	1964	?
Asian		
Africa Samachar (Gujerati)	1954	16,000
Kenya Daily Mail (Gujerati)	1927	3,500
*Kenya Daily Mail (Gujerati)	1927	2,500
Observer (Urdu and English)	1946	2,500
Africa Times (Gujerati)	1963	?
Vernacular		
Kiri-Nyaga (Kikuyu)	1959	10,000
Twi ba Meru (Meru)	1961	7,000
Nyanza Times (Luo and English)	1946	4,000
Wathiomo Mokinya (Kikuyu) (M)	1920	3,600
Piny Owacho	1963	?

(*) = Daily   (F) = Fortnightly   (M) = Monthly

Source: Registrar of Newspapers, Government of Kenya.

masses in the period after World War II, especially during the Mau Mau Emergency.[21]

---

[21] The role of the vernacular press in Mau Mau is examined perfunctorily in Colony and Protectorate of Kenya, *The Origins and Growth of Mau Mau: An Historical Survey* (1960), pp. 191–99. This survey is also known as the Corfield Report.

Figure 17 portrays the average weekly distribution of the leading English and Swahili newspapers in 1963.[22] The pattern is again similar to that for most measures of social communications in Kenya, with a marked concentration in the major towns and in the central and Nyanza regions. There is a tendency for Swahili newspaper circulation to be larger in the former reserve districts and English newspaper circulation to be larger in the major areas of European settlement, but this contrast is not as pronounced as might be expected. Swahili papers have been distributed primarily as an adjunct to the English language press and have only recently begun to establish distinct markets for themselves. Increasing circulation has been particularly rapid in the area north of Kisumu in recent years as the Swahili press has expanded into the less accessible but densely populated rural areas. This trend is likely to continue in the future.

Table 6 indicates the ten centers with the largest circulation of Swahili and English newspapers. In both cases, these ten centers account for about 70 per cent of the total circulation.

TABLE 6

NUMBER OF NEWSPAPERS PER WEEK

Swahili		English	
Nairobi	46,497	Nairobi	168,747
Mombasa	31,656	Mombasa	46,313
Nakuru	12,081	Nakuru	13,411
Kisumu	8,315	Kisumu	9,337
Nyeri	3,873	Eldoret	4,988
Kitale	3,180	Thika	4,201
Eldoret	3,100	Kitale	4,180
Kericho	2,845	Nyeri	3,350
Limuru	2,345	Gilgil	2,512
Kisii	2,266	Kericho	2,300

Source: Circulation Departments, East African Newspapers and East African Standard.

---

[22] The papers used were *Baraza* (weekly), *Taifa Leo* (six issues per week), *Taifa Kenya* (weekly), *East African Standard* (one weekly, five daily issues), *Sunday Nation* (weekly), *Daily Nation* (six issues per week), and the *Mombasa Times* (six issues per week). The *Mombasa Times* ceased publication in 1966. The figures were derived from detailed accounts of distribution supplied by the Circulation Departments of the newspapers involved. For the East African Newspapers group, these consisted of route slips given to the distributors who, by road, rail, and air, delivered papers throughout Kenya. The same data provides the basis for Table 6.

FIGURE 17

NEWSPAPER CIRCULATION: ENGLISH

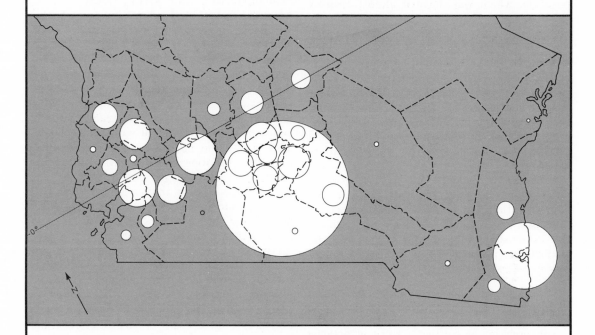

NEWSPAPER CIRCULATION: SWAHILI

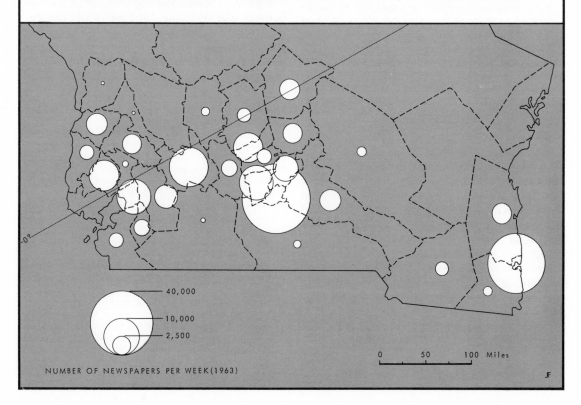

40,000

10,000

2,500

0   50   100 Miles

NUMBER OF NEWSPAPERS PER WEEK (1963)

Radio and Television

Broadcasting began in Kenya in 1929 with the British East Africa Broadcasting Corporation, which was devoted almost entirely to serving the small European population. In 1959, long after the African Broadcasting Service came into being, the two groups joined to form the Kenya Broadcasting Service, a government-controlled body. Three years later, K. B. S. was taken over by the Kenya Broadcasting Corporation, an independent consortium working in conjunction with the government, and in the same year television service, the first in East Africa, was introduced.[23]

In 1964, the independent African government again brought broadcasting under its administration and renamed the organization the Voice of Kenya. The explanation given for the establishment of V. O. K. reveals the critical role given to the mass media by the new states and deserves to be quoted:

> Kenya is a nation on her own and Government accepts that in a young country like Kenya, in her formative stages of development and faced with problems of creating a spirit of national unity among its different communities, the powerful media of radio and television, with their great influence on public opinion, should not be administered by an organization independent of the government. This might be permissible where such an organization was not tied to foreign interests and was completely free to interpret the feeling and aspirations of the nation as expected by the people and the country. The government is not convinced that the K. B. C., as presently constituted, could fully meet this expectation.[24]

The African government proceeded to set in motion plans to expand services throughout the country aimed at providing medium wave coverage for all the more densely populated parts of Kenya. At present, there are three main transmission centers, at Nairobi, Mombasa, and Kisumu, each broadcasting regional as well as national programs. The approximate range of these stations is shown on Figure 18. Nakuru, in its important position between the Nairobi- and Kisumu-focused clusters of pop-

ulation, is a small station with only fringe medium wave reception. Under the new plan, Timboroa, Nakuru, and Nyeri will be used as "launching pads" for V.H.F. transmission to proposed relay stations at Kisumu, Embu, Kericho, Eldama Ravine, Thomson's Falls, Nanyuki, Meru, Isiolo, Eldoret, Kitale, Bungoma, Mtito Andei, Voi, and Mombasa.[25]

In 1963, over forty thousand wireless and nearly five thousand television licenses were issued, and programs were broadcast in English, certain Asian languages, Arabic, Swahili, and nearly all the major vernacular languages. The radio has now become a powerful tool for promoting political participation and national integration in Kenya. Bennett and Rosberg have noted that during the 1960–61 election campaign, "It was consistently reported that the radio was able to reach more persons than were the newspapers." A K.B.S. survey had revealed that there were at least 52,000 African households with radio sets and an estimated African audience potential of over 275,000.[26] A recent AID survey of Elgon Nyanza reported that the radio was second only to the chief's *baraza,* or meeting, as a source of information on current events in Kenya and the rest of the world.[27]

Figure 19 shows the distribution of wireless licenses issued during 1963–64, while the distribution of television licenses for the same year is shown in Figure 18 along with existing and proposed broadcasting facilities. There are probably many more "bootleg" radios, especially transistors,[28] than are included on

[23] *East African Standard,* June 25, 1964.
[24] Government of Kenya, *Government Observation on the Report of the Lutta Commission of Inquiry into the Financial Position and Administration of the Kenya Broadcasting Company,* March, 1964, p. 5.

[25] *East African Standard,* July 3, 1964.
[26] G. Bennett and C. Rosberg, *The Kenyatta Election: Kenya 1960–1961* (1961), p. 219.
[27] *Elgon Nyanza,* survey conducted for the Agency for International Development by Marco Surveys, Ltd. (1962), pp. 54–56. The *baraza* is an extremely important source of information for the bulk of Kenya's population and an institution worthy of much more intensive study. The AID Survey, however, indicates that the *baraza* is most important as a source for local and district news but is surpassed by the mass media (newspapers and radio) for national and world news, particularly in the more economically developed and urban areas and where the level of education is high. It has not been possible to obtain detailed data on the spatial variation in the impact of the *baraza* and, with regret, it has been omitted from further analysis.
[28] For example, it was estimated by one source that in 1965 there were between 350,000 and 400,000 radios in Kenya. See William A. Hachten, "The Press in a One-Party State: Kenya Since Independence," *Journalism Quarterly* (1965), pp. 262–66.

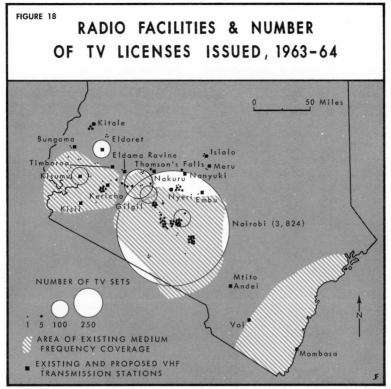

FIGURE 18

RADIO FACILITIES & NUMBER OF TV LICENSES ISSUED, 1963–64

0   50 Miles

Kitale
Bungoma
Eldoret
Eldama Ravine   Isiolo
Timboroa   Thomson's Falls Meru
Kisumu   Nakuru   Nanyuki
Kericho   Nyeri Embu
Kisii   Gilgil

Nairobi (3,824)

Mtito
Andei

Voi

Mombasa

NUMBER OF TV SETS

·   ·   ○   ◯
1   5   100   250

AREA OF EXISTING MEDIUM
FREQUENCY COVERAGE

EXISTING AND PROPOSED VHF
TRANSMISSION STATIONS

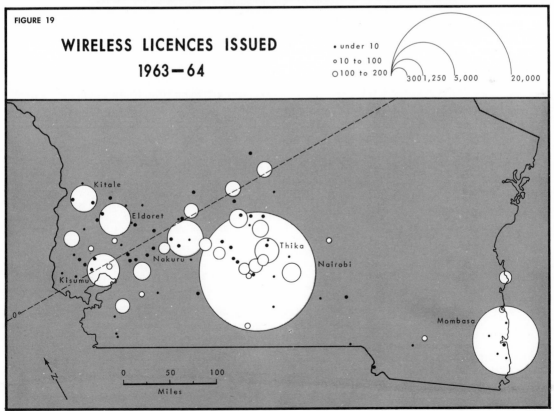

FIGURE 19

WIRELESS LICENCES ISSUED
1963—64

·under 10
○10 to 100
◯100 to 200

300 1,250 5,000   20,000

Kitale

Eldoret

Thika

Nakuru

Nairobi

Kisumu

Mombasa

0   50   100
Miles

the map, though the figures for television sets are much more reliable. The map is also somewhat misleading since there are a great many more radios scattered throughout the rural areas—all licenses are purchased and recorded at the major post offices, not at the place of residence.[29]

Television service is very much centered on the Nairobi area, the capital city having nearly 80 per cent of all sets in use. Relatively weak reception exists in western Kenya and none at all along the coast.[30] Table 7 shows the ten largest radio and television centers by number of licenses issued.

TABLE 7
DISTRIBUTION OF RADIO AND TELEVISION
LICENSES (MAJOR TOWNS)

Radio		Television	
Nairobi	18,847	Nairobi	3,824
Mombasa	7,150	Nakuru	246
Nakuru	1,800	Thika	128
Kisumu	1,617	Eldoret	108
Eldoret	1,242	Gilgil	104
Kitale	883	Kisumu	95
Thika	799	Machakos	57
Kericho	555	Ruiru	47
Nyeri	511	Limuru	37
Machakos	403	Kericho	34
Total issued (1963–64): 40,487		Total issued (1963–64): 4,900	

Source: Licensing Office, Government of Kenya.

THE SPATIAL STRUCTURE
OF COMMUNICATIONS

An additional dimension of importance in the spatial pattern of communications is its structure: the hierarchy of nodes, the degree of interaction among them, and the regional organization of nodal hinterlands. As a step toward describing communications structure

and nodality in Kenya, origin and destination data for telephone calls were used to construct a simple map in which the nodal flow of sixty centers is represented (Figure 20).[31]

There are only two independent or terminal points in the network: Nairobi and Voi. Nairobi is the dominant node in the entire network and is the center of a nodal region which essentially encompasses the entire area of Kenya with telephone service. Although not shown on the map, the nodal flow of telegraph traffic from the administrative centers of northern Kenya (Garissa, Moyale, Wajir, Maralal, and Marsabit) is also directed to Nairobi. In addition, the nodal flow from Kampala and Dar es Salaam is to the Kenya capital, indicative of the primacy of Nairobi within the communications system of all of East Africa.[32]

The heavy lines in Figure 20 show the most intense linkages within the telephone network (greater than one hundred calls between the two nodes). This maximum linkage subsystem shows even more clearly the position of Nairobi as the core area of Kenya. All the nodes for subregions of the second order (Mombasa, Nyeri, Nanyuki, Kisumu, Nakuru, and Eldoret) have their nodal flow to Nairobi, and only Lamu of the third order nodes is poorly connected with the capital.[33]

Voi is an entirely different kind of terminal point. It is located in a communications vacuum between the hinterlands of Nairobi and Mombasa—a position most likely to lead to a high degree of independence. The maximum flow from Voi is to Mwatate, a smaller center which in turn has a nodal flow to Voi. The latter appears to be the center of an iso-

---

[29] These figures, however, are much more reliable than any previous ones. The "Regional" Constitution of 1963 put license revenue under the control of local authorities, and all licenses had to be registered at the nearest major center within the district of residence. Formerly, most licenses were issued at the place of purchase, usually Nairobi or some other large town.

[30] It is interesting to note that both television and radio reception from V.O.K. are good in the Moshi-Arusha area of northern Tanganyika and that Mombasa's regional service can be heard as far south as Tanga and Pangani. If relations between Kenya and Tanzania should become sufficiently strained in the future, radio and television could prove to be effective instruments of propaganda on behalf of the Kenya government in an area which historically has had very close ties with Nairobi.

[31] Nodal flow is defined as the largest outgoing flow of transactions (in this case, telephone calls) from a single subordinate center (one whose maximum flow is to a larger center). An independent city, or terminal point, has its maximum flow to a smaller center (measured in terms of total telephone traffic) and thus does not itself have a nodal flow. The terms and method used here have been derived from a study of communications nodality in the state of Washington, using telephone traffic data, by John D. Nystuen and Michael F. Dacey, "A Graph Theory Interpretation of Nodal Regions," *Papers and Proceedings of the Regional Science Association* (1961), pp. 29–42.

[32] The data used here are from the same nine-hour sample of telephone traffic used in constructing Figure 16. The author wishes to thank the East African Posts and Telecommunications Administration for making the data available to him.

[33] Total traffic between Nairobi and Kitale is 78; Kericho, 68; Thomson's Falls, 32; Molo, 16; and Lamu, 0.

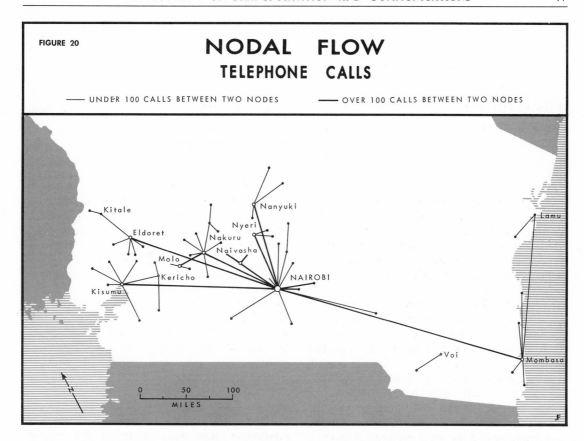

FIGURE 20

NODAL FLOW
TELEPHONE CALLS

—— UNDER 100 CALLS BETWEEN TWO NODES   —— OVER 100 CALLS BETWEEN TWO NODES

Kitale

Eldoret

Nanyuki

Nyeri

Nakuru

Molo

Naivasha

Kericho

Kisumu

NAIROBI

Lamu

Voi

Mombasa

0   50   100
MILES

lated subregion encompassing most of Taita District (the extreme western portion is more closely tied to Moshi, in Tanzania) and gravitating slightly more toward Mombasa, where many Taita are employed, than Nairobi.

The existence of such an unattached subregion reflects the strength of the communications gap between the coast and Nairobi, a kind of "insulation" that has hindered integration of the coastal area with the rest of Kenya. Lamu, for example, is the only large town in Kenya which made no phone calls to Nairobi during the sample period. In fact, the entire Lamu subregion, which includes several smaller surrounding centers, made no calls at all outside the coast.

V

The Human Factor: Social, Economic, and Political Characteristics of the Population

The previous chapter stressed the importance of the physical structure of the network of social communications, but there still exists another set of phenomena that guides the flow of information in any behavorial system. Whereas roads and railways, newspapers and radios, provide the facilities for human interaction, their location does not necessarily determine who does the interacting, with whom and why. Put in another way, the existence of a post office or an all-weather road may have entirely different implications for social mobilization in an area with a dense, literate population engaged in cash crop agriculture than in a backward, sparsely settled pastoral region.

The purpose of this chapter is to examine those characteristics which affect communicative behavior and the areal patterns of modernization. The discussion will be divided into five major sections: (1) urbanization, (2) labor migration and ethnic mixture, (3) the development of a money economy, (4) education and literacy, and (5) voluntary associations.

URBANIZATION

The network of transportation and communications just outlined—in essence, the circulatory system of Kenya—provided the avenues for a wholesale redistribution of population which stands as perhaps the most dramatic and tangible consequence of modernization in Kenya. In addition to the general increase in numbers, especially in the agricultural areas where the impact of improved health facilities was felt most strongly, this population redistribution took two related forms: (1) the movement of people out of their homelands into urban centers and European farming areas; and (2) the consequent increase in cross-ethnic contact and the development of distinct areas which were not considered the domain of a single group but instead contained a mixture of peoples from all over Kenya.

There is no tradition of urban life in Kenya outside the coast. North and east of Lake Victoria, agglomerations of huts occasionally grew to some size around the residence of a powerful local leader, but these were ephemeral settlements and displayed few of the typical functions and structures of urban centers. The beginnings of urbanization, or at least of significant nodal concentrations of settlement, came with the caravan trade, but as previously noted these Arab trading posts were superseded by the new centers growing out of railway construction and the spread of effective British administration.

Nearly all the important centers existing today were established during the first decades of British colonization. Administrative and mission stations were set up in the African areas while Asians—restricted from agriculture except in a few small areas—established trading posts in the more remote sections of the country and also succeeded in gaining control of retail trade in the larger centers serving the European population. No new large center came into being after 1930.

Although Africans soon formed the bulk of the urban population, the existence of a large *permanent* African urban community is a recent development. Until the rise of a national elite during the drive toward independence, the African had only begun to become integrated into urban society. A large proportion of Africans in towns were—and many still are—target workers who returned to their rural homes after a period of urban employment sufficient to achieve a particular monetary goal: a bicycle, transistor radio, or school fees for their children.

This lack of participation by Africans in urban culture is reflected in the morphology of towns in Kenya. Nearly all have well-constructed core areas consisting of administrative buildings and Asian- and European-owned shops surrounded primarily by Asian residential districts. On the periphery, except for suburban European developments, are the African areas which, with some minor exceptions, consist of ramshackle structures with exceptionally poor sanitary conditions. Only recently have these conditions begun to change, with a trickle of African businessmen entering the downtown areas and new housing projects being constructed to serve the growing African population.

The sex ratio also reflects the lack of a large permanent African population in the major towns. Table 8 shows that few centers have more than six females for every ten males, owing to the high proportion of urban migrants who are unaccompanied by their wives and families. This sexual imbalance, though typical of many urban centers in the developing countries, is exceptionally marked in Kenya as a result of the government and racial restrictions placed upon African urbanization during the colonial period.

TABLE 8
AFRICAN SEX RATIO IN MAJOR TOWNS

Town	Adult Males	Adult Females	Sex Ratio
Nairobi City	75,947	30,378	40.0
Mombasa	48,004	27,865	58.0
Nakuru	12,110	6,269	51.7
Kisumu	5,960	2,863	48.0
Eldoret	5,970	3,085	51.6
Thika	4,781	2,417	50.5
Nanyuki	3,791	1,940	51.2
Kitale	2,532	1,516	59.9
Nyeri	2,858	1,355	47.4
Kericho	2,505	1,247	49.8
Gilgil	1,726	863	50.0
Lamu	683	540	79.1
Malindi	1,314	627	47.7
Athi River	2,710	869	32.1

Source: Kenya Population Census, 1962.

Figure 21 indicates the extent of urbanization in Kenya in 1962. There were 34 towns with a population greater than 2,000 and 18 greater than 5,000. Using the latter figure as a breaking point, the total urban population in 1962 was 621,943, or 7.2 per cent—higher than Uganda (4.0 in 1959) and Tanganyika (3.5 in 1957) but well below that for other large African countries (Ghana and Congo-Kinshasa, for example, are over 20 per cent urbanized). In addition, the rate of urban growth over the past few decades has not been particularly high in comparision with many other developing countries.

Nearly two-thirds of the urban population is concentrated in Nairobi and Mombasa and almost 36 per cent is non-African. More than 90 per cent of the Asian population lives in towns of over 5,000 people, while nearly all the rest resides in smaller towns and trading centers. Corresponding figures for European, Arab, and African are 61 percent, 75 per cent, and 4.8 per cent, respectively.[1]

The lack of African participation in urban culture was largely the outgrowth of colonial policy. The Report of the Royal Commission of 1953–55 notes:

> The theory of indirect rule as well as the personal inclinations of many administrators led to a concentration on the development of rural tribal societies rather than the training of an educated urban *elite,* and also to the view that the town was not a suitable habitat for a permanent African society. . . . The towns have, therefore, been regarded rather as bases for administrative and commercial activities than as centers of civilizing influences, still less of permanent African population.[2]

Education in particular was emphasized in the "tribal areas" and consequently greatly neglected in the towns and the European farming areas.

The impact of urbanization on the African, however, was much greater than can be inferred from figures and government statements. The towns may have been regarded as primarily extra-African, but no government policy could prevent them from becoming the major generators and diffusers of change, a role cities have played throughout history.

The idea that African development can be guided and maneuvered within a series of airtight compartments, while other areas are conveniently set aside for non-Africans, in isolation and without important repercussions in the African regions, has been one of the most common and unfortunate fallacies of colonial rule in Africa. It has been the interaction between African and European which

---

[1] *Kenya Population Census, 1962.* Advance Reports of Volumes I and II, and Volume I, published in 1964 by the Economics and Statistics Division of the Ministry of Finance and Economic Planning, Government of Kenya.

[2] P. 201.

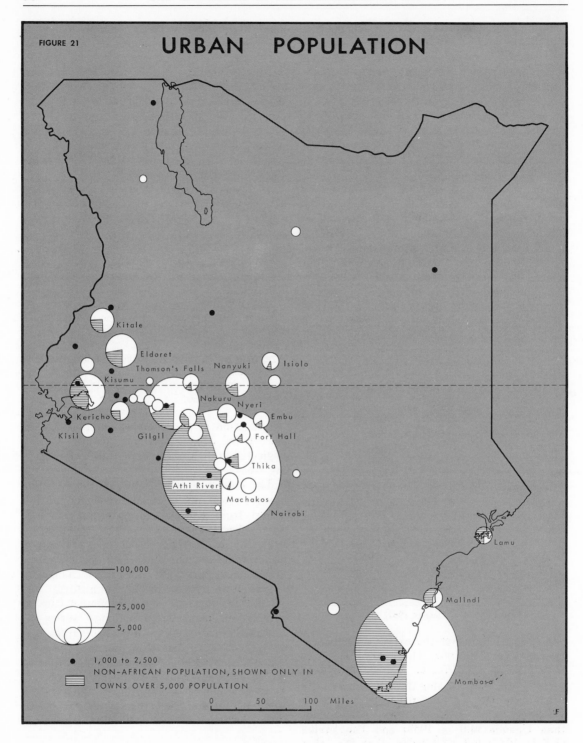

FIGURE 21

URBAN POPULATION

has developed such countries as Kenya, South Africa, and Rhodesia, and the existence of thriving farms and factories in the "European" areas has been paralleled by equally significant developments in the African compartments.

A policy of separate development, in order to function at all, must be expanded to its theoretical limits. There must be little or no interaction between the two component areas —they must become *separate systems.* In

Kenya, as in southern Africa, this has been impossible to achieve. Instead, there have developed two distinct subsystems, which, although they have a slightly different mix of modernizing forces, do indeed interact. A "duality" has emerged, but both sectors have remained part of a single larger system.

The temporary status of most Africans in the towns and their retention of close ties with the rural areas, for example, has permitted the dissemination of at least a portion of urban culture to large sectors of the population, thus increasing the extent of social mobilization. The most outstanding result of this subsystem interaction has been the growth of large quasi-urban populations—particularly near Nairobi and Kisumu, where major urban centers grew adjacent to densely populated African areas.

These two quasi-urban areas—in southern Kiambu and in the area surrounding the railway line north of Kisumu—have been the seedbeds of African nationalism. If measured only by the arbitary size limit of five thousand; these areas are barely urbanized at all. But if measured functionally, they display many features of urban behavior: high newspaper circulation, postal traffic, radio ownership, membership in voluntary associations, and political participation.

The birthplace of Kikuyu political parties was not only in Nairobi proper but also in the Nairobi-focused southern fringe of Kiambu. The dominant party of Kenya today, the Kenya African National Union (KANU), emerged in the Nairobi-Kiambu area as well. The Young Kavirondo Association (one of the earliest Luo and Luhya parties) had its beginnings in the area around Maseno, and it was not entirely coincidental that the Kenya African Democratic Union (KADU) was formally established at Ngong, just south of Nairobi.

It appears then that the combination of urbanization and education, each characteristic of different areal subsystems, produced the impetus needed for African political activity. Where these two forces were in closest juxtaposition—in the hinterlands of Nairobi and Kisumu—change occurred most rapidly. Alliance High School, near the town of Kikuyu; St. Mary's at Yala, north of Kisumu; and the mission school at Maseno were leaders in the production of an educated African elite—an elite which, because of physical proximity, was essentially "urbanized."

The size and density of population in the quasi-urban areas are astounding by any measure. Kiambu, Kikuyu, and Limuru divisions of Kiambu District; Maseno division of Central Nyanza; and Vihiga division of North Nyanza together have an area of 617 square miles and a population of 562,800, with a resulting density of over 911 per square mile. In six of the ten locations[3] in Kiambu, the population density is over 1,300 to the square mile, among the highest rural densities in the world. In comparison, the density of the Nairobi Extra-Provincial District is 1387.

The only gazetted townships in these areas prior to independence were Kiambu (2,533), Maseno (1,177), and Limuru (360), each of which shows up prominently on the transportation and communication maps of the previous chapter. If the quasi-urban areas plus Nairobi and Kisumu were grouped together as two urban regions, they would contain over 10 per cent of the population of Kenya in .4 per cent of the area. And if the remainder of Kiambu District, plus Thika District, and the Winam division surrounding Kisumu were added, these two regions on the eastern and western edge of the former White Highlands would contain over 1,450,000 people. The almost complete domination of Kenya politics by the Luo, Luhya, Kamba, and particularly Kikuyu—even more specifically by certain sectors of these groups—is in no small way linked to the existence of these structurally rural but behaviorally urban-oriented regions.

A visual indication of the contrast between these quasi-urban areas and another densely populated section of Kenya is given in Figure 22. Note the greater density of nucleated settlements, good roads, postal facilities, and schools in the Kiambu sector as opposed to the portion of Kisii District. Many other measures show a similar contrast (e.g., road traffic flow, number of radio and television receivers, postal traffic, and paid employment).

An additional force which has brought about a greater degree of urbanization in the broad sense was the program of "villagization" imposed upon the Kikuyu as an administrative measure during the Mau Mau Emergency, 1952–60. In a few years, the pattern of dispersed homesteads, typical among the Kikuyu,

---

[3] Most districts outside of the old White Highlands are divided into divisions, locations, and sub-locations.

FIGURE 22

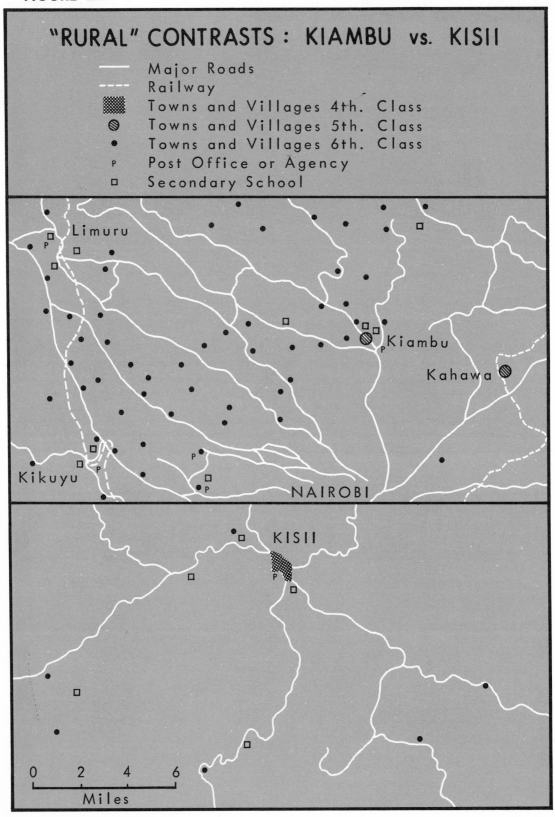

"RURAL" CONTRASTS: KIAMBU vs. KISII

—— Major Roads
- - - Railway
▨ Towns and Villages 4th. Class
◍ Towns and Villages 5th. Class
• Towns and Villages 6th. Class
P Post Office or Agency
□ Secondary School

Limuru

Kiambu

Kahawa

Kikuyu

NAIROBI

KISII

0   2   4   6
Miles

was transformed almost entirely into one of nucleated settlements. Facilities were provided in the new "villages" and access roads were built, thereby improving social communications among the Kikuyu and tying them even more closely to the Nairobi core area. Many of the Emergency villages are now slowly disintegrating as many Kikuyu are returning to live on their plots of land, but the nucleated structure remains and will probably provide the framework for urban growth in the future.

LABOR MIGRATION AND ETHNIC MIXTURE

In addition to urban migration, large numbers of Africans moved into the areas of European settlement as squatters and laborers as soon as effective administration was established and land alienation begun. Whereas only a small settled agricultural population existed in the White Highlands prior to the construction of the Kenya-Uganda railway, after 1902 the area became one of the major demographic frontiers in Africa.

Elimination of the threat of raids by the Masai and other pastoral groups and the labor requirements of European farmers were the major forces behind the African occupation of the Rift Valley and surrounding highlands —areas which were formerly Masai grazing grounds, buffer zones, or no man's lands. The Agricultural Census of 1934 counter over 114,- 000 squatters on European farms, and by 1948 the number of Africans in Trans-Nzoia, Uasin Gishu, Nakuru, Laikipia and Nanyuki districts alone had jumped to nearly 410,000. According to the 1962 population census, the figure had increased to almost 610,000, more than half of which were Kikuyu.

Furthermore, the 1962 census revealed that the former White Highlands, which could not have contained much more than 100,000 people in 1900, supported more than one million Africans, about 115,000 Asians, and 45,000 Europeans. There were thirteen centers with 5,000 or more inhabitants in or on the margins of the Highlands with a total urban population of over 425,000, making the area one of the more highly urbanized in tropical Africa.

Thus, the white "island" from its initial establishment was occupied predominantly by Africans. But since it was considered a separate compartment administratively, it developed along different lines from the reserves. African education was neglected, and no African cash crop agriculture was permitted since Africans could not own land. At the same time, the major accouterments of modern European society were introduced: urban centers; roads and railways, postal facilities; European hotels, hospitals, schools, clubs; and mass media facilities—radio, newspapers, and later television. The white population settled into the Highlands and attempted to recreate a little bit of Europe in Africa.

Another feature which distinguished the European from the African subsystem was the evolution in the former of multi-ethnic settlement and greater ethnic heterogeneity than Kenya has ever known. It would be incorrect to suggest that there was no cross-societal interchange prior to European penetration—the complexity of the peoples of Kenya indicates that a great deal of interaction and exchange has always characterized the relations between some neighboring groups. But the growth of towns and European settlement brought about a degree of contact between all the diverse ethnic groups of Kenya that far surpassed the primarily peripheral contacts of the past.

It must be emphasized that this commingling was areally concentrated. Outside the former European and Asian areas of the Highlands and to a lesser extent along the coast, ethnic homogeneity within defined areas—the Native Reserves—actually increased. In addition, there was a strong tendency for various ethnic groups within the Highlands to retain links with their traditional homelands and thus to prevent real social mixing from developing. Nevertheless, the European subsystem provided the basis for widening individual attitudes and ambitions; it weakened indigenous authority and parochialism and probably supplied the most important initial stimulant to modernization among the African people of Kenya.

This stimulant was increased in potency by the interaction which developed *between* the two subsystems. It is impossible to estimate what portion of the African population had lived and worked at one time or another in the White Highlands. Considering, however, that nearly 12 per cent now live in the area and that thousands—hundreds of thousands—had done so in the past, it is clear that whatever changes were associated with African-Euro-

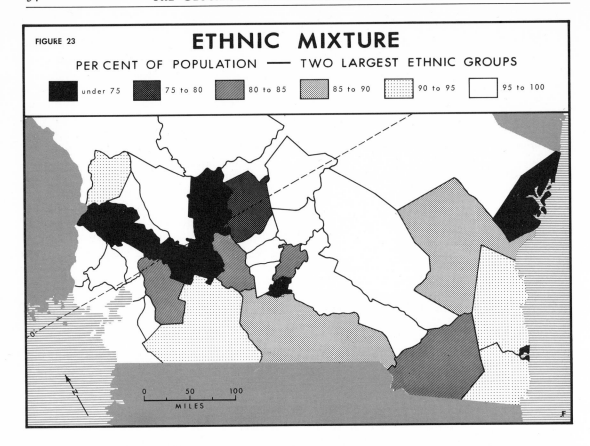

FIGURE 23

ETHNIC MIXTURE

PER CENT OF POPULATION — TWO LARGEST ETHNIC GROUPS

under 75 | 75 to 80 | 80 to 85 | 85 to 90 | 90 to 95 | 95 to 100

pean contact in the Highlands were diffused directly and indirectly to a very large sector of the population.

Figure 23 attempts to portray the areal patterns of ethnic heterogeneity in Kenya and as such depicts broadly the two subsystems of modernization. For each district, the population of the two largest ethnic groups is expressed as a percentage of the total. The most homogeneous districts are Fort Hall (99.6 per cent, essentially all Kikuyu) and Kisii (99.2 per cent, nearly all Kisii). The least homogenous are Mombasa (33 per cent Mijikenda and Kamba), Nairobi (36 per cent Kikuyu and Kamba), and Uasin Gishu (55 per cent Kikuyu and Luhya).[4]

The Kikuyu appeared as either the first or second most populous group in 14 out of 36 districts, the Kamba in 9, Luhya, in 7, and Luo in 5. Clearly, the Kikuyu have dominated the African element in the European subsystem. In 1948, fully one third of the Kikuyu

population lived outside their home districts of FortHall, Kiambu, and Nyeri. Other groups had large proportions of their population not living in their traditional home areas, but the combined total of *all* others barely surpassed the nearly 330,000 Kikuyu "migrants."

By 1962, despite the forced movement of many Rift Valley squatters back to the reserves during the Emergency, the figure for Kikuyu outside their homeland rose dramatically to more than 715,000, or approximately 44 per cent of the entire Kikuyu population. Figure 24 shows the approximate distribution of Kikuyu beyond the limits of their pre-European homeland as of the last census and indicates clearly the Kikuyu role in internal population redistribution. At least half a million are now settled in areas that Kikuyu living in 1900 probably never saw or knew existed.[5]

---

[4] The exact figures for all districts are presented in Appendix A. For the names of the various districts shown, see Figure 35.

[5] It is interesting to note that an African president of the present Rift Valley region at one time wished to place restrictions on Kikuyu expansion (*East African Standard*, February 22, 1964). Interviews with officials administrating resettlement in the Highlands also indicated that if no restrictions were placed upon the Kikuyu, legal or otherwise, they would virtually flood the highland districts.

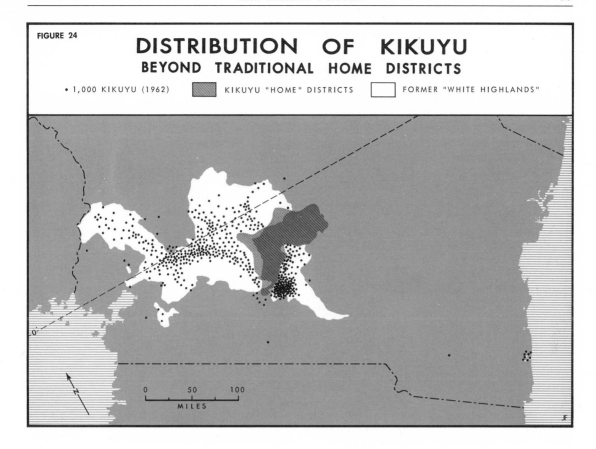

FIGURE 24

DISTRIBUTION OF KIKUYU
BEYOND TRADITIONAL HOME DISTRICTS

• 1,000 KIKUYU (1962)　　KIKUYU "HOME" DISTRICTS　　FORMER "WHITE HIGHLANDS"

Data for district of origin are not available for 1962, but the 1948 census revealed facts regarding the source areas of Kikuyu migrants. About 42 per cent of Kiambu Kikuyu—those from the district nearest Nairobi and served by the best circulatory network—lived outside the district. The figure for Nyeri district was 32 per cent (close to the Kikuyu average) and for Fort Hall, in the heart of Kikuyuland but with poorer communication links, 22 per cent. Relative location, communications development, and traditional migratory patterns have thus all had a powerful effect on modern population movements.

This threefold difference among the Kikuyu holds true for nearly all conventional measures of modernization. It is an outstanding example of the differentiation *within* ethnic groups caused by the unevenness of modernization. Similar contrasts are found among the Kamba (Machakos vs. Kitui), Luo (Central vs. South Nyanza), and Luhya (Maragoli and Bunyore locations vs. all others). In all cases, geographic location has been an important differentiating factor—usually more important than traditional internal differences.

The groups closest to the Kikuyu in number of migrants within Kenya are the Luhya (272,000, including 85,000 in nearby Central Nyanza in an extension of the traditionally occupied area) and Luo (160,000 outside Central and South Nyanza). The figure for the latter, however, is misleading since the Luo have become intimately involved in railway activities and, like the Kamba during the days of caravan trade, have spread throughout East Africa. There are at least 24,000 Luo in Uganda (1959) and nearly 60,000 in Tanganyika (1957), including a large extension along Lake Victoria from South Nyanza. In contrast, there were only 599 Kikuyu in Uganda and 856 in Tanganyika during the same years. The important role of the Luo in both internal and external migration is closely linked to their equally important role, probably second only to the Kikuyu, in the development of African politics.

Summarizing the two preceding sections, the growth of the White Highlands created two distinct subsystems of modernization, one focusing upon the African reserves and the other on the major towns and European farming areas. In each, a different mix of modernizing forces was effective. But since the two formed part of a single over-all system, a great deal of interaction took place which led to a wholesale redistribution of population and to a development of "feedback" between the two subsystems. The pattern of this inter-action was closely associated with the location of densely populated African areas in reference to the major centers of European society. More specifically, the African hinterlands of Nairobi and Kisumu were affected most strongly as the Kikuyu, Luo, Luhya, and Kamba found themselves playing key roles in both subsystems. This differentiation, related closely to geographical location, had a great impact upon the nature of the participants in African political development.

THE DEVELOPMENT OF A MONEY ECONOMY

The shift from a subsistence to an exchange economy has been basic to the modernization process throughout the world. Among Africans in Kenya, like the patterns of demographic change, the rise of a cash economy has been influenced by the two broad subsystems of modernization. In the former European districts—today called the Scheduled Areas—the African has until the past several years been almost exclusively a paid laborer or squatter. Cash crop production by Africans has been virtually non-existent. In the Non-scheduled Areas, formerly the Native Reserves, however, Africans have developed a commercial agriculture which contributes significantly to the national economy. Consequently, each phase must be discussed separately.

Over 480,700 Africans—25 per cent of the adult population—were engaged in paid employment in 1963. Of these, 45 per cent were in agriculture and forestry, 29 per cent in private industry and commerce, and 26 per cent in the public service. Over 157,000, nearly a third of the total, were employed in the fourteen largest towns.[6]

Figure 25 is a cartogram in which area is proportionate to the number of Africans employed in each district and the major towns in 1961, the last date for which detailed data

based on the district boundaries used in this study were available. The prominence of the urban areas is clearly represented. Also prominent are the Scheduled Areas: the mixed farms of the Rift Valley districts, the tea estates in Kericho, and the coffee and sisal plantations of Kiambu and Thika.

The shadings in the cartogram represent average African salaries (total emoluments divided by the number of paid laborers). The rural areas of the former White Highlands continue to stand out, having the lowest salaries in Kenya. Most of those employed are agricultural laborers on European farms who receive some land for the production of food crops in addition to their salaries. This explains, in part, the very low wage level.

The highest average salaries are found primarily in the major towns, where a minimum wage law is in effect, and in several areas where paid employment is small. Many of the latter areas are isolated—the Northern Frontier, Turkana, Tana River, Kajiado—and most of those employed hold relatively high positions, primarily in government and civil service.

Industry is still poorly developed in Kenya and contributes not much more than 10 per cent to the Gross Domestic Product, although this percentage is higher than that for Uganda and Tanzania. Nairobi is the major manufacturing center, employing over 50 per cent of the African urban labor force and about 17 per cent of the total in paid employment. The larger portion of the urban employed are engaged in administration, commerce, communications, transportation, and domestic services.[7]

Figure 26 is a similar cartogram outlining the extent of African cash income from agriculture and animal husbandry. Since data for the number and distribution of Africans engaged in commercial agriculture are impossible to obtain, area here is in proportion to farm income reported in the 1962 District Reports. The leading cash products are included for most of the districts. A comparison with Figure 25 will reveal the distinct contrast between the two modernization subsystems. A combination of the two, however, provides a relatively accurate description of the spatial pattern of African wealth in the

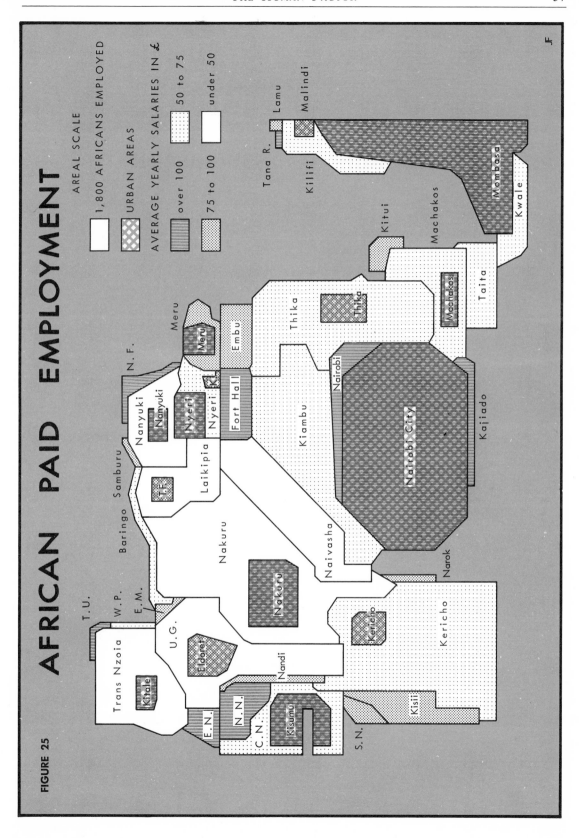

FIGURE 25

AFRICAN PAID EMPLOYMENT

AREAL SCALE

1,800 AFRICANS EMPLOYED

URBAN AREAS

AVERAGE YEARLY SALARIES IN £

over 100

75 to 100

50 to 75

under 50

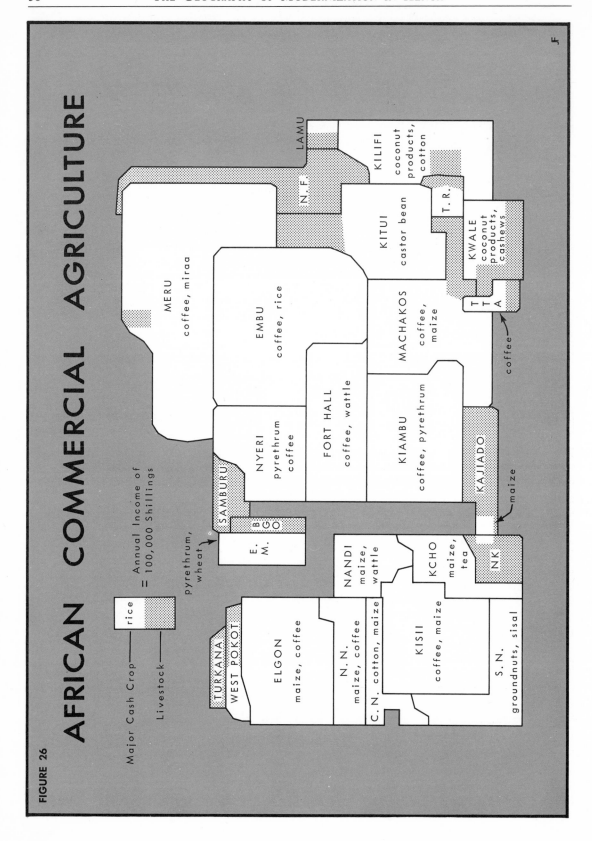

FIGURE 26

AFRICAN COMMERCIAL AGRICULTURE

absence of data on the distribution of the Gross Domestic Product.

Coffee is the dominant African cash crop in terms of income. The production of tea has been increasing in recent years[8] but has not yet reached primary status in any district. Maize was the first major crop grown for sale by Africans and was a key factor in the construction of the railway branch from Kisumu to Butere, the only line built specifically to tap an African area. It remains the leading cash crop in terms of allotted acreage.

African commercial agriculture has been a relatively recent development, especially in the areas closest to the Highlands and those supplying the largest number of laborers. The greater part of commercial production still comes from European and Asian holdings, which numbered about 3,600 in 1961. In that year, for example, the estimated gross revenue from the Scheduled Areas was £35.9 million, while the corresponding figure for the Non-scheduled Areas was £10.4 million.[9] Coffee, tea, and sisal were the leading export crops.

Despite this recent start—Africans began growing coffee extensively fifteen to twenty years ago and tea only in the past five—African commercial agriculture has increased rapidly, particularly in the former Central and Nyanza Provinces. The key factors stimulating this growth have been the work of the African Land Development Board, established in 1945, and the implementation of the Swynnerton Plan.[10]

The Swynnerton Plan, officially entitled "A Plan to Intensify the Development of African Agriculture in Kenya," commenced at the height of the Mau Mau Emergency in 1954. It involved the consolidation of African landholdings, the introduction of individual tenure and a series of schemes for reclamation, increased water supplies, and the general expansion of cash crop and livestock production.

Its partly political nature led to a greater focus on the Kikuyu-Embu-Meru areas and complemented the strategic program of villagization going on there. These two forces

working together produced the most outstanding example of rural modernization in Kenya. Prior to these changes, Kikuyu landholdings were highly fragmented and inefficiently scattered over large areas. In addition, the colonial government refused to recognize the degree of individual land ownership existing among the Kikuyu, with the result that "... no African had security of land tenure or negotiable title to his agricultural loans for the development of his holdings; and his rights to the land were constantly under challenge in the courts."[11]

With the introduction of land reform, individual titles were recognized and fragmented plots consolidated into contiguous holdings. Concurrently, with a greater concentration in villages rather than scattered and isolated homesteads, the forces of modernization were more strongly felt. New road links were built to bring produce to market, children to school, and cattle to water. The areas involved thus became more closely drawn into the evolving system of modernity.[12]

Consolidation spread from the Kikuyu areas to other sections of the country. By the middle of 1961, nearly a million acres were enclosed in Central Province, 560,000 in Nyanza Province, and 440,000 in the African districts of Rift Valley Province.[13] Registration of individual titles, however, proceeded much less rapidly and revealed the degree of conservatism in some of the African areas. In Kiambu and Nyeri, *all* consolidated farms were registered. The next highest percentages were in Embu and Fort Hall; those in Meru and the Rift Valley districts were lower; while none of the enclosed farms in Nyanza Province had been registered by midyear, 1961.

Thus far this discussion of the extent of the money economy has emphasized the contrasts between the two subsystems of modernization,

[8] D. R. F. Taylor, "New Tea Growing Areas in Kenya," *Geography* (1965), pp. 373–75.

[9] International Bank for Reconstruction and Development, *The Economic Development of Kenya*, (1963), p. 63. Figures are no longer kept on a racial basis.

[10] See Colony and Protectorate on Kenya, *African Land Development in Kenya, 1946–1962* (1962).

[11] *The Economic Development of Kenya*, p. 66.

[12] An excellent analysis of agricultural change in Kenya during this period can be found in E. S. Clayton, *Agrarian Development in Peasant Economies* (1964). See also G. J. W. Pedraza, "Land Consolidation in the Kikuyu Areas of Kenya," *Journal of African Administration* (1956), pp. 82–87; and G. B. Masefield, "A Comparison Between Settlement in Villages and Isolated Homesteads," *ibid.* (1955), pp. 64–68.

[13] F. D. Homan, "Consolidation, Enclosure and Registration of Title in Kenya," *Journal of Local Administration Overseas* (1962), pp. 11–12, (formerly the *Journal of African Administration*).

one characterized by paid employment and the other by African cash crop agriculture. In 1961, however, a program was initiated by the Kenya government to purchase over one million acres of European farmland and make it available by sale to Africans. This vast settlement and land reform project plans to introduce by 1967 "the most rapid change in the economic and human geography of an area of this size ever experienced in East Africa,"[14] a change which will greatly alter the economic patterns just described by bringing closer together the characteristics of the two modernization subsystems.

The basic aims of the program are to transfer land ownership from European to African hands without reducing production and to provide farms for the landless, destitute, and unemployed. By 1965, the major outlines of settlement had been well established and a considerable acreage already purchased and occupied. When completed, the distinction between the two modernization subsystems will be reduced significantly.[15]

The areas affected thus far have been on the margins of the former African Land Units in the mixed farming districts of the Scheduled Areas. Most of these were considered zones of "tribal overspill" and were attached to the nearby African districts under the regional delimitation of 1963. The major European plantations of tea, coffee, and sisal, however, remain and are not planned for government purchase in the near future.

It is still too early to measure the accomplishments of these schemes, but there can be no doubt that their success or failure—both in sustaining production and promoting national unity and economic growth—will be a major factor in Kenya's future well-being.

Finally, mention must be made of another important dimension of the Kenya economy: trade. Figure 27 shows the distribution, by value, of trade licenses issued in 1962–63.[16]

Note the heavy concentration in Nairobi, Mombasa, and several of the other major towns (Nakuru, Kismu, Kericho, Eldoret, and Nyeri). This distribution is very highly correlated with the number of Asians in each district (a rank correlation coefficient of .96), reflecting the dominance of the immigrant group in Kenya's internal trade. The railways, also shown on the map, are another important factor in the pattern of trade licenses issued.

EDUCATION AND LITERACY

Western education in Kenya began with the establishment of mission stations during the last half of the nineteenth century. The first sites were along the coast, especially in the hinterland of Mombasa, but soon afterward the missionary effort spread inland to Kikuyu country and the Nyanza area. Figure 28 shows the distribution of mission schools at about the time the Education Department was formed (1911), after which the government began to play a more active role in African education.

As a result of the missionary effort and the support of the government, primary education facilities were made available throughout most of the densely populated sections of Kenya, particularly those fringing the Highlands. Secondary education, in contrast, was slow to develop. The first African secondary school was opened in 1926, but by 1955 there were still only eighteen secondary schools for Africans with a total enrollment of 2,167—as opposed to a primary enrollment of nearly 400,000. In 1963, the figures were 12,872 and 840,000 respectively.[17]

The post-primary bottleneck has been one of the major problems facing the developing countries, reflecting again the often dysfunctional relationship between the aims of the colonial powers and the needs of the new states. It has been noted that the ". . . broad spread of elementary education with relatively slight development at higher levels which now characterizes African educational systems had its roots in the character and purposes of mis-

[14] D. G. R. Belshaw, "Agricultural Settlement Schemes in the Kenya Highlands," *East African Geographical Review* (1964), p. 30.

[15] See *ibid.*, pp. 30–36; D. M. Etherington, "Land Settlement in Kenya: Policy and Practice," *East African Economic Review* (1963), pp. 22–34; Department of Settlement, Kenya, *Annual Report*, 1963–64 and 1964–65; and N. S. Carey Jones, "The Decolonization of the 'White Highlands' of Kenya," *Geographical Journal* (1965), pp. 186–201.

[16] The price of licenses varies with the estimated size of stock. The scale is discussed under TRADE in Appendix A.

[17] Guy Hunter, *Education for a Developing Region: A Study in East Africa* (1963), p. 15; and Government of Kenya, *Statistical Abstract, 1964*, p. 119.

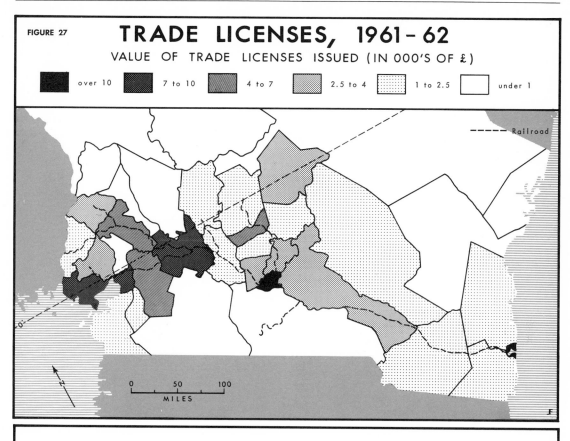

FIGURE 27

TRADE LICENSES, 1961–62

VALUE OF TRADE LICENSES ISSUED (IN 000'S OF £)

over 10   7 to 10   4 to 7   2.5 to 4   1 to 2.5   under 1

Railroad

0   50   100
MILES

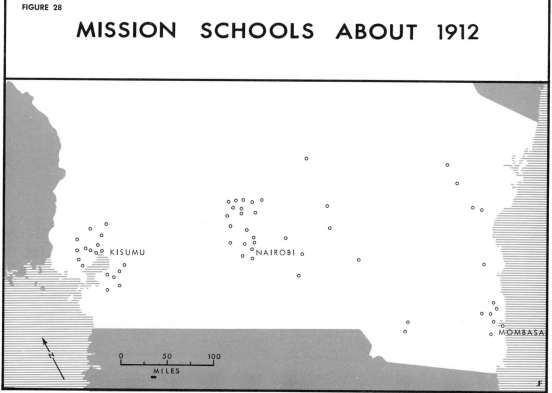

FIGURE 28

MISSION SCHOOLS ABOUT 1912

KISUMU

NAIROBI

MOMBASA

0   50   100
MILES

sion education."[18] Little effort was expended in producing an educated elite, but instead the emphasis was on creating a stable, loyal, "civilized" mass. Although secondary and post-secondary education has increased in recent years, it remains one of the strongest indictments of British colonial policy in Kenya that, in the ten years preceding independence, more capital was invested in British and Asian education—serving 3 per cent of the people in Kenya—than in education for the 97 per cent of the population which is African.[19]

The distribution of secondary schools in 1964 is shown in Figure 29. Note the concentration outside the Scheduled Areas, particularly in the Kikuyu-Meru-Embu areas and in the hinterland of Kisumu. Similar patterns are shown in Figures 30 to·32, which are based on preliminary and as yet unpublished data collected in the 1962 Census of Population.

The Kikuyu areas have been able to build upon their early start and stand out today as the most highly literate and educated sections of Kenya. This fact is brought out most clearly in Table 9, which is an attempt to summarize the data used for the maps on an ethnic basis. Although no really accurate comparisons are possible since education statistics are not collected on ethnic lines, Table 9 represents the best estimates available.[20]

Even with the exclusion of Nairobi, Nakuru, and other districts where they form a large proportion of the population, the Kikuyu re-

TABLE 9
ETHNIC BREAKDOWN
OF AFRICAN EDUCATIONAL ACHIEVEMENT

Primary Education		Minimal Literacy		Post-Secondary	
Kikuyu	56.0	Kikuyu	51.2	Kikuyu	645
Nandi	50.8	Kisii	40.5	Kisii	332
Taita	44.8	Luhya	38.5	Luhya	329
Embu	41.0	Kipsigis	36.2	Kamba	214
Luo	37.7	Embu	34.7	Luo	205
Kipsigis	36.2	Luo	33.0	Meru	154
Kisii	34.6	Taita	33.0	Nandi	144
Luhya	34.0	Nandi	31.8	Tugen-	
Meru	32.0	Meru	28.5	Njemps	119
Elgeyo-		Kamba	21.3	Kipsigis	111
Marakwet	24.1	Tugen-		Mijikenda	110
Kamba	20.5	Njemps	21.8	Embu	61
Tugen-		Elgeyo-		Elgeyo-	
Njemps	17.7	Marakwet	21.8	Marakwet	44
Pokot (Suk)	15.2	Mijikenda	15.5	Taita	26
Mijikenda	14.9	Pokot (Suk)	9.1	Masai	24
Masai	13.0	Masai	7.7	Potok (Suk)	11

Primary Education: percentage of males *plus* percentage of females between the ages of 5 and 9 with some schooling.

Minimal Literacy: percentage of males over 20 with some schooling.

Post-Secondary: number with 13 or more years of education.

Source: Kenya Population Census, 1962 (preliminary data, publication forthcoming).

main ahead of all other groups in each category used. Perhaps the most interesting figure is for post-secondary education, the Kikuyu having nearly twice the number of the next closest competitor.[21]

Outside the Kikuyu districts, other areas with high levels of educational achievement include Nairobi, Mombasa, Nakuru (owing largely to immigration of educated Africans to the towns), and several districts fringing Lake Victoria (Central and North Nyanza and Kisii). The lowest levels are found in the

[18] Francis X. Sutton, "Education and the Making of Modern Nations," in J. S. Coleman (ed.), *Education and Political Development* (1965), p. 61.

[19] Government of Kenya, *Education Committee Report*, Part I (1964), p. 21.

[20] The figures for the various ethnic groups listed in Table 9 were obtained directly from the census data by district. The more highly mixed districts, including Nairobi, were not used, while the total figures for the other districts were assigned to the major group occupying the area. Thus, all of Central Nyanza was considered Luo, all of Kericho was classed as Kipsigis, etc. Districts used were: Kikuyu = Kiambu, Fort Hall, and Nyeri; Nandi = Nandi; Taita = Taita; Embu = Embu; Luo = Central and South Nyanza; Kipsigis = Kericho; Kisii = Kisii; Luhya = North and Elgon Nyanza; Meru = Meru; Elgeyo-Marakwet = Elgeyo-Marakwet; Kamba = Machakos and Kitui; Tugen-Njemps = Baringo; Pokot (Suk) = West Pokot; Mijikenda = Kilifi and Kwale; Masai = Kajiado and Narok. Districts excluded were: Nairobi, Mombasa, Nakuru, Uasin Gishu, Trans-Nzoia, Naivasha, Laikipia, Nanyuki, Thika, Samburu, Northern Frontier, Tana River, Lamu, and Turkana.

[21] It is difficult to judge the impact of the Independent School Movement on these figures. This movement evolved primarily in Kikuyu-occupied areas between the two world wars. Sparked by a dispute over female circumcision, the Kikuyu began to develop independent educational institutions which stood in opposition to mission and government influence. By 1936, there were already nearly 4,000 pupils in 44 of these Independent Schools located throughout Central Province and parts of the Rift Valley. At the peak of the movement, it was claimed that 60,000 pupils were being taught in 342 schools, a highly significant number even if cut in half to conform with government estimates. It is still not clear, however, to what extent groups other than the Kikuyu participated in this movement. The major published source on this subject is *The Origins and Growth of Mau Mau*, which has supplied the statistics referred to. This report, however, is today considered extremely biased in its approach to all aspects of the Mau Mau question.

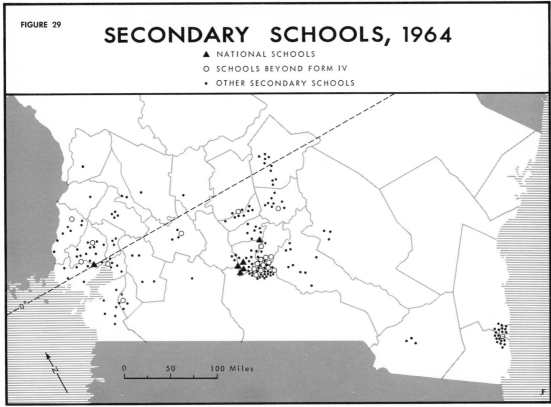

FIGURE 29

SECONDARY SCHOOLS, 1964

▲ NATIONAL SCHOOLS
O SCHOOLS BEYOND FORM IV
• OTHER SECONDARY SCHOOLS

0   50   100 Miles

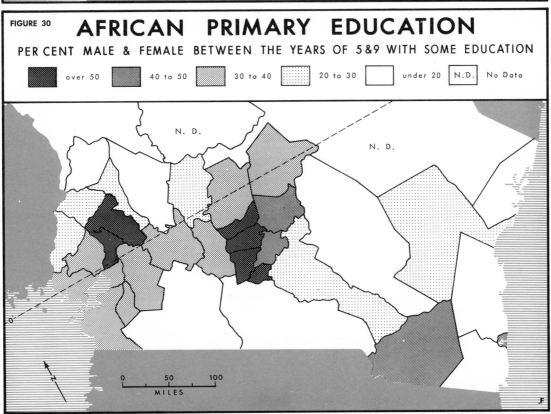

FIGURE 30

AFRICAN PRIMARY EDUCATION

PER CENT MALE & FEMALE BETWEEN THE YEARS OF 5 & 9 WITH SOME EDUCATION

over 50   40 to 50   30 to 40   20 to 30   under 20   N.D. No Data

N. D.   N. D.

0   50   100
MILES

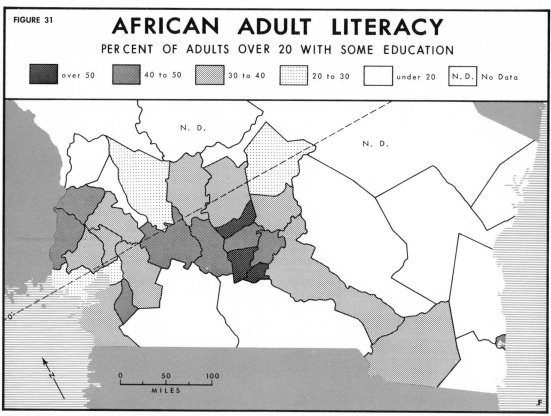

FIGURE 31

AFRICAN ADULT LITERACY
PERCENT OF ADULTS OVER 20 WITH SOME EDUCATION

over 50 | 40 to 50 | 30 to 40 | 20 to 30 | under 20 | N.D. No Data

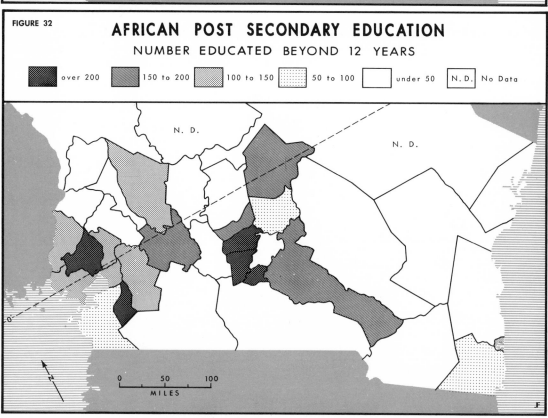

FIGURE 32

AFRICAN POST SECONDARY EDUCATION
NUMBER EDUCATED BEYOND 12 YEARS

over 200 | 150 to 200 | 100 to 150 | 50 to 100 | under 50 | N.D. No Data

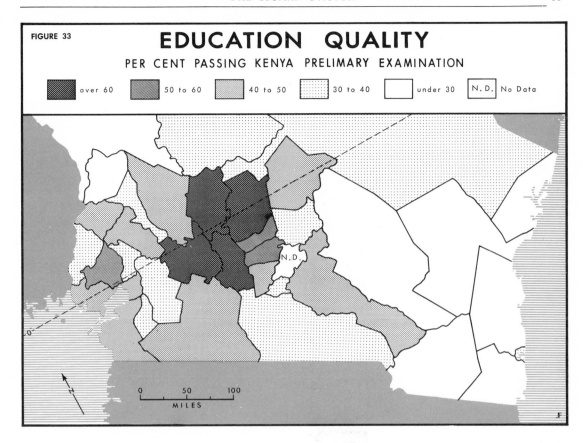

FIGURE 33

EDUCATION QUALITY
PER CENT PASSING KENYA PRELIMARY EXAMINATION

over 60 | 50 to 60 | 40 to 50 | 30 to 40 | under 30 | N.D. No Data

pastoral districts of the Masai and Suk, although most of the coastal districts also score low. No figures were available for Turkana and the Northern Frontier, but it is most likely that they score still lower.

Most of the Scheduled Areas show up favorably in primary education because of recent increases in facilities and the availability of cash income to pay school taxes. This showing may also result from a tendency among migrants to have greater interest in educating their children. More importantly, the quality of education, as measured by the percentage passing the Kenya Preliminary Examination for entry into secondary schools, tends to be high, a phenomenon which may prove significant in the future development of the Rift Valley area (see Figure 33). But the policy of neglecting African education in the supposed white reserve and the associated barriers to cultural assimilation are reflected in the small number of Africans with thirteen or more years of schooling.

The geography of education, therefore, still mirrors the attitudes and objectives of mission education and colonial policy. Primary edu-

cation is widespread, but secondary and post-secondary educated Africans are few in number and highly concentrated in the major towns and in the Central and Nyanza Province clusters of population. Different policies have been operative in the two subsystems and, in addition, only certain areas within each have attained high levels of education while others remain backward. The Kikuyu lead all others in educational achievement, and all indications point to their continued leadership in the future. This is particularly true for the Kiambu and Nyeri Kikuyu and those in the major urban centers.[22]

VOLUNTARY ASSOCIATIONS

It has not been possible to obtain accurate distributional data on the extent and importance of voluntary associations in Kenya at a

---

[22] Distinctions must always be made within ethnic groups, for frequently internal contrasts are extremely sharp. For example, the Machakos Kamba have a 31 per cent level of minimal literacy, have 196 educated beyond 12 years, and supplied 255 students to Kenya secondary schools in 1964. The comparable figures for the Kitui Kamba are 12 per cent, 18, and 61.

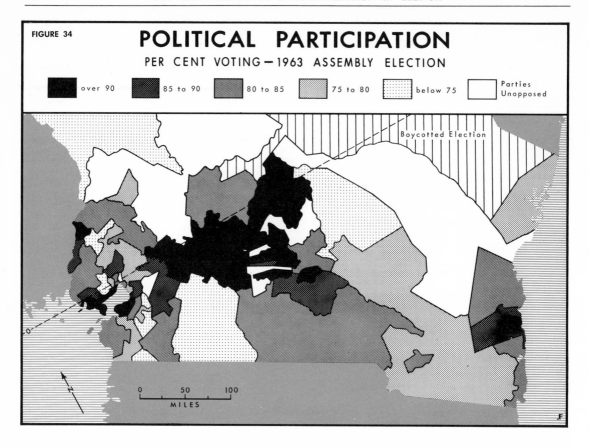

FIGURE 34

POLITICAL PARTICIPATION
PER CENT VOTING — 1963 ASSEMBLY ELECTION

over 90   85 to 90   80 to 85   75 to 80   below 75   Parties Unopposed

Boycotted Election

0   50   100
MILES

level comparable to other measures used in this study. Agricultural cooperatives are still in their early stages of formation, although this situation is changing with the large-scale settlement schemes now underway. Data on trade union and political party membership—much less distribution—are not available. Thus, for this important component of the modernization process—the growth and areal distribution of voluntary associations based on nontraditional interests—only a small number of indirect measures are available for examination.

Election results, which presumably could give some indication of party affiliation and level of political participation, prove disappointing for present objectives. In the only general election which permitted some estimate of the size and strength of African political parties in all the constituencies of Kenya, that which was held just prior to independence in 1963, either the Kenya African National Union (KANU) or the Kenya African Democratic Union (KADU) ran unopposed in several areas. This fact hinders the use of a district by district index based on

the percentage of eligible voters casting a ballot for measuring spatial variations in political participation.

Nevertheless, some broad patterns can be perceived from Figure 34, in which the percentage of those eligible who voted in the 1963 election for the House of Representatives is mapped by constituency.[23] The most outstanding feature of the map is the extremely high percentage voting (over 90 per cent of those eligible) in the Kikuyu, Meru, and Embu areas of Central and Rift Valley provinces and in many of the Luo areas of Central Nyanza, despite the fact that in many of these constituencies the outcome of the election was never in doubt. This pattern conforms closely with previous discussions on the role of these two groups in Kenya politics. High percentages are also found in parts of the Kamba district of Machakos (note the contrast with Kitui), in some of the Luhya areas, among the Kipsigis of Kericho District, and in sections of the coastal region. At the other extreme,

[23] Data for the map were obtained from the *East African Standard*, May 30, 1963.

the Somali-dominated northeast boycotted the 1963 election.[24]

Two measures of the geographical unevenness in the growth of voluntary associations are shown in Table 10. The first column shows the number of registered political organizations of all types by district in early 1964.[25]

Of the more than 3,600 societies, about one third were located in Nairobi, with large numbers also in Nakuru and Mombasa Districts. This pattern of concentration reflects the large and heterogeneous populations and generally high level of modernization in these areas. Other districts with more than one hundred such organizations include Central Nyanza, with its highly mobilized Luo and Asian populations, Kiambu, North Nyanza, and Thika. The last named is second only to Nairobi in ratio of societies to population.

The second column provides a measure of the diffusion of KANU, the major political party of Kenya. The figures indicate the number of days after the initial registration of KANU as a political party (November 6, 1960) that a branch office was registered in each district. This measure is not as closely associated with the urban and quasi-urban areas as the first. Although there are some exceptions (e.g., Kitui and Elgon Nyanza), the Kikuyu districts were the first to which KANU spread. The Meru, Embu, and Kamba districts followed, along with Mombasa, while

---

[24] When elections were eventually held in the Northeastern Region in February, 1964, nearly all members were returned unopposed and no statistics on percentage voting were available. The Northeastern Region consists of the primarily Somali areas of the former Northern Frontier District. It was established under the administrative reorganization which followed independence. It should be stressed again that the present study is based upon the district boundaries which existed prior to this reorganization.

[25] Political organizations include all groups of ten or more persons registered under the Societies Act (revised, 1962) and expressing specifically political interests. These include not only the branches of the national political parties but also such groups as the Indian Association, the Luo Union, and externally directed organizations such as the Movement for South African Freedom. Appreciation is expressed to the Registrar, Government of Kenya, for making these figures available.

TABLE 10
VOLUNTARY ASSOCIATIONS AND
THE GROWTH OF KANU

District	No. of Registered Political Orgs.	Growth of KANU
1. Nairobi	1221	November 6, 1960*
2. Mombasa	493	217 (7)
3. Central Nyanza	322	380 (18)
4. Nakuru	201	167 (2)
5. Kiambu	182	209 (6)
6. North Nyanza	148	332 (16)
7. Thika	109	254 (11)
8. Uasin Gishu	91	261 (13)
9. Kisii	78	475 (20)
10. Kericho	77	547 (23)
11. Nyeri	74	204 (5)
12. Machakos	70	255 (12)
13. South Nyanza	62	399 (19)
14. Trans-Nzoia	56	581 (24)
15. Kitui	48	187 (3)
16. Elgon Nyanza	44	194 (4)
17. Kilifi	43	716 (29)
18. Nanyuki	40	758 (28)
19. Meru	32	251 (10)
20. Embu	30	287 (15)
21. Fort Hall	29	232 (9)
22. Naivasha	26	218 (8)
23. Laikipia	23	266 (14)
24. Taita	20	357 (17)
25. Kwale	19	763 (26)
26. Kajiado	17	546 (22)
27. Nandi	16	504 (21)
28. Lamu	9	1675 (35)
29. Northern Frontier	7	1385 (34)
30. Tana River	6	1380 (33)
31. Samburu	4	848 (30)
32. Narok	4	698 (25)
33. West Pokot	3	718 (27)
34. Elgeyo-Marakwet	2	1680 (36)
35. Baringo	2	951 (31)
36. Turkana	1	1316 (32)

*Date of official registration of KANU as a political party. All other figures in this column represent the number days after this date that a branch office was established and registered for the given district. Rank order is shown in parentheses.

Source: Registrar's Office, Government of Kenya.

the Taita, Luhya, and Luo came afterward. The coast and the major pastoral regions—the strongholds of the major opposition party, KADU—came much later.

VI

Multivariate Dimensions of Modernization in Kenya: Methods of Measurement and Analysis

In Chapters IV and V, various measures of modernization were identified, examined individually, and linked to contemporary spatial patterns. Close correlations were observed between many of these measurements, and comments were made on the relationships between the growth and spread of social communications and the development of African politics. The analysis was placed within an historical framework hinging upon the patterns of European contact and settlement in Kenya.

Such a survey, however, raises more questions than it answers. What does the composite picture look like? Which of the measurements are the most effective indicators of the over-all patterns of social mobilization? How can the measurements be weighted? Is there an identifiable cluster—or clusters—of features closely associated with one another which "summarize" the processes of transition? Can one identify stages of development? More generally, can a geography of modernization be accurately represented through an analysis of a large number of relevant indices weighted according to their contribution to the over-all pattern?

The fundamental aim of the second half of this study is to examine these questions through the use of a multivariate statistical technique known as principal components analysis and to use the results to shed some light on the process of modernization in Kenya, particularly but not wholly as it is spatially manifested. Special emphasis will be placed upon the interrelationships between process and pattern.

THE CHOICE OF METHOD

Principal components analysis—a branch of factor analysis—is a technique designed primarily to synthesize a large number of variables into a smaller number of general components which retain a maximum amount of descriptive ability.[1] It permits a more economical description of the phenomenon being measured by suggesting certain underlying elements, or *dimensions*, which account for the statistical interrelationships of the variables. Although originally developed to deal with the traits of individuals (e.g., personality and intelligence), it has come to be applied to groups and areal units as well.

In recent years, principal components analysis has been used frequently in geography, particularly in dealing with such complex, multidimensional concepts as economic development, economic health, and poverty.[2] The method has been chosen here, where a similar roughly defined multivariate phenomenon—modernization—is the focus of interest. It should be emphasized, however, that the principal components technique is used here as a crude exploratory tool, a structured search for order in a highly complex process, and not as a hypothesis-testing, proof-supplying formula.

Principal components analysis has also been used by political scientists, sociologists, and economists to examine various facets of mod-

---

[1] Basic reference works in factor analysis include Harry H. Harman, *Modern Factor Analysis* (1960); Benjamin Fruchter, *Introduction to Factor Analysis* (1954); M. G. Kendall, *A Course in Multivariate Analysis* (1961); and D. N. Lawley and A. E. Maxwell, *Factor Analysis as a Statistical Method* (1963).

[2] See Brian Berry, "Basic Patterns of Economic Development," in Ginsburg (ed.), *Atlas of Economic Development* (1961), pp. 110–19 and "An Inductive Approach to the Regionalization of Economic Development," in Ginsburg (ed.), *Essays on Geography and Economic Development* (1960), pp. 78–107; John Thompson, *et al.*, "Toward a Geography of Economic Health: The Case of New York State," *Annals of the Association of American Geographers* (1962), pp. 1–20; Michael Ray and Brian Berry, *Multivariate Socio-Economic Regionalization: A Pilot Study in Central Canada* (1964); and Mary Megee, "Economic Factors and Economic Regionalization in the United States," *Geografiska Annaler* (1965) pp. 125–37.

ernization at the international level.[3] Whether the generalizations derived from these examinations are applicable at the *intrastate level*, however, has not been sufficiently investigated. Since the state is the major system within which modernization takes place—the locus where decisions are formulated, made, and put into effect, where institutions are built and patterns emerge—this gap in the literature is unfortunate.[4] Just as independent states can be placed within broadly defined clusters along the many avenues between traditional and modern society,[5] so may the areal divisions within a state. The present analysis is therefore an attempt to apply a methodology used most frequently at the international level to the component areal units within a single state.

THE DATA SET

The variables used in this study are simple measurements of the component elements of modernization discussed in the previous two chapters. The choice of indices was guided by (a) the availability and reliability of complete data for Kenya at the district level and (b) conceptual linkages with existing studies using similar techniques. A list of the variables is included in Table 11, while the method of measurement, date, source, and reliability are discussed in Appendix A.

The thirty-five enumeration areas are shown in Figure 35. Of the northern districts of Kenya, Samburu and Turkana are treated separately, but all data for Garissa, Isiolo, Marsabit, Wajir, Mandera, and Moyale have been averaged and included as the Northern Frontier District because of the sparsity of

detailed data for this area. The districts are those which existed prior to the boundary changes of 1963.[6]

Ideally, the absolute measures for each variable, properly transformed to fulfill certain prerequisites of principal components analysis, would have been most desirable. The data set actually used, however, was based upon rank-ordered statistics. The use of ranked data is in no way inappropriate to the objectives of this study and in fact is a simple way of guaranteeing the initial requirements of homogeneity of variance and linear relationship which are important assumptions for interpretation. In addition, ranking is thought to reduce systematic error distortion and permits a more rational and facile framework for estimating missing data, which can be a major barrier to the geographer using factor analytical techniques.[7]

PRINCIPAL COMPONENTS ANALYSIS AND FACTOR ROTATION: BASIC CONCEPTS

The matrix of Spearman Rank Correlation Coefficients derived from the data set of 36 districts and 25 variables (Table 12) provides the basic material upon which the principal components analysis operates. The method draws out underlying factors, or *dimensions*, in order based upon their contribution in accounting for the total variance within the 25-variable data space. The objective is to determine whether the variations within the data can be described sufficiently by a number of reference dimensions smaller than the number of variables with which the investigation began, in other words to achieve some parsimony of description.

The dimensions—or principal components—represent clusters of interrelated variables which delineate general patterns of covariation within the data set. Each of the variables is weighted according to its degree of importance in defining the principal components. These weights are called *factor loadings*

---

[3] Leo Schnore, "The Statistical Measurement of Urbanization and Economic Development," *Land Economics* (1961), pp. 229–45; Raymond Cattell *et al.*, "An Attempt at More Refined Definition of the Cultural Dimensions of Syntality in Modern Nations," *American Sociological Review* (1952), pp. 408–21; Bruce Russett, "Delineating International Regions," in J. D. Singer (ed.), *Quantitative International Politics: Insights and Evidence* (1967).

[4] There are several case studies of individual countries (e.g., Lucian Pye's study of Burma in *Politics, Personality, and Nation Building*, and Lerner's analysis of countries in the Middle East in *The Passing of Traditional Society*, but none known to the author treats all sections of the state as a statistical population, similar to the population of independent states, upon which to build and test hypotheses concerning modernization.

[5] As in Berry (1961), *op. cit.*; and Russett *et al.*, *World Handbook of Political and Social Indicators* (1964), pp. 293–310.

[6] A map of the administrative districts existing in 1967 is included in Appendix C.

[7] Missing original data, although not preventing the estimation of correlation coefficients upon which the technique operates, does produce obstacles in the determination of factor scores, which will be discussed below. Since these scores are of great importance to the geographer as a basis for the analysis of *pattern* from the dimensions of process, completeness of observations is essential.

TABLE 11
VARIABLES USED IN THE STUDY

Demographic Characteristics

1. PODEN: Population density(R)
2. EUROP: European population (#)
3. ASIAN: Asian population (#)
4. MIXTU: Degree of ethnic mixture (%)
5. TOWNP: Degree of urbanization (#)

Education (African Only)

6. COLED: Post-Secondary education (#)
7. LITER: Adult literacy (%)
8. PRIMA: Primary school attendance (%)
9. KPEXA: Education quality (% passing entry exam for secondary school)

Communications and Transport

10. TOPOS: Total postal traffic (#)
11. PPLET: Per capita postal traffic (R)
12. SWAPA: Swahili newspaper circulation per capita (R)
13. ENGPA: English newspaper cirulation per capita (R)
14. RADIO: Number of radio licenses issued (#)
15. NOTEL: Total number of telephones (#)
16. TRAFF: Road traffic density (R)

Connectivity with Nairobi

17. DISTA: Road distance to Nairobi from district Headquarters (#)
18. NBIFO: Percentage of total phone calls made to Nairobi (%)

Economic Development

19. TAXPP: Per capita taxes (Africans only) (R)
20. TRADE: Value of trade licenses issued (#)
21. PEMPL: Percentage of Africans employed (%)
22. AVSAL: Average African salaries (R)
23. ACASH: African cash income (#)

Political Development

24. SOCIE: Number of registered political societies (#)
25. KANUS: Date of establishment of KANU branch office (#)

NOTE: Symbols in parentheses denote how variable was measured (R = ratio, # = total number, and % = percentage).

and provide the basis for identifying and interpreting the nature of the underlying dimensions.

The first component extracted will account for a maximum portion of the total variance (which in this case will be 25, one unit for each of the variables). A residual matrix is then calculated, portraying the remainder of the total variance after the removal of Factor 1 (F1). From it is extracted a second component, F2, which will be orthogonal to and therefore independent from F1. The process can be repeated until all the variance is accounted for.

It can be shown that if each variable were completely uncorrelated with all the others, every factor would account for the same proportion of the total variance. In such a case, no more economy of description would be provided than existed with the original data set. But since the variables used in this study were thought to measure a similar phenomenon—the level of modernization in Kenya—a high degree of interdependence would be expected, and consequently the first

several dimensions extracted should absorb a large portion of the total variance.

A geometric interpretation may facilitate understanding the nature of this technique. The variables can be viewed as unit vectors, their ends represented as a scatter of points within a 25-dimensional space (one dimension for each variable) and the cosines of the angles between them indicative of their coefficient of correlation (e.g., a 90° angle for r = 0). The more circular the distribution of these terminal points, the less interdependent are the variables, or their vectors. If perfectly circular—with no apparent clustering—25 equally important dimensions would be required to account for the total variance, 25 defining axes would have to be drawn with each passing through a single vector space.

The more ellipsoidal the distribution, or the more it is flattened out, however, the more the variables are interrelated and the greater the variance that the first dimension will account for. With a perfectly straight distribution, only one axis would be needed for

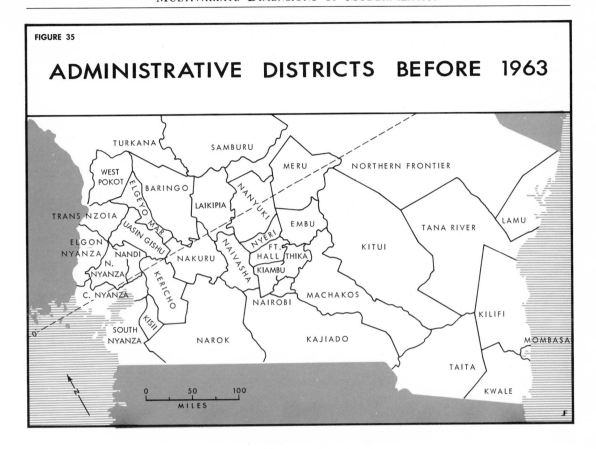

FIGURE 35

ADMINISTRATIVE DISTRICTS BEFORE 1963

TABLE 12: MATRIX OF CORRELATION COEFFICIENTS
(Decimal Points Omitted)

	1	2	3	4	5	6	7	8	9	10	11	12	13	14	15	16	17	18	19	20	21	22	23	24	25
1. PODEN	—	50	61	−04	42	85	74	72	37	72	34	53	42	60	61	76	32	39	00	69	20	11	75	72	61
2. EUROP		—	90	58	76	46	68	56	46	87	81	92	93	87	92	82	44	52	28	84	83	−43	81	77	59
3. ASIAN			—	44	88	57	71	62	44	92	79	89	89	96	94	84	43	62	25	96	75	−25	91	90	60
4. MIXTU				—	50	−14	28	24	05	40	75	60	62	50	54	42	03	15	39	35	72	−32	21	27	08
5. TOWNP					—	33	61	52	38	83	84	81	86	89	86	72	35	56	23	85	75	−25	75	75	53
6. COLED						—	69	69	40	66	29	45	38	54	55	67	37	38	01	64	23	11	73	67	57
7. LITER							—	82	60	79	66	76	71	76	77	88	46	44	14	74	57	−19	73	72	69
8. PRIMA								—	48	75	63	71	64	66	69	81	43	42	22	64	49	−08	65	66	63
9. KPEXA									—	55	39	52	46	51	53	56	58	54	−10	46	34	−36	39	37	43
10. TOPOS										—	82	88	86	93	86	78	46	59	16	93	70	−23	87	90	69
11. PPLET											—	87	91	84	94	90	34	49	33	71	87	−30	59	66	49
12. SWAPA												—	96	92	93	86	47	59	34	83	84	−37	78	77	66
13. ENGPA													—	91	92	82	47	57	37	82	89	−41	76	74	63
14. RADIO														—	96	86	49	64	26	93	78	−29	88	86	71
15. NOTEL															—	88	44	60	24	91	80	−34	86	83	67
16. TRAFF																—	46	53	13	83	69	−22	80	79	65
17. DISTA																	—	71	33	40	45	−22	54	35	60
18. NBIFO																		—	18	56	50	−03	60	46	55
19. TAXPP																			—	21	33	13	27	24	35
20. TRADE																				—	64	−16	92	93	68
21. PEMPL																					—	−52	60	52	41
22. AVSAL																						—	−17	−08	00
23. ACASH																							—	87	75
24. SOCIE																								—	72
25. KANUS																									—

its description. Put in another way, the patterns of covariation between all the variables could then be expressed in terms of a single dimension.

Between the extremes of a single dimension and a number of equally weighted dimensions of the same number as there are variables lies an infinite variety of possible solutions for the factor analyst. The principal components technique, however, produces a unique and duplicatable solution in that it extracts the maximum amount of variance for each successive dimension.

The greater the intercorrelation between the variables, therefore, the fewer the axes needed to "soak up" a large proportion of the variance. The first component will account for a large amount of this variance if there appears to be a major underlying dimension—an extremely elongated distribution. The next component, independent from the first, will absorb a maximum of what remains. This will be large or small depending upon the nature of the residual distribution—the extent of elongation within a plane orthogonal to F1. With a highly interrelated set of variables, only the first several components may be needed to describe the patterns of covariation within the original data matrix.

As previously mentioned, the loadings for each variable on the given dimension provide clues for its interpretation. Further information is found in the *factor scores*, which, in the present case, enables one to evaluate the relative level of any *district* on each dimension. Scores are obtained by summing the products of the ranks of a district and the loadings on a dimension.

Although the principal components technique produces a more parsimonious description of the covariant pattern of the original data set, it is often difficult to identify and label the dimensions extracted because of the frequent appearance of medium-sized factor loadings. For example, a loading of .92 for a given variable indicates that it is a major delineating element for the dimension. But it becomes much more difficult to deal with several other variables loading, let us say, .41, .49, and .58.

This problem has led to the procedure known as *rotation*, whereby the dimensions can be made to coincide more closely with groups of variables without the restriction that each consecutive factor always extracts the maximum amount of variance. In the present study, for example, it was expected that the first factor extracted would reflect the interrelated nature of the original variables and thus account for a very large proportion of the total variance. It would, almost invariably, be labeled a summary dimension of modernization. The succeeding factors may provide additional information on other aspects of the modernization process, but after one or two the loadings would be so low as to prevent any reliable interpretation. Although helpful in getting an over-all view, this information would tell little about the specific groupings of closely related variables, each of which may load highly on the same component but be quite distinct and "distant" from one another within the vector space.

Varimax rotation[8] simplifies the columns of factor loadings by producing closer correspondence between the dimensions and the variables. It does so by approximating "simple structure," a pattern in which the number of high and low loadings is maximized, thereby reducing the number of distressing intermediate loadings and aiding interpretation. Varimax rotation tends to react less to the entire distribution than to major clusters of related variables within it. The original orthogonal axes are accordingly shifted to coincide more closely with these clustered vectors, thus creating a set of more easily interpretable components which are not as sensitive to changes in the number of variables as is the original solution. Consequently, where there are groupings of significantly interrelated variables, these will continue to be identified even if new variables are included in the analysis (a characteristic known as factorial invariance).[9]

From the preceding description, it is clear that the technique used in this study has its drawbacks as well as its advantages. Principal components analysis—like many forms of multivariate analysis—is primarily a probing tool most useful when a highly complex, multifaceted phenomenon is being studied. It produces some economy of description and provides valuable information on the basic

[8] The Varimax method is one of many types of rotation aimed at increasing the interpretability of the matrix of factor loadings. See Henry F. Kaiser, "The Varimax Criterion for Analytical Rotation in Factor Analysis," *Psychometrika* (1958), pp. 187–200.

[9] For a further discussion of the Varimax method and its qualities of simplicity (simple structure) and factorial invariance, see Harman, *op. cit.*, pp. 289–308.

dimensions underlying the processes involved. It gives some degree of order to them. The technique has been selected here to fulfill these objectives.

SIMPLE BIVARIATE CORRELATIONS

Before proceeding to the principal components analysis, it may be helpful to examine some of the simple bivariate rank correlations to see with which of the others each individual variable is most highly associated. The highest correlates of each variable are italicized. All others can be found in Table 12.

Communications and Transportation

1. *Newspaper Circulation:* The circulations of English and Swahili papers are, as expected, most closely correlated with one another ($r = .96$) since both are distributed to the same areas, primarily the urban centers. Only recently have Swahili papers entered the more isolated African areas. Each is also closely correlated with *European population,* the *number of telephones* and radios, per capita postal traffic, and Asian population.

2. *Number of Radios Licensed:* High correlations (over .90) exist with *number of telephones, Asian population,* trade licenses issued, total postal traffic, and newspaper circulation. Somewhat lower correlations are found with urban and European populations, suggesting perhaps that the radio is slightly more important than the newspaper for the non-European population as a measure of communications development—particularly for the Asians. But it must be noted that Asian newspapers were not included in the previous pair of variables.

3. *Number of Telephones:* Similar high correlations are found with other communications variables (*number of radios,* total mail traffic, and newspaper circulation) as well as with European and Asian populations, trade licenses issued, and road traffic density. This variable has the highest average correlation with all others, suggesting that it probably is a key index of over-all development.

4. *Total Mail Traffic:* Again, *number of telephones,* radios, Asians, and trade licenses score highest, along with road traffic density, number of political societies, and newspaper circulation. The strong association between the Asian trading population and communications development is repeated here. The high correlation with registered political societies

poses an interesting question: Does it result from the societies accounting for a large proportion of mail traffic, or are both indicative of developed social communications? The latter appears most likely.

5. *Per Capita Mail Traffic: Newspaper circulation* per capita is most closely associated with this variable, English slightly more so than Swahili, followed by percentage of Africans employed and total numbers of telephones, radios, and urban dwellers. Note the high intercorrelations among all communications variables whether based on per capita or total measures.

6. *Road Traffic Density:* This index scores most highly with *total mail traffic,* literacy, number of telephones, Swahili papers, and radios. High correlations exist with nearly all the communications variables. The relationship with literacy will be mentioned under that variable.

African Education

1. *Post-Secondary Education:* The number of Africans with thirteen or more years of education is most closely related to *population density* and African cash income. This indicates the greater emphasis placed upon education in the densely populated African reserves as opposed to the Scheduled Areas and the greater chance of receiving post-secondary education in the wealthier sections of the country.

2. *Literacy:* The percentage of African males over twenty years of age with some education is associated most highly with *road traffic density* and percentage of school-aged children attending primary school. It appears that road accessibility is a key element in school attendance and education, confirming the importance of transportation in the modernization process.

3. *Primary School Attendance:* This variable is most highly correlated with *literacy* and road traffic density. In general, it closely resembles literacy in its associations.

4. *Education Quality:* The percentage of Africans passing the Kenya Preliminary Examination (KPE) for entry into secondary schools is not highly correlated with any other variable. *Literacy,* as might be expected, has the highest correlation, followed by proximity to Nairobi measured both by road mileage and proportion of telephone calls made. Thus quality of education appears moderately re-

lated to a well-established educational system and close contacts with Nairobi.

Demographic Characteristics

1. *Population Density:* Population density is most closely associated with the *number of Africans with post-secondary education.* Also related are road traffic density, total African cash income, and literacy. The associated variables are measured in several different ways (total figures, density per square mile, percentages) and seem to reflect the general importance of population density in the patterns of modernization. This supports the thesis that the settled agricultural tribes have modernized more rapidly than the pastoralists. Whether these relationships hold true in a more uniformly agricultural population needs further investigation.

2. *European Population:* European population is most closely correlated with *newspaper circulation,* English only slightly more than Swahili. High correlations also exist with various communications indices (radio, telephone, mail), Asian population, trade, and percentage of Africans employed. Also interesting is the moderately high negative correlation with average African salaries, reflecting the low average wages paid to laborers in the European farming districts.

3. *Asian Population:* This variable correlates most closely with *trade licenses issued,* clearly showing the Asian domination of trade in Kenya. About as high is radio ownership, followed by indices similar to those related to the number of Europeans. The high correlations between both immigrant populations and most of the frequently used measurements of economic development is noteworthy. These relationships are indicative of the great importace of the two groups in the development of Kenya but may distort any attempt to map the level of modernization among Africans. High modernization scores for certain districts may reflect not African development but the presence of these immigrant communities.

4. *Ethnic Mixture:* Ethnic heterogeneity is most closely associated with *per capita mail traffic,* percentage of Africans employed, and newspaper circulation. Although not included in the figures presented, ethnic mixture and its associated variables are each highly correlated with a dichotomous variable based on location on the railway (1 = yes, 0 = no), support-

ing the view that the railway has been a great stimulus to internal migration, African paid employment, and communications development.

5. *Urban Population:* As measured by the population of the largest center in each district, this variable is most highly related to the *number of radios,* the Asian population, telephone distribution, newspaper circulation, and trade, all easily understandable. Note that European population correlates less with this variable than Asian (.76 to .88), owing most likely to the larger, nonurban European farming population.

Economic Development

1. *Tax Per Capita:* This index is not even moderately correlated with any other (i.e., above .40). *Ethnic mixture* has the highest coefficient (.39). The low correlations may be a result of the relatively higher taxes paid by the less well-developed pastoral groups (the evaluation of cattle for tax purposes is high), but even more so to the uneven distribution of tax delinquency. This is perhaps the least useful index of all in measuring spatial variations in modernization, but it has been included in the analysis because it does take into account wealth in cattle and land that does not normally enter into the exchange economy figures.

2. *Trade:* As expected, *Asian population* has the highest correlation, followed by total number of radios, mail traffic, registered political societies, cash income, telephones, and town population. The low correlation (not above .40) with ethnic mixture and connectivity with Nairobi by road probably reflects the penetration of the Asian trader into some of the more remote African areas.

3. *Percentage of Africans Employed: English newspaper circulation,* followed closely by per capita mail volume, Swahili papers, and number of Europeans correlate highest on this variable. Just as Asians dominate trade in Kenya, Europeans control African paid employment or are at least highly correlated with it spatially. The highest negative association between any two variables (−.52) was with percentage employed and average salary, indicating the low average income of paid African laborers in the major centers of employment and, conversely, the high salaries of those working in the more isolated districts of the north and east.

4. *Average African Salaries:* Because of

the tendency for average salaries to be lowest where the number employed and modernization in general are highest, this variable is negatively correlated with almost all others. The coefficients are also quite small, the largest being with *percentage employed* and European population (−.43). The fact that African laborers in the former White Highlands also produce crops for their own subsistence partly explains their lower average wages.

5. *African Cash Income:* This variable, taking into account both paid employment and commercial agriculture, scores highest with the number of *trade licenses issued* and *Asian population*, followed by several communications indices. The coefficient for Asian population is higher than that for European (.91 to .81), suggesting further the importance of the Asian trader in the over-all patterns of development. It should be stressed, however, that these correlations do not reveal cause and effect relationships. The role of the Asian trader in the modernization of Kenya is a very complex one and deserves much closer examination. The high correlation here, for example, may arise from the trader's choosing the wealthiest African areas to establish his business.

Political Development

1. *Number of Political Associations:* The distribution of registered political societies is related most closely to *trade* and *Asian population*, and also to African cash income and radio distribution, pointing out the influence of economic and communications development in stimulating political organization. A surprisingly low correlation (.27) is found with ethnic mixture, thus showing little tendency to form voluntary associations in areas with the greatest ethnic heterogeneity—a finding which does not support the commonly held view for Africa in general. This may, in part, be a result of restrictions placed upon political organization in the Scheduled Areas prior to independence, leading to relatively weak political development in the old White Highland districts, where ethnic mixture is greatest. The coefficient of .75 with town population, however, does suggest a close association between political organization and urbanization.

2. *Growth of KANU:* The diffusion of KANU branch offices appears most closely associated with *African cash income*, the number of registered political societies, radio distribution, total postal traffic, and literacy—a provocative list of related variables. Even as crudely measured here (districts were ranked according to the number of days after the initial registration of KANU as a political party that the district branch was established), the growth of KANU appears closely related to wealth, communications development, and literacy.

Connectivity with the Nairobi Core Area

1. *Road Distance:* Road distance to Nairobi from the district administrative center is most highly correlated with the *proportion of telephone calls made to Nairobi*, an interesting indication of the similarity between these two measures of core connectivity. Next are the growth of KANU and education quality, the former reflecting the role of Nairobi as center for the diffusion of KANU.

2. *Telephone Connectivity: Road distance* reciprocates here as the highest correlated variable, but is followed by Asian population, number of telephones, and African cash income, each of which can be seen as promoting connectivity with Nairobi regardless of physical distance. Like road distance, however, no variable is very highly correlated with this measure: the largest coefficient other than that between the two core-connectivity measures is .64.

Table 13 presents the average rank correlation coefficient of each variable with all others and thus gives a rough approximation of their associativeness within the data set. Five of the first six are measures of communications: total number of radios, telephones, postal traffic, and per capita newspaper circulation. The importance of communications indices in

TABLE 13
AVERAGE INTERCORRELATIONS

1. RADIO	.732		14. LITER	.629
2. NOTEL	.731		15. PEMPL	.603
3. TOPOS	.723		16. PRIMA	.573
4. SWAPA	.719		17. KANUS	.555
5. ASIAN	.714		18. PODEN	.501
6. ENGPA	.706		19. NBIFO	.483
7. TRAFF	.694		20. COLED	.472
8. TRADE	.693		21. DISTA	.437
9. EUROP	.690		22. KPEXA	.427
10. ACASH	.672		23. MIXTU	.359
11. SOCIE	.647		24. AVSAL	.232
12. PPLET	.640		25. TAXPP	.228
13. TOWNP	.633			

the over-all measurement of development has been found by many other investigators. Cutright, for example, used an index based upon newspaper circulation, newsprint production, radio receivers, and domestic mail per capita in measuring political development, while Lerner used a similar index based on newspaper circulation, radio receivers, and cinema seating capacity in his studies of transitional societies.[10]

Lerner states that "... a communications system is both index and agent of change in a total social system" and links communications development closely with the evolution of the "participant style" which characterizes modern society.[11] The "Dimensionality of Nations" project, conducted by a number of scholars at Northwestern and other universities, supports further the role of communications in measuring modernization. Working with 236 variables and up to 82 independent states—using data from the mid-1950's—this research team discovered fifteen factors, or dimensions, of international significance which describe the most important ways states differ from one another. Their first dimension, labeled "Development," accounted for twenty per cent of the total variance after rotation and clustered together a group of variables similar to those used in the present study of modernization in Kenya.[12]

—————

[10] Phillips Cutright, "National Political Development: Measurement and Analysis," *American Sociological Review* (1963), pp. 253–64; and Daniel Lerner, "Communications Systems and Social Systems: A Statistical Exploration in History and Policy," *Behavioral Science* (1957), pp. 266–75; and Lerner, *The Passing of Traditional Society, passim.*

[11] "Communications Systems," p. 266. The participant style in modern societies is also discussed in Gabriel Almond and Sydney Verba, *The Civic Culture: Political Attitudes and Democracy in Five Nations* (1963).

[12] R. J. Rummel, H. Guetzkow, H. Sawyer, and R. Tanter, *Dimensionality of Nations* (forthcoming).

This Development Dimension suggests that the most important element distinguishing states from one another is social, economic, and political development. Other dimensions included, after Development, were Political Orientation, Size, Catholic Culture, Foreign Conflict Behavior, Density, Oriental Culture, and Domestic Conflict Behavior. What is important for the present study, however, were the high loadings on the Development Dimension of per capita telephones, radio receivers, newspaper circulation, and domestic mail.

Other highly associative variables include the size of the immigrant population, Asian slightly higher than European, the development of trade, and road traffic density. The first nine variables taken together form a highly intercorrelated cluster (all coefficients over .80) which appear to identify a major dimension of modernization in Kenya obtainable through bivariate analysis alone.

Thus cluster, however, points out a shortcoming of the data used in this study. For no variable of the nine can the African component be clearly identified—who owns the phones, who uses the roads—and therefore a scaling of districts according to the list of average correlations would result in a pattern which heavily reflected the existence of the much more modernized immigrant communities. This would distort any attempt to derive implications concerning *African* social mobilization.

In consequence, many of the conventionally used indices of modernization are potentially misleading in any area where there is a large and advanced minority community. Proximity to a more modernized population is an important element in stimulating change, but the distinction in levels of modernization measured by most indices must clearly take into account the potential distortions caused by this juxtaposition of cultures. This injunction is applicable both to the bivariate comparisons and to the principal components analysis.

VII

Principal Components Analysis: Results and Interpretation

Many broad patterns of modernization in Kenya have already been identified in the preceding chapters, first through an historical geographic interpretation of the contact situation and then with the analysis of some of the key variables associated with the modernization process. In the following two chapters, the results of principal components analysis are presented in an attempt to ascertain some of the underlying dimensions of modernization and to describe and explain their spatial expressions. Moreover, these chapters represent a detailed, multivariate description of spatial variations in the transition from traditional to modern ways of life at a critical point in Kenya's history—the time of independence in late 1963.

DIMENSION I: "DEVELOPMENT"

Eight factors were extracted through the principal components method. Factor 1 accounted for 63 per cent of the total variance, F2 for 11 per cent, F3 for 5.8 per cent, and F4 for 5.5 per cent—a total of more than 85 per cent on the first four dimensions. The remaining components explained less than 4 per cent each, or less than would be accounted for if a single variable defined a component perfectly with all others loading 0.00.[1] No economy of description seemed to be added after the fourth dimension, and consequently only F1–4 have been interpreted.

The first component, as expected, grouped together most of the variables into a large sum-mary dimension similar to ones obtained by other scholars working at the international level, particularly in terms of the high loadings for nearly all the communications indices.[2] This finding lends further support to the contention that modernization is systemic, in that a large number of interrelated events occur together as an area moves from traditional to modern ways of life. It also upholds the key role assigned to communications development in the modernization process.

F1 has been labeled the *Development Dimension* in order to retain a conceptual link with previous studies and to reserve the use of modernization for more specific purposes. Development is viewed here as the more general term and one with fewer direct behavioral connotations than modernization.

Factor loadings were high (greater than .75) for sixteen of the twenty-five variables and moderately high (.50 to .75) for six others (see Table 14). The only low loadings (below .30) were for tax per capita (.29) and average salary (−.28), supporting the view discussed in the previous sections that these variables have little to do with the major patterns of modernization.

The highest loadings were scored on the communications variables, and the ranking of the indices is almost exactly the same as their ranking by average bivariate rank correlation in Table 13. This is not unexpected given the nature of the principal components technique. The determination of factor scores, however, permits a more accurate weighing of these variables by district. All the factor scores are listed in Appendix B and mapped in Figure 36, which may be considered a highly generalized portrayal of the geography of modernization in Kenya. It should be stressed, however, that this map represents the same potential distortion

---

[1] The percentage of the total variance explained by a given dimension is derived from the sum of the squared factor loadings divided by the total variance (which, in this case, is 25, reflecting the number of variables). Thus, if one variable loads at 1.00 and all others at 0.00, the explained variance would be 1/25 or 4 per cent. This threshold provides a convenient break for interpretation, for above this level there exists a clustering of related variables which can be described in one dimension that "soaks up" more of the variance than would a single variable. Thus, the "economy" aimed for in factor analysis is achieved.

[2] See Rummel *et al.*, and Schnore, *op. cit.*

TABLE 14
DIMENSION I: "DEVELOPMENT"

Variable	Loading	Brief Label
RADIO	.97	Large number of radio licenses issued
NOTEL	.97	Large number of telephone receivers
TOPOS	.96	Many letters received and posted
ASIAN	.96	Large Asian population
SWAPA	.95	High per capita circulation of Swahili newspapers
TRADE	.93	Well-developed trade
ENGPA	.93	High per capita circulation of English newspapers
TRAFF	.92	Well developed and utilized road network
EUROP	.91	Large European population
ACASH	.90	High total income for Africans from agriculture and paid employment
SOCIE	.87	Large number of political associations
TOWNP	.85	Large urban population
PPLET	.85	High level of postal traffic per capita
LITER	.84	Large proportion of adult Africans with some education
PEMPL	.79	High percentage of Africans employed
PRIMA	.76	Large proportion of African children attending primary school
KANUS	.74	Early development of Kenya African National Union

Variance accounted for: 63 per cent.

Range of factor scores: Nairobi 33.6 (most "developed") to Turkana 643.6 (least "developed").

with respect to the African population that was mentioned previously.

The range of factor scores extends from 33.6 for Nairobi to nearly 650 for the isolated, sparsely populated, pastoral district of Turkana in the northwest. Nairobi is followed, after a gap of nearly 60 points, by Mombasa and Nakuru. Mombasa District, like the Nairobi Extra-Provincial District, is almost entirely urban. The city is the second largest in Kenya and the major port in East Africa. For this reason, a high ranking would be expected. But the similarly high rank for Nakuru district, which contains in addition to the town of Nakuru (only a third the size of Mombasa) almost 2,500 square miles of farming country, is more surprising. The score for Nakuru seems to reflect the greater emphasis placed upon the highland areas vis-a-vis the coast throughout the colonial period in Kenya.

Even more than Nairobi, Nakuru symbolized the "White Highlands" and because of its central position was considered its "capital." Nakuru is also one of the most accessible areas within the East African road and rail network. It has the shortest total road distance among towns of more than 4,000 people, connecting it with all other towns of the same size in East Africa. Nairobi scores sixth and Mombasa twenty-third. It also leads all other towns when roads are weighted according to quality and, interestingly enough, has a greater urban population (towns of 4,000 or more) within a 100-mile radius than any other East African town. Nakuru is not only the pivot of the transport and communications network in Kenya but is in a similar position with respect to all of East Africa.[3]

In part, this high relative ranking for Nakuru District may be the result of its greater total population when compared to Mombasa (237,-385 to 179,575) and thus higher resultant scores on variables based on total numbers (e.g., RADIO, NOTEL, TOPOS). But it should be noted that for none of these high loading variables does Nakuru rank higher than Mombasa. It achieves its position on the list of factor scores by being consistently highly ranked on nearly all of the most important variables in this dimension.[4]

Scoring between 125 and 250 are nearly all the districts wholly within the Scheduled Areas (Thika, Uasin Gishu, Naivasha, Trans-Nzoia, and Nanyuki) and those districts (Kiambu, Nyeri, Central Nyanza, and Kericho) which are part Scheduled and part Non-Scheduled area. This illustrates two major points about the spatial pattern of modernization in Kenya.

First, the Scheduled Areas, because they contain nearly all the resident non-African population, both European and Asian, are clearly the most modernized sections of Kenya as gauged by the general Development Di-

[3] I wish to thank Marilyn Tschannen, a graduate student in geography at Northwestern University, for compiling these indices for use in this study.

[4] As a reminder, factor scores are determined by multiplying the column vector for the dimension (in this case, the factor loadings on F1) by the row vector of the original ranked data matrix for each district (in this case, Nakuru). The higher the ranks (i.e., the closer to 1) the smaller will be the factor score. In the discussion, however, low scores will be highly ranked (i.e., closer to unity).

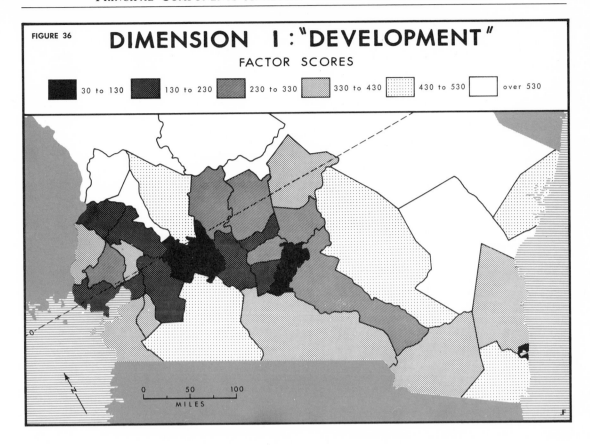

FIGURE 36

DIMENSION I: "DEVELOPMENT"
FACTOR SCORES

30 to 130   130 to 230   230 to 330   330 to 430   430 to 530   over 530

0   50   100
MILES

mension. This is not surprising, since this dimension is heavily dependent upon such accouterments of the European farmer and administrator and Asian trader as radios, telephones, postal facilities, newspapers, and a good road network. Note also the high loadings on European and Asian population variables.

Secondly, the most "favored" African areas are those in closest proximity to the major centers of immigrant communities. Thus Kiambu, surrounding Nairobi in the north, ranks fifth in factor scores. Nyeri, along another line of contact with Nanyuki and other sections of the old European highland areas, ranks seventh. Both these Kikuyu districts have been major centers of African political development. Fort Hall, the third district of the former Kikuyu Reserve, contains the more conservative core area of the Kikuyu, has had less direct contact with the European farming areas and the towns, has generally been more resistant to change, and ranks thirteenth on the list of factor scores.

Central Nyanza, containing Kisumu, another major center of African politics and node of the second largest population cluster, also ranks high (eighth). This district contains the only important agricultural area reserved in the past for the Asian population as well as a section of the former Highlands. Kisumu is also very accessible within the East African transport network, especially when Lake Victoria traffic is taken into account. The Kiambu, Nyeri, and Kisumu areas (the latter containing not only the Luo but the Maragoli and other nearby Luhya groups of North Nyanza as well) were the major sources of laborers for the towns, the railways, and the European and Asian farming areas.

Also included in this range is Kericho District (ninth), where a large portion of the well-developed European tea estates is located. The major African group occupying this district is the Kipsigis, formerly an almost purely pastoral people who became a showpiece for the colonial government because of the ease with which they have taken to modern commercial agriculture.[5] Many reasons have been offered to explain this transition, but it is clear that proximity to the European farming areas within the same district was a vital stimulant to the changes which occurred.

By calling such districts as Kiambu, Central Nyanza, and Kericho "favored," it is not meant to imply that there was a purposeful attempt by the colonial government to develop these areas. It has been through their locational advantage and the ease and intensity of interaction with the non-African population— which in turn was affected by their traditional social and economic organization as well as location—that these districts have achieved relatively high levels of development.

Naivasha (tenth) and Trans-Nzoia (eleventh) follow Kericho on the ranked list of factor scores, after which a gap of about 33 points occurs before Nanyuki and another gap of 31 points between Nanyuki and Fort Hall. Starting with Fort Hall, between 270 and 400, there is a group of moderately developed districts headed by Fort Hall, Machakos, North Nyanza, Laikipia, and Embu (thirteenth through seventeenth).

Laikipia never lived up to the dreams of the early European settlers after it was removed from the Masai Reserve and placed almost entirely within the White Highlands. Except for some sections in the south, particularly around Thomson's Falls, it has remained poorly developed and sparsely populated. It has the lowest rank of any district wholly or in large part in the Scheduled Areas.

Machakos (Kamba), North Nyanza (Luhya), and Embu (Kikuyu, Embu, and other related groups), with close contacts with either Nairobi or Kisumu, have been important secondary centers in the evolution of African politics in Kenya.

Toward the middle of this range of moderately modernized areas are several districts, including Meru (eighteenth), Kisii (nineteenth), and Elgon Nyanza (22), which were among the earliest centers for African cash crop development and remain among the most productive agricultural areas today. Meru led all districts in African cash crop income in 1962 (£1,224,000), followed by Embu (£1,034,000),

Kisii (£588,000), and Elgon Nyanza (£585,-000).[6]

This suggests that African commercial agriculture has not had a very significant impact on the general patterns of modernization in Kenya. These agriculturally advanced districts have not played a particularly important political role until recently, suggesting further that economic "satisfaction" may have actually hindered political development in some sections of Kenya.

This is in keeping with the discussion in Chapter IV, where it was mentioned that commercial agriculture was permitted in certain areas largely because they were somewhat isolated and did not provide a major component of the labor force on European farms. This relationship between economic satisfaction and political development presents a focus for much needed behavioralist research in Kenya and elsewhere in Africa.

The least well developed districts (scoring over 400) include most of the more isolated and sparsely populated pastoral areas of northern, eastern, and southern (Masai) Kenya. The major exception is South Nyanza, a fairly densely populated (90 percent Luo) district which is largely agricultural and contains an important commercial sector. South Nyanza has always been isolated—it has no railway link and very few good roads and depends heavily upon Lake Victoria transport for outside contact. Much of this district has only recently been occupied by the Luo, and perhaps a great deal of the aggressive energy of these people has been channeled into this internal expansion at the expense of participation in the over-all processes of modernization. In addition, the major route of demographic movement crosses the border into northern Tanzania, where a large Luo community resides today. This division between two modernization systems may have also hindered the development of South Nyanza.[7]

---

[5] For a description of these changes, see C. W. Barwell, "A Note on Some Changes in the Economy of the Kipsigis Tribe," *Journal of African Administration* (1956, 95–101.

[6] Figures are from *District Annual Reports*, Department of Agriculture, 1963.

[7] It should be noted that the Central Nyanza Luo are also somewhat divided between two modernization systems, or perhaps three: there are at least 37,000 Luo in Uganda and part of the Tanzanian Luo are also from Central Nyanza. But this has been an entirely different type of migration—primarily a movement of Luo workers into the major towns—and has been directed to some of the focal points of modernization in East Africa. There is no accurate breakdown of district of origin among the Uganda Luo, but is very likely that by far the larger proportion are from Central Nyanza.

South Nyanza is one of the most interesting districts in contemporary Kenya. Its great difference in factor scores with Central Nyanza (230 points), also primarily a Luo area, clearly reveals the gap created by the uneven spatial impact of modernization within a single ethnic group. The Luo in Central Nyanza were in closer contact from the beginning of the colonial period with the major centers of development along the railway, in the Highlands, and in Kisumu town—the largest center between Nakuru and Jinja (Uganda). More than their southern brothers, they supplied large numbers of laborers both in Kenya and, as railway workers, throughout East Africa.[8]

Given the nature of its population (agricultural Luo), its size (over 480,000 people), and its location (on the relatively well watered and fertile fringes of Lake Victoria), South Nyanza deviates from normal expectations more than any other district in Kenya. At the same time, it probably has the potential to rise most rapidly along the scale of modernization in the future—a potential which is not only recognized by development planners, who now realize how much the district has been ignored in the past, but also by Kenya politicians who have made South Nyanza an important ideological battleground in the attempt to direct the large, weakly mobilized population to their support.

The Masai Districts of Kajiado and Narok are also included within the list of poorly developed areas. In many ways, the Masai Reserve acted as an almost separate political unit during the colonial period—a "reserve" in every sense of the word. The Masai resisted the few attempts made to induce change and have remained one of the most tradition-bound peoples of Kenya. Like the Luo, they have been split in two by the Kenya-Tanzania boundary and, like parts of South Nyanza, these districts have been generally isolated from the mainstream of Kenya politics.

Although most of the Masai territory lies just south of the main railway line and thus borders the southern section of the Sched-uled Areas and Nairobi, the advantages of physical proximity have been outweighed by social distance and the impact of one of the most forceful internal boundaries in Africa. One need only look at a population distribution map to trace the Masai Reserve boundary, especially near Kiambu and Kisii districts, where densely populated agricultural areas end abruptly and the sparsely inhabited pastoral country of the nomadic Masai begins —with no significant change in the physical environment.[9]

Physical proximity, however, has had some effect on the Masai areas, particularly for the sections of Kajiado closest to Nairobi. Ngong, just on the outskirts of the capital city,[10] was the administrative center for Southern Province (which included the Kamba districts of Machakos and Kitui as well as the Masai areas until the recent boundary changes) and was the site for the formal establishment of the now-dissolved Kenya African Democratic Union (KADU). The Great North Road, an all-weather route running southward from Nairobi through Tanzania, Zambia, and on to South Africa, cuts through Kajiado to link the core area of Kenya with the well-developed Arusha-Kilimanjaro area of northern Tanzania. Plans also exist for the construction of a trunk railway approximately parallel to this route.[11] A branch railway already exists to Magadi, site of one of the world's largest soda deposits and the leading mineral-producing area in Kenya. As a result of its location and important mineral resource, Kajiado scores nearly eighty points higher than the more isolated district of Narok.

It should be noted that nearly all the coastal districts have medium to low factor scores. Had a similar study of the patterns of development been made at the turn of the century, there is no doubt that the coast would have scored much higher relative to the in-

[8] For example, in the 1948 Census, where some district of origin data are available, it was shown that there were nearly 13,000 Central Nyanza Luo in Nairobi as compared with 4,000 from South Nyanza. For Thika District, the figures were 5,000 to 2,000; for Nakuru, almost 8,000 stated that they were from Central Nyanza while another 5,500 were unspecified. Kericho contained the largest number of South Nyanza migrants, about 8,500, but there were also over 13,000 from Central Nyanza.

[9] See, for example, Philip W. Porter, "East Africa—Population Distribution," Map Supplement Number 6, *Annals of the Association of American Geographers* (March, 1966).

[10] The Ngong Road is one of the major thoroughfares of suburban Nairobi, but it ends suddenly at the city limits, where the asphalt turns into murram through the settlement of Ngong and then into a nearly impassable dirt track beyond it. This is a good example of how the landscape reveals the impact of internal boundaries, particularly when they separate two areas with great differences in levels of modernization.

[11] *Development Plan, 1964–1970, op. cit.,* p. 95.

terior. Mombasa would still have led the coastal area, but Lamu District with its important port and road and telegraph connections, would have been close behind.

The coast, as mentioned previously, was isolated as development became concentrated in the highlands. Mombasa became the port for the interior and did not act as a generator of modernization for its surrounding areas to the extent that Nairobi and Kisumu did for their hinterlands, a fact made amply clear from the maps in Chapters IV and V. If it were not for Mombasa itself, this area would probably be the least developed coastal region relative to the interior of any ocean-fringing African state exccept those focusing on the Nile (Sudan and the United Arab Republic).

DIMENSION II: "MODERNIZATION SUBSYSTEMS"

The broad scope of the first dimension does not give an entirely appropriate picture of the African component in modernization and political development. As previously mentioned, many of the relevant indices do not distinguish between the African and non-African, and it becomes extremely difficult to interpret the factor scores on the Development Dimension in terms of specifically African economic, social, and political behavior.

For example, it has been shown that African politics did not emerge from the European farming districts, nearly all of which score highly on F1. Clearly then there is little direct correlation between the existence of many physical concomitants of modernization, such as telephones, newspapers, and roads, and the extent and depth of African political activity.

Furthermore, one cannot assume that the African population of, let us say, Uasin Gishu District (ranked sixth on F1) is inherently more modernized than that of Fort Hall (thirteenth). The higher score for Uasin Gishu probably reflects the more than 1,200 Europeans and 3,800 Asians residing in the district, as contrasted to the 150 Europeans and 800 Asians in Fort Hall.

Reference to Dimension II, however, introduces another important measure of variation which helps to bring the distinctly African element into better perspective. It provides a set of descriptive characteristics which distinguishes the two modernization subsystems discussed in Chapter V: one in which the

level of development strongly reflects the existence of resident immigrant communities and another where the direct influence of non-African residents is much less but, owing to interaction and feedback from the minority-dominated areas, significant behavioral changes within the African community have occurred. For convenience, the former is labeled the European Subsystem and the latter the African Subsystem.

Dimension II, which accounts for 11 percent of the total variance, is at first difficult to analyze and label. As can be seen from Table 15, no variable loads higher than .75 and only five are between .50 and .75. The largest loadings are for degree of ethnic mixture, number of post-secondary school educated, population density, percentage employed, and average African salaries.

In general, the districts with the highest positive scores are sparsely populated, have a high degree of ethnic mixture and percentage of Africans employed, have high rates of newspaper circulation per capita, and tend to be more urbanized. At the same time, however, the African population of these districts is poorly educated (note positive loadings for COLED, PRIMA, LITER), has low average

TABLE 15
DIMENSION II: MODERNIZATION SUBSYSTEMS

Variable	Loading	Brief Label (Lowest Negative Scores)
MIXTU	−.74	Great ethnic homogeneity
COLED	.65	Many Africans with post-secondary education
PODEN	.62	High population density
PEMPL	−.51	Small percentage of Africans employed
AVSAL	.50	High average African salaries
PPLET	−.39	Low per capita postal traffic.
KANUS	.31	Early establishment of KANU branch office
ENGPA	−.30	Few English newspapers per capita
PRIMA	.27	African primary education widespread
TAXPP	−.26	Low tax per capita
LITER	.24	High literacy
ACASH	.23	High total cash income for Africans
EUROP	−.23	Low European population
TOWNP	−.22	Low urban population
SWAPA	−.20	Few Swahili newspapers per capita

Variance accounted for: 11 per cent.

Range of factor scores: Fort Hall −42.0 (African Subsystem) to Laikipia 55.6 (European Subsystem).

salaries, established a KANU branch office rather late, and has rather low total cash income despite the high percentage employed. The districts at this end of the scale are either sections of the Scheduled Areas (Laikipia, Nanyuki) or parts of Coast Province (Lamu, Kilifi). The full list of factor scores is included in Appendix B.

The lowest negative scores reflect the other extreme: high densities, great ethnic homogeneity, a high level of educational development, an early start in the growth of political parties, and relative African wealth. These include some of the major African "reserve" districts of interior Kenya: Fort Hall, Kisii, North Nyanza.

Intermediate scores group together such diverse areas as Nairobi and Turkana, Mombasa and the Northern Frontier District, Central Nyanza and Narok—districts which scored at the extremes on F1. They fall in the middle here, however, since they score consistently high or low on the key F2 variables and thus achieve a balance resulting from the mixture of positive and negative scores.

Since F1 and F2 are orthogonal and thus independent, it would be incorrect to assume that either extreme on F2 represents a higher or lower level of modernization. Conceptually, Dimension II describes the major ways in which districts differ after the variations of the Development Dimension are extracted or "held constant."

When the two sets of factor scores are plotted together, however, the interpretation of the second dimension becomes much easier. In Figure 37, Development increases toward the bottom of the graph, while positive scores on F2 are to the right and negative to the left. As a matter of convenience, the axes pass through the median score on each dimension.

From the graph, it appears that F2 divides the Development Dimension into two major sectors which reflect the characteristics of the modernization subsystems previously discussed. Quadrant I, for example, contains *all* the districts wholly within the Scheduled Areas, plus Mombasa and Kericho (which is a mixed district). In contrast, Quadrant II includes the major centers of African nationalism and social change, headed by Nairobi, Kiambu, Nyeri, and Central Nyanza.

Many of the characteristics of the two subsystems and the linkages between them have already been noted: the contrast between the main areas of African paid employment and commercial agriculture, the geography of African education, the emergence of quasi-urban areas in the hinterlands of Nairobi and Kisumu, and the patterns of interaction growing out of internal labor migrations. Dimension II helps to isolate these subsystems more clearly, to weigh the major differentiating variables, and to determine with some precision the spatial variations of development in each.

DIMENSIONS I AND II: SYNTHESIS AND INTERPRETATION

It may be valuable, at this point, to synthesize some of the earlier findings of this study so that the causes and consequences of the emergence of the two modernization subsystems can be more clearly understood. The division is not simply the outgrowth of the dual economies thought to characterize many former colonial areas, for this interpretation tends to neglect the complex and intensive interaction between the two sectors, particularly their strong interdependence. Moreover, the forces operating are not only economic but have equally important political, social, and psychological overtones.

The formidable administrative and social barriers associated with the growth of the White Highlands produced a compartmentalization which has had profound effects on the geographical patterns of modernization in Kenya. The European farming districts became a recognizable subsystem characterized by a relatively high infrastructural development and proportion of non-African residents. In addition, however, the demands of the minority-dominated economy led to a close interaction with adjacent centers of African population and the filling in of the formerly sparsely populated sections of the Highlands by peoples from all over Kenya. (Note the high negative loading for MIXTU on F2.)

Interaction with the White Highlands thus created another subsystem which included those districts in closest association with European commercial and administrative activities. A greater opportunity to receive an education, a significant amount of income primarily from agriculture, and more developed African

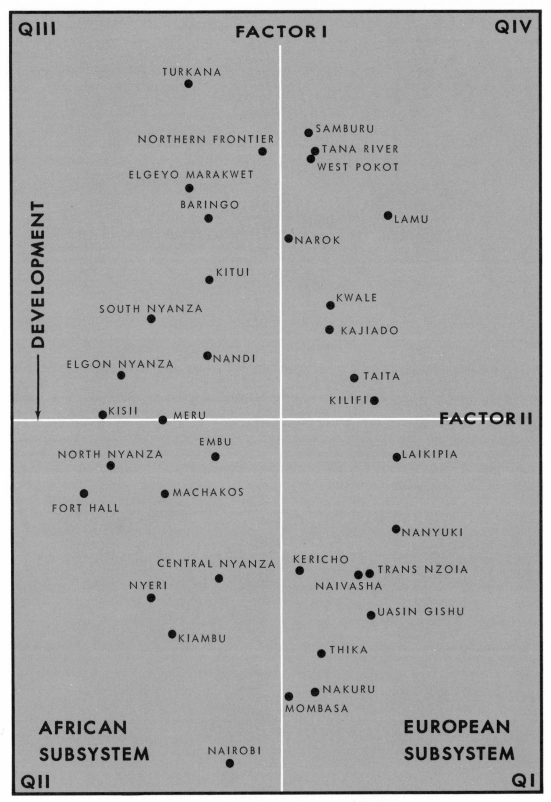

FIGURE 37. MODERNIZATION SUBSYSTEMS

political participation distinguished this subsystem from the first.

The second subsystem did not include all the rest of Kenya on an equal basis but involved certain districts more than others. Some areas, in fact, appeared not to be affected very strongly by either subsystem. The key elements controlling this differentiation were many and complex, but a number of important ones can be recognized.

First was *geographical proximity*. The greater the distance away from the Highlands, the less the districts were affected. The clearest example is the coastal region, which never recovered from the cessation of the slave trade and the shift of economic focus into the interior. Mombasa has become a relatively modernized exclave of the Kenya Highlands and has failed to act as a generator of modernization for the surrounding coastal districts to the extent that Nairobi and Kisumu have for their hinterlands. Kamba, Luo, Kikuyu and other interior peoples have played an economic and political role in Mombasa far greater than their numbers relative to the Mijikenda, Taita, and other coastal groups would suggest.

Similar distance relationships can be seen, although to a lesser degree, in the interior. Peripheral agricultural districts such as Meru, Kisii, and South Nyanza (and to a certain extent, Embu and Elgon Nyanza) have been less involved in this second modernization subsystem than might have been expected, given their early start in commercial agriculture and relative wealth. As has already been suggested, economic satisfaction or complacency in these areas may have reduced the intensity of interaction with the more modernized sections of Kenya. These districts are part of the African Subsystem but clearly subsidiary to such areas as Kiambu, Nyeri, and Central Nyanza.

A second factor of importance has been *the nature of traditional society*, particularly the contrasts between pastoralist and agriculturalist and their different reactions to European contact. A sedentary, primarily agricultural population like the Kikuyu, Luhya, and Luo is more amenable to the forces of social mobilization than nomadic pastoralists, such as the Masai or Samburu. Even within the same ethnic group, where it is divided into pastoral and agricultural segments as among

the Kamba, Suk, Elgeyo, and Marakwet, the agriculturalists have modernized more rapidly. (Note the contrast between the primarily agricultural Kamba district of Machakos and the largely pastoral Kamba district of Kitui in the factor scores for F1.) It is also no coincidence that modernization among once essentially pastoral groups such as the Kipsigis and Nandi has been closely associated with the emergence of a settled agricultural economy.

A related variable is *population density*. With a greater concentration of population, larger numbers of people are accessible to the instruments of modernization: schools, cities, the mass media. In addition, modernization has resulted in population growth in the most affected areas, especially in the quasi-urban hinterlands of Nairobi and Kisumu, where "rural" population densities occasionally surpass 1,200 to the square mile. High population density thus appears to be both stimulus and response to the modernization process.

Were it not for the relatively sparse population of the former European farming districts, it is likely that PODEN would have loaded much higher on F1 than it did (.68). Its close association with the high scoring districts of the African Subsystem, however, indicates its important relationship to the over-all patterns of African modernization.

Another factor affecting the extent and intensity of interaction with the European Subsystem has been the *patterns of internal migration*. Before effective colonial administration froze the dynamic traditional milieu, a number of important migratory thrusts had been under way. The Kikuyu were expanding southward and, to a lesser extent, to the north and northwest; the Luo were steadily occupying the lowlands fringing Lake Victoria; the Kamba had expanded throughout a large area of East Africa, owing to their early contacts with the caravan trade; and the Somali were pressing beyond the Tana River from the northeast. A number of smaller movements were occurring to the northwestern highlands as the surrounding population began slowly to fill the no man's land in the Uasin Gishu and Trans-Nzoia areas.

In most cases, colonial administration put an end to these internal migrations. The "Somali Line," for example, was established to guarantee the isolation of these expanding pastoralists, and the delimitation of Native Reserves secured limits to the free movement of the major ethnic groups.

At the same time, however, new outlets for population movement were provided in the urban centers and on European farms which accommodated many of the pressures that initiated the pre-colonial migrations—overpopulation and the need for new land, dissatisfaction with traditional social organization, internal conflicts.

The degree to which these alternate outlets affected the various migrant communities was controlled largely by the geography of European contact. Nairobi, for example, lay across the major corridor of Kikuyu population expansion and also acted as the center for the spread of European farmers into the Highlands. The Kikuyu, whose migrants were already oriented in this direction, were quick to involve themselves in the new outlets and soon became the dominant African group not only in Nairobi but in nearly all the European farming areas.

Nairobi also attracted large numbers of Kamba from nearby Machakos District, while Kisumu acted as a similar gateway for the Luo and Luhya of Nyanza Province. These four groups—Kikuyu, Kamba, Luo, and Luhya —formed the bulk of the African labor force in the European Subsystem and through the two-way flow of men and money led in the creation of a new modernization subsystem in the primarily agricultural, densely populated Native Reserve districts fringing the White Highlands on the east and west.

The processes involved in the creation of this second subsystem can be linked to what Karl Deutsch has termed the "lift-pump" effect. It is worthwhile to quote Deutsch at length on this point for he produces invaluable insights into the basis for African modernization and political development in Kenya:

> Where large economic or industrial developments have taken place, they have had a "lift-pump" effect on the underlying populations. They have induced migrations of populations to the regions of settlement, employment, and opportunity, and put these newcomers into intensive economic and political contact with the locally predominant peoples, and with each other. This physical, political, and economic contact had one of two cultural and linguistic consequences: either it led to national assimilation, or, if national assimilation to the dominant group could not keep pace with the growing need for some wider

group membership for the newcomer, then the "lift-pump" effect would tend to lead eventually to a new growth of nationalism among the newly mobilized populations. Eventually, it might result in the assimilation of some previously separate groups, not to the still-dominant minority, but to the "awakening" bulk of the population.

> This rebellious nationalism of the newly mobilized population rejects the language or culture of the dominant nationality. Yet it shares many of its values and it desires to share or acquire its wealth and opportunities. The motives for this secessionist nationalism are thus to a significant extent the same motives that would lead, under different circumstances, to national assimilation. Nationalism and assimilation are, therefore, ambivalent in the economic as well as in the psychological sense. The same wealth and prestige are pursued by either method: in national assimilation they are to be attained through sharing, while in national resistance they are to be attained through power.

> Both national assimilation and national resurgence thus respond in a "lift-pump" situation to the power of the "pump." The intensity and appeal of nationalism in a world of sharply differentiated income and living standards perhaps may tend to be *inversely proportional to the barriers to mobility between regions and classes* and *directly proportional to the barriers against cultural assimilation, and to the extent of the economic and prestige differences between classes, cultures, and regions.*[12]

Since the barriers to assimilation within the White Highlands were so great, the major centers of African development and change grew in those areas which were physically and economically most closely associated with the European Subsystem but outside of it. The population of these areas experienced the impact of the "lift-pump" effect with fewer societal restrictions than those who resided outside the traditional territory. Obtaining an education was easier; wealth, both from wages sent back by laborers and from indigenous agricultural development, was relatively abundant; political parties, at least on the district level, were more easily established; and proximity afforded the necessary infrastructural basis for modernization (cities, roads, railways, the mass media).

The relative "closedness" of the European "island" thus stimulated the emergence of

---

[12] Karl W. Deutsch, "The Growth of Nations: Some Recurrent Patterns of Political and Social Integration," *World Politics* (1953), pp. 179–80.

another subsystem articulated to the few openings existing in the first. This subsystem included the major centers of African political development, educational achievement, wealth, and change. Reference to Dimension II, therefore, produces a clearer picture of the patterns of African modernization in Kenya than that obtained through the use of the general Development Dimension alone.

The position of Nairobi is revealing. It forms the focal point for both subsystems, but is placed farther to the left in Figure 37 than any area of the former White Highlands except for a few mixed districts like Kiambu and Central Nyanza and is therefore included within the African Subsystem. One wonders whether it would have been similarly placed several decades ago, before its population grew so rapidly and it began to increase as the focus for educated Africans, industrial development, and African political activity. Nairobi has probably been shifting closer to the characteristics of the African Subsystem and away from those of the European as African modernization has increased.

The European Subsystem is headed by Mombasa, Nakuru, and Thika, but it achieves its purest characteristics in Nanyuki and Laikipia, fairly isolated districts in which the patterns of development have been most heavily dominated by the resident European community. Kericho is offset to the left in Figure 37—closer to the characteristics of the African Subsystem—reflecting the large part of the district that is outside the Scheduled Areas and occupied by the Kipsigis. A similar displacement within the African Subsystem is seen for Central Nyanza, another mixed district but one in which the African component is dominant. As previously noted, Quadrant I contains every district wholly within the Scheduled Areas and, as shown in Figure 38, its geographical outlines are nearly coincident with those of the former White Highlands.

Among the less well developed areas attached to the European Subsystem (Quadrant IV) are the remainder of Coast Province (Kilifi, Taita, Kwale, Lamu, and Tana River), the Masai districts of Kajiado and Narok,

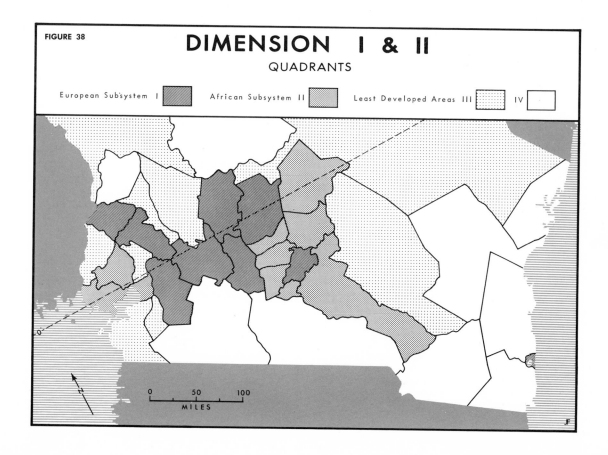

FIGURE 38

DIMENSION I & II

QUADRANTS

European Subsystem I   African Subsystem II   Least Developed Areas III   IV

0   50   100
MILES

and two districts very much like the Masai areas, Samburu and West Pokot. Because of isolation, traditional economic systems, and the geography of colonization, these districts have not experienced the "lift-pump" effect to the same extent as those with similar F1 scores in the African Subsystem. Put in another way, the level of modernization which does exist is largely a reflection of the presence of immigrant communities—the European and Asian plantation and resort areas along the coast, the sisal estates near Voi (Taita), the Magadi Soda Company in Kajiado—and has little basis in behavioral change within the African population of the districts.

The African Subsystem is headed by Nairobi and the major Kikuyu (Kiambu, Nyeri, Fort Hall, and the largely Kikuyu-occupied Embu), Luo (Central Nyanza), Luhya (North Nyanza), and Kamba (Machakos) districts. Among the less developed areas forming part of this subsystem are Meru, Kisii, Elgon Nyanza, South Nyanza, and Kitui, all of which have participated significantly in the economic, social, and political mainstream of modernization in Kenya despite their relatively low levels of development.

A good argument can be made to consider the least developed districts of both subsystems (Narok, Lamu, West Pokot, Tana River, and Samburu from the European and Baringo, Elgeyo-Marakwet, the Northern Frontier, and Turkana from the African) as effectively outside of either. In Deutsch's terms, their populations are unmobilized and provide a reservoir of potential support for the leading mobilizational groups.[13]

DIMENSIONS III AND IV

The third and fourth dimensions, each explaining only between 5 and 6 per cent of the total variance, are heavily loaded on those variables least represented on F1 and F2: KPEXA, AVSAL, TAXPP, DISTA, NBIFO, and somewhat less on SOCIE, KANUS, and

---

[13] A party revolt in the Kenya Parliament during April, 1966, included representatives from many of these areas. Even more important for the present study, however, are the representatives who, soon after the revolt, reversed their decision and asked to be reaccepted into the government. They included members from West Pokot, Baringo, and parts of the former Northern Frontier District, thus indicating the ambivalence of these poorly developed areas with respect to the emerging ideological conflicts within the Kenya government.

TABLE 16
DIMENSIONS III AND IV

Identification	Loading	III Brief Label (Lowest Negative Scores)
KPEXA	.67	High percentage passing KPE
AVSAL	−.57	Low average salaries
DISTA	.48	Close to Nairobi
TAXPP	−.41	Low tax per capita
NBIFO	.27	High interaction with Nairobi (telephone)
SOCIE	−.25	Few political societies
MIXTU	−.22	Ethnic homogeneity

Variance accounted for: 5.8 per cent.

Range of factor scores: Naivasha (−46.9) to Mombasa (28.7).

Identification	Loading	IV Brief Label (Lowest and Negative Scores)
TAXPP	.70	High tax per capita
DISTA	.58	Close to Nairobi
NBIFO	.45	High interaction with Nairobi (telephone)
AVSAL	.33	High average salaries
KANUS	.32	Early growth of KANU

Variance accounted for: 5.5 per cent.

Range of factor scores: Kajiado (−14.8) to Trans-Nzoia (48.8).

MIXTU. Table 16 shows the pattern of highest loadings. The full list of loadings is in Appendix B.

On F3, low KPE scores, high average salaries, high per capita taxes, few political societies, and ethnic heterogeneity are *inversely* associated with the degree of connectivity with Nairobi, i.e., the greater the "distance" from Nairobi (in road mileage and proportion of telephone calls), the more intense these characteristics tend to become. The highest positive scores ("far" from Nairobi, low KPE scores, etc.) include Mombasa and most of the coastal districts, several areas in Nyanza Province and, somewhat anomalously, Nairobi itself. The capital has a positive score primarily because of its unusually low rank on KPEXA, the highest loading positive variable on F3.

The districts with the greatest negative scores include most of former Rift Valley and Central provinces plus Machakos. Apart from the exceptional case of Nairobi, the negative scores cluster in the center of Kenya, the highest positive scores on the eastern and western fringes (Figure 39).

On F4, however, connectivity with Nairobi is *directly* associated with some of the same variables (AVSAL, TAXPP), while others have very low loadings (MIXTU, SOCIE,

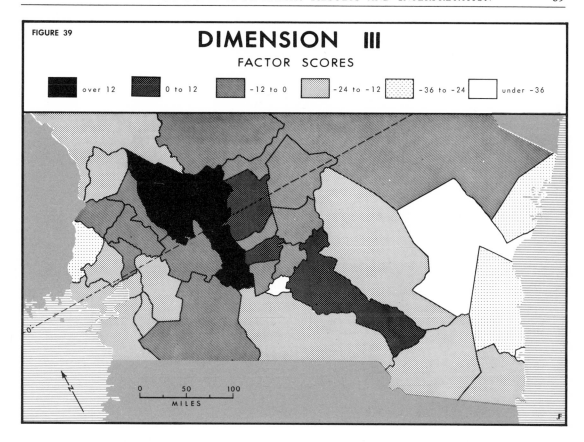

KPEXA). Nairobi here has a low score (1.0) and is characterized by high taxes per capita, an early start for KANU, and high average salaries. The map of factor scores (Figure 40) again reveals a similar pattern, with high positive scores being located in bands along the eastern and western borders and negative and low positive scores in the center.

This complex and perplexing pattern has several possible explanations: (*a*) that connectivity with Nairobi is central to both dimensions, and the associated variables reflect different aspects of its impact; (*b*) that the two dimensions are basically measuring the same thing, but because of the complex array of related variables the nature of this dual dimension is impossible to interpret; (*c*) that they are measuring totally unrelated dimensions, each associated differently with NBIFO and DISTA but too complex to characterize; (*d*) that F1 and F2 "milked" the data of nearly all its underlying generality and that the succeeding factors merely reflect freak distributions within the field or error elements within the data set.

If the last three possibilities are accepted, and indeed (*d*) appears likely from the data, no further discussion is needed. The first, however, suggests that connectivity to the national core area may be another important dimension to the modernization process. NBIFO and DISTA load fairly high on F1 (.65 and .55) as well as on F3 (.27 and .45), and F4 (.48 and .58), indicating that not only is core connectivity associated with Development but that the former, or its lack, may be helpful in explaining other aspects of modernization or some of the more unusual data distributions.

For example, KPEXA is not only moderately related to Development (.56) but seems to be even more closely associated with proximity to Nairobi (.67 on F3). As previously mentioned, most of the districts with the highest positive scores on F3 (generally ranking low on KPEXA) are located in peripheral areas. The major exception is Nairobi itself, which has KPE scores relatively low for its locational advantage. This may be due to the nature of Nairobi—attracting people from all over the country and from all levels of de-

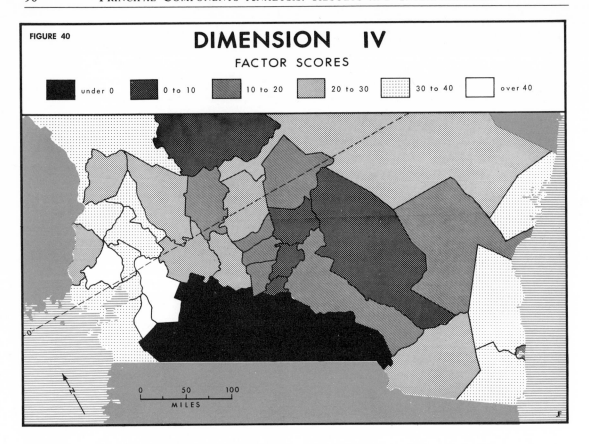

FIGURE 40

DIMENSION IV
FACTOR SCORES

under 0   0 to 10   10 to 20   20 to 30   30 to 40   over 40

0   50   100
MILES

velopment, the attendant overcrowding and unemployment, and perhaps the more lasting impact of racial discrimination in the schools. It could be that the core area or primate city of any developing country will display a number of anomalous characteristics which reflect its role as the focal point for the entire system.

The high loadings of TAXPP and DISTA on F4—both load highest on this dimension —seem to suggest that taxes per capita are highest in those areas closest to Nairobi. Is proximity to Nairobi an underlying force in the success of tax collectors? TAXPP is not closely associated with Development (.29 vs. .55 for DISTA), and it may be that this variable does not measure the inherent wealth of an area but rather the relative success of tax collection.

The change from direct to inverse relationships between core connectivity and several other variables on Dimensions III and IV could possibly be a reflection of Nairobi's position as the focal center for both modernization subsystems. But it must be stressed again that this and other interpretations of F3 and F4 are extremely conjectural and perhaps untenable. They have been made only to suggest further lines of investigation, particularly in relation to the core area, its field of influence, and the nature of its impact, and to introduce some relationships which may become clearer in the following chapter.

VIII

Principal Components Analysis: Rotated Version

In the preceding chapter, principal components analysis produced a number of descriptive dimensions of modernization. The largest, explaining 63 per cent of the total variance, was an aggregate measure of Development on which a large proportion of the variables loaded highly, particularly those found to be major indicators of modernization in other studies. The second dimension served primarily to distinguish two subsystems affecting the patterns and processes of modernization, a duality of development which has had significant repercussions on economy, polity, and society in Kenya. Although the third and fourth dimensions did not account for a large proportion of the variance, they pointed to the possible importance of core connectivity within the larger system.

In this chapter, attention is given to the results of factor rotation. The eight original factors extracted from the principal components analysis were orthogonally rotated, and a new set of eight dimensions was obtained. Rotation redistributed the total variance among the dimensions so that the new factors account for the following percentages:

*F1 = 30.4%		*F5 = 5.6
*F2 = 19.7		*F6 = 4.9
*F3 = 18.5		*F7 = 4.3
*F4 = 9.2		*F8 = 2.3

(The rotated factors are represented in shortened form by asterisks to distinguish them from the unrotated factors, e.g., *F1).

GENERAL INTERPRETATION OF ROTATED DIMENSIONS

*F5–8 are based almost entirely on single variables which contribute little to describing the major patterns of modernization (Table 17). Some of the distortion caused by these variables in the unrotated version is ameliorated here by their isolation on separate dimensions. TAXPP and AVSAL appear to be unrelated

TABLE 17
ROTATED DIMENSIONS V–VIII

Dimension	Variance Explained	Key Variable	Loading	Next Highest Loading
V	5.6%	AVSAL	−.92	.34
VI	4.9%	KPEXA	−.81	less than .30
VII	4.3%	TAXPP	−.93	less than .30
VIII	2.3%	KANUS	−.51	less than .30

to any major pattern, KPEXA only somewhat less so. This lack of associativeness is shown by the very high loading of each on their separate dimensions and the absence of other closely related variables. If the analysis were to be rerun, TAXPP, AVSAL, and KPEXA would be excluded as having little bearing on the broad spatial patterns of modernization. KANUS does have some medium-sized loadings on *F1 and *F2 (see below), but its importance as a measure of modernization appears less than initially expected.

Principal components analysis has thus served one of its major functions by sifting through a set of variables conceived of as measuring a similar phenomenon and identifying those with the least significance to the over-all patterns. By examining Table 13, page 75, it can be seen that these variables could not have been as clearly identified by simply using their average intercorrelations. Note particularly the position of MIXTU, a variable which figures prominently in the larger analysis despite its very low position in Table 13.

The first four rotated factors now absorb nearly 78 per cent of the total variance, 7 per cent less than for the unrotated version. But with the original restriction of successive absorptions of maximum remaining variance relaxed, the rotated components provide a more discriminatory picture of the major dimensions of modernization. Much of the influence of the distorting variables has been removed, and attention is focused more directly on the underlying interrelationships characterizing the data. The rigid orthogonal structure has been repositioned to fit more closely the major clusters of highly associated variables. No longer is there a monolithic Development Dimension, but instead a series of four rotated components which reflect various facets of the over-all pattern.

The rotated dimensions are labeled as follows: I, Urbanism-Asian Trade; II, African Education and Literacy; III, Mixture, Migration, and European Settlement; and IV, Core Connectivity. The rotated matrix of factor loadings is given in Table 18 and the list of factor scores in Table 19. It is significant that Nairobi clearly leads all other districts on each of the rotated dimensions, indicative of its

important role in all aspects of modernization in Kenya.

URBANISM-ASIAN TRADE DIMENSION

*F1 has been labeled the Urbanism-Asian Trade Dimension because of its high loadings on TRADE (.84), ASIAN (.83), and TOWNP (.76). The list of associated variables further supports this decision (Table 20).

Most of the political associations, radios, telephones, newspaper readers, and postal facilities are concentrated in the towns of Kenya, as are trade and the immigrant populations. The towns also supply a major share of African cash income and have played a central role in the growth of KANU. Clearly, the thread of urbanization ties this cluster of variables together.

The factor scores are mapped in Figure 41, which is presented as the urban dimension in the modernization of Kenya. Urbanization here is not measured simply in terms of the number of people living in towns over a certain size. Instead, attention is focused upon a set of functional characteristics of urban life —well-developed trade, large non-African communities, high media and communications development, political activity, and organizational growth—which permit the identification of a wide range of variation. It is primarily for this reason that "urbanism" rather than "urbanization" was chosen in labeling the dimension.

The districts of Nairobi, Mombasa, and Nakuru stand out clearly in Figure 41 as does the dominance of the highland districts relative to the coast and north. These are areas of large towns, many Asians, well-developed trade, a large number of political societies, etc. Also significant is the degree to which the pattern is associated with the railway network and the early cores of European settlement, two forces which strongly influenced the development of the urban system in Kenya.

Note that Kiambu, although it does not have a single town over 5,000, is among the most "urban" districts of Kenya as measured by *F1. This is in keeping with the earlier discussion of quasi-urban areas in Kenya. Kiambu does not itself have any large urban centers, but its position relative to Nairobi has enabled it to share the latter's urbanism and to experience the major social, economic, political, and psychological changes associated with the urbanization process. A high degree

TABLE 18
THE ROTATED MATRIX OF FACTOR LOADINGS
(The highest loading for each variable is underlined.)

Variable	Loading 1	Loading 2	Loading 3	Loading 4
TRADE	.84	.40	.26	.14
ASIAN	.83	.33	.36	.21
SOCIE	.81	.47	.16	.03
ACASH	.76	.51	.11	.30
TOWNP	.76	.10	.50	.18
RADIO	.75	.34	.43	.25
TOPOS	.71	.49	.38	.19
NOTEL	.70	.38	.50	.20
EUROP	.67	.30	.49	.18
ENGPA	.61	.24	.61	.23
SWAPA	.59	.35	.57	.21
KANUS	.51	.45	.01	.33
COLED	.37	.85	−.22	.17
PODEN	.43	.84	−.05	.09
PRIMA	.21	.78	.36	.14
LITER	.36	.71	.33	.13
TRAFF	.49	.64	.46	.18
MIXTU	.19	−.08	.89	−.11
PPLET	.47	.21	.79	.13
PEMPL	.42	.13	.74	.30
DISTA	.15	.25	.03	.83
NBIFO	.40	.14	.22	.82

(The following variables have their highest loadings on subsequent rotated dimensions which are not included on table.)

TAXPP	.12	−.02	.26	.13.....F7 = .93
AVSAL	−.12	.09	−.26	−.02.....F5 = .92
KPEXA	.20	.29	.10	.37.....F6 = .81

Variance accounted for:	
Urbanism-Asian Trade	30.4%
African Education and Literacy	19.7%
Mixture, Migration, and European Settlement	18.5%
Core Connectivity	9.2%

TABLE 19
FACTOR SCORES ON THE ROTATED DIMENSIONS

Rank	*Factor 1		*Factor 2		*Factor 3		*Factor 4	
1	Nairobi	17.8	Nairobi	11.2	Nairobi	11.8	Nairobi	13.9
2	Mombasa	47.3	Kiambu	55.3	Mombasa	25.7	Thika	36.0
3	Nakuru	57.0	Mombasa	56.8	Nakuru	31.7	Nakuru	39.6
4	Thika	89.6	Nakuru	63.4	Thika	42.1	Kiambu	41.4
5	Kiambu	100.9	Nyeri	71.1	Uasin Gishu	44.4	Nyeri	49.4
6	Uasin Gishu	103.4	Thika	81.7	Trans-Nzoia	65.7	Naivasha	54.4
7	Central Nyanza	112.4	Central Nyanza	101.8	Naivasha	69.7	Mombasa	57.4
8	Nyeri	118.8	Uasin Gishu	102.7	Nanyuki	74.9	Machakos	62.0
9	Kericho	124.4	Fort Hall	103.4	Kericho	81.6	Fort Hall	62.3
10	Trans-Nzoia	133.7	Kericho	109.2	Kiambu	82.8	Uasin Gishu	67.2
11	Naivasha	145.3	North Nyanza	116.0	Nyeri	98.3	Central Nyanza	67.3
12	Nanyuki	165.3	Trans-Nzoia	124.7	Central Nyanza	98.6	Nanyuki	74.4
13	Machakos	173.1	Naivasha	127.9	Laikipia	105.9	Kericho	79.1
14	Fort Hall	185.7	Machakos	131.8	Taita	140.0	Embu	81.2
15	North Nyanza	191.3	Kisii	134.3	Embu	147.9	Trans-Nzoia	82.4
16	Embu	205.6	Embu	144.0	Kilifi	148.1	Laikipia	86.2
17	Laikipia	208.2	Nanyuki	146.9	Machakos	149.3	Meru	89.6
18	Meru	217.6	Meru	156.2	Fort Hall	149.5	Kajiado	98.9
19	Kilifi	218.9	Elgon Nyanza	157.5	North Nyanza	157.2	North Nyanza	100.7
20	Kisii	219.3	Nandi	171.8	Kajiado	169.4	Kisii	109.8
21	Elgon Nyanza	247.2	Laikipia	180.5	Nandi	174.0	Taita	121.5
22	Taita	255.4	South Nyanza	182.5	Meru	178.0	Elgon Nyanza	121.6
23	Nandi	276.3	Taita	197.0	Kwale	180.0	Narok	121.7
24	Kajiado	281.5	Kilifi	200.3	Kisii	183.3	Nandi	124.0
25	South Nyanza	284.5	Kwale	222.9	Elgon Nyanza	192.7	Kilifi	127.6
26	Kitui	299.6	Kitui	228.3	Lamu	195.4	Kitui	128.0
27	Kwale	306.4	Kajiado	229.6	South Nyanza	207.2	Baringo	137.6
28	Narok	336.3	Baringo	242.6	Narok	216.7	South Nyanza	137.7
29	Lamu	341.7	Elgeyo-Marakwet	245.7	Kitui	225.6	Kwale	146.5
30	Baringo	355.3	Narok	260.1	Tana River	233.1	Northern Frontier	160.0
31	Elgeyo-Marakwet	370.4	Lamu	276.0	Baringo	240.7	Elgeyo-Marakwet	160.6
32	Northern Frontier	379.5	West Pokot	285.5	West Pokot	241.4	Samburu	166.1
33	West Pokot	385.3	Tana River	287.8	Elgeyo-Marakwet	250.4	West Pokot	171.6
34	Tana River	391.9	Northern Frontier	291.9	Northern Frontier	253.0	Lamu	175.0
35	Samburu	397.4	Samburu	302.9	Samburu	258.4	Tana River	175.1
36	Turkana	417.0	Turkana	314.3	Turkana	286.5	Turkana	188.3

TABLE 20
ROTATED DIMENSION I: URBANISM-ASIAN
TRADE

Identification	Loading	Brief Label (Lowest Scores)
TRADE	.84	Many trade licenses issued
ASIAN	.83	Large Asian population
SOCIE	.81	Large number of political societies registered
ACASH	.76	High African cash incomes
TOWNP	.76	Large town population
RADIO	.75	Many radios
TOPOS	.71	Heavy postal traffic.
NOTEL	.70	Large number of telephones
EUROP	.67	Large European population
ENGPA	.61	High circulation of European newspapers
SWAPA	.59	High circulation of Swahili newspapers
KANUS	.51	Early growth of KANU
TRAFF	.49	High road traffic density
PPLET	.47	High per capita postal traffic

of rural-urban feedback has probably developed in this almost entirely Kikuyu district.

Nearly all the other high-scoring districts either include one of the larger urban centers in the Highlands (Thika, Eldoret, Kisumu, Nyeri, Kericho) or are within or near the quasi-urban hinterlands of Nairobi and Kisumu (Fort Hall, Machakos, North Nyanza).

Urbanism has been used as a label for the first dimension in part to highlight its generic character. A parallel dimension of primary importance stressing the growth and impact of urban centers would probably be found if a similar analysis were made in most developing countries. The role of the Asian trader, however, evokes the more specific aspects of modernization in Kenya. His distribution is more closely associated with *F1 than that for any other variable.

The prominence of the Asian trading population in the development pattern can be explained in several ways. First, the Asian trader has played a very important role in bringing large sections of Kenya into contact with modern society. In many of the more isolated districts, the Asian *duka,* or shop, was the major interface between the African population and the outside world. Further-

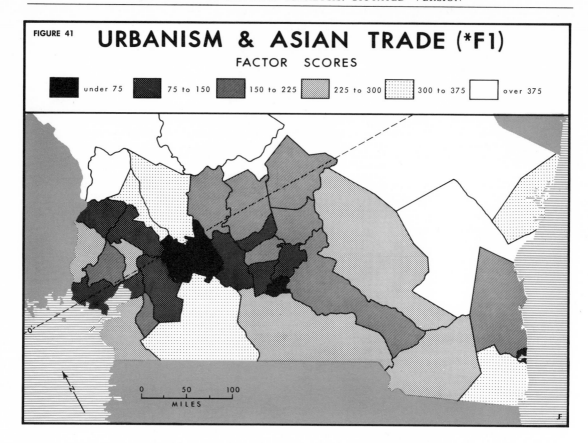

FIGURE 41
URBANISM & ASIAN TRADE (*F1)
FACTOR SCORES

under 75 | 75 to 150 | 150 to 225 | 225 to 300 | 300 to 375 | over 375

more, the racial and administrative barriers which isolated the Europeans from the masses placed the Asians in the position of agents for the diffusion of modern ideas and, perhaps more important, modern aspirations.

Secondly, the Asians are the most highly urbanized group in Kenya and are therefore heavily concentrated in the most developed parts of the country. Indeed, with minor exceptions, the distribution of Asians provides a more accurate measure of urbanization, in terms of settlement focality and the existence of urban functions such as markets, than the relatively crude index used in this study (the size of the largest center in each district). Consequently, Asian traders have come to dominate the urban system in Kenya, from the largest towns to the smallest trading centers, and have monopolized the role of middleman in the patterns of culture contact.

It might be assumed, at first, that the distribution of Europeans would be more closely associated with *F1 than is acutally the case: EUROP loads at .67 as compared with .83 for ASIAN. But it must be remembered that

many Europeans were and are farmers who, except for providing Africans with employment and cash income, did not interact very closely with the African population within the Scheduled Areas and did little *there* to stimulate rapid African mobilization. As the discussion of the two modernization subsystems indicated, the major impact of European contact was on the fringes of the former White Highlands where few Europeans resided.

Consequently, in terms of distributional association, the specific character of the urban phase in Kenya's modernization is more closely linked to the Asian trading population than to European settlers and administrators. The web of cause and effect, however, is much more complex, for the impact of the Asian has been immediate, personal, and extensive and that of the European indirect and restricted.

The domination of this phase of development by the Asian population has important implications for contemporary Kenya. The Asian still retains his strong influence in urban society, and the African government maintains that this has prevented the full participation of the African population in modern urban life. Commercialization and urbanization have not increased social and political integration everywhere in Kenya, nor have they led to the emergence of a large African middle class. It may be that the attempt to build a cohesive nation will require government action to bring more Africans into key urban positions.

AFRICAN EDUCATION AND LITERACY DIMENSION

The second dimension is clearly based upon African education and literacy. The highest loadings include total numbers of Africans with thirteen or more years of education, the percentage (male plus female) of school-aged children attending primary schools, and the percentage of males over 20 with some education (Table 21). PODEN also loads highly on this dimension, indicative of the greater attention paid to education in the densely populated African districts.

TABLE 21
ROTATED DIMENSION II: AFRICAN
EDUCATION AND LITERACY

Identification	Loading	Brief Label (Lowest Scores)
COLED	.85	Many Africans with post-secondary education
PODEN	.84	High population density
PRIMA	.78	High percentage of African children in primary schools
LITER	.71	High literacy among Africans
TRAFF	.64	High road traffic density
ACASH	.51	High African cash income
TOPOS	.49	Heavy postal traffic
SOCIE	.47	Many registered political societies
KANUS	.45	Early growth of KANU

Other high-loading variables include road traffic density, total postal traffic, African cash income, the number of political societies, and the growth of KANU, showing the association of education on one hand and communications development, wealth, and political organization on the other.[1] It is also interesting to note that SWAPA loads significantly higher than ENGPA, *F2 being the only one of the four rotated dimensions for which this is true, thus emphasizing the "African-ness" of this dimension.

---

[1] It must be remembered, however, that population density is also associated with these variables and may be part of the reason for their inclusion on this dimension.

Figure 42 shows the spatial variation in factor scores. Nairobi is again the leading district, but is followed by Kiambu, which has reached a higher level of educational development than the next two districts, Mombasa and Nakuru. This is another indication of the key position of Kiambu District in the over-all patterns of modernization. Other districts which increase their rank significantly from *F1 to *F2 include Nyeri, Fort Hall, North Nyanza, and Kisii, all of which have been identified as major parts of the African Subsystem.

MIXTURE, MIGRATION, AND EUROPEAN SETTLEMENT DIMENSION

Just as urbanism and education appear to provide the motif for the first two rotated dimensions, the impact of European settlement ties together the cluster of variables associated with the third. Accordingly, this dimension is called Mixture, Migration, and European Settlement. The highest loading—higher than any other on the first four dimensions—is for the measure of ethnic mixture (Table 22). This variable is followed by per capita postal traffic, percentage of Africans employed, English and Swahili newspaper circulation, number of telephones, town population, and the distribution of Europeans.

TABLE 22
ROTATED DIMENSION III:
MIXTURE, MIGRATION, AND
EUROPEAN SETTLEMENT

Identification	Loading	Brief Label (Lowest Scores)
MIXTU	.89	Ethnic heterogeneity
PPLET	.79	High per capita postal traffic
PEMPL	.74	High percentage of Africans employed
ENGPA	.61	High circulation of European newspapers
SWAPA	.57	High circulation of Swahili newspapers
NOTEL	.50	Large number of telephones
TOWNP	.50	Large town population
EUROP	.49	Large European population
TRAFF	.46	High road traffic density

That this dimension revolves closely around European settlement in Kenya can be seen in Figure 43, in which a remarkably accurate outline of the former White Highlands is represented by the highest scoring districts.

Communications and mass media are well developed in the areas with high scores, but equally significant are the employment opportunities available to the African population

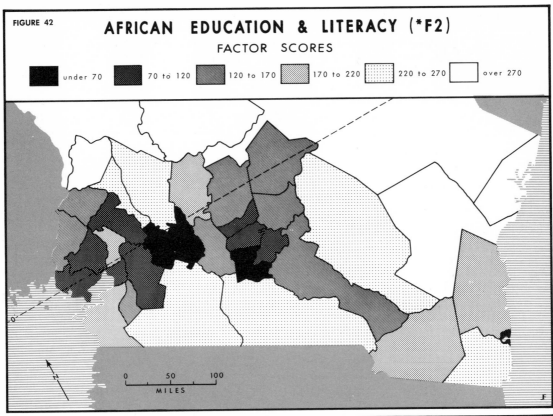

FIGURE 42

AFRICAN EDUCATION & LITERACY (*F2)
FACTOR SCORES

under 70   70 to 120   120 to 170   170 to 220   220 to 270   over 270

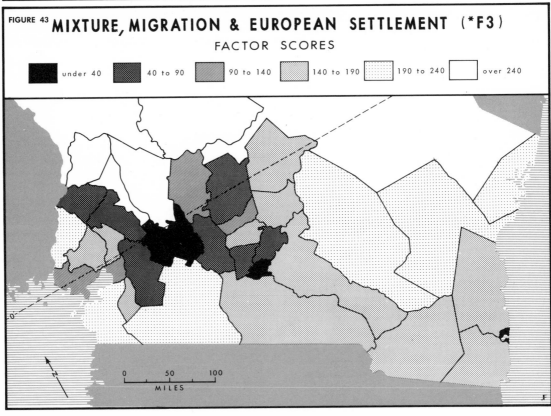

FIGURE 43

MIXTURE, MIGRATION & EUROPEAN SETTLEMENT (*F3)
FACTOR SCORES

under 40   40 to 90   90 to 140   140 to 190   190 to 240   over 240

and the attendant attraction of peoples from all over Kenya. Hence the high loadings for MIXTU and PEMPL. This attraction also helps to explain the high loading for PPLET, for not only is there a large letter-writing European population but the large number of African migrant laborers write many letters as well to maintain contact with their home areas—further evidence of the interaction which created the two modernization subsystems.

Like *F1, this dimension has a strong urban component, but one in which the European rather than the Asian population is more important. Whereas the Asian penetrated far into the Native Reserves and came to dominate urban life in both the European and African Subsystems, the European has been more parochial and more heavily concentrated in the white "island" carved out of the presumed empty spaces in the Kenya Highlands.

CORE CONNECTIVITY DIMENSION

The only high loadings on *F4 are for DISTA and NBIFO, the two measures of connectivity with Nairobi. These variables do not load very high on the other dimensions, and few other measures are closely associated with them on *F4 (Table 23). Only percentage passing the KPE (.37), the growth of KANU (.30), African cash income (.30), and number of radios (.25) score at .25 or higher. Core Connectivity, then, appears as a separate dimension of modernization.

Because of the nature of *F4, the factor scores have not been mapped in the same way as for the preceding three dimensions. Instead, they have been used to construct the cartogram presented in Figure 44. Distance from the capital is in proportion to the difference in factor scores between a given district and Nairobi. The lines radiating from Nairobi

show the major channels of communication and transportation linking the major district centers with the core area. In a crude way, the cartogram portrays the circulatory structure within the field of Nairobi's influence. Note the importance of paved roads, shown by the darker lines, in this circulatory structure.

Since the dimension is not based entirely on DISTA or NBIFO, but on a combination of these variables along with others in proportion to their factor loadings, many districts appear "closer" to Nairobi than would be expected if only road mileage or percentage of telephone calls were taken into account. Mombasa, for example, ranks thirtieth on DISTA, fifth on NBIFO, and seventh on *F4. The corresponding ranks for Nakuru are ten, seventeen, and three. At the other extreme, Kajiado District ranks fifth on DISTA, third on NBIFO, but eighteenth on Core Connectivity.

Most of these discrepancies are accounted for by the contribution of other variables which affect Core Connectivity. Interaction with Nairobi is not dependent upon physical distance and telephone connectivity alone. Many newspaper readers, heavy postal traffic, well-developed commercial agriculture, the existence of an important political party branch office, and other attributes increase the number and intensity of contracts with the core area. *F4 therefore provides a multivariate measure of Core Connectivity which depends heavily upon DISTA and NBIFO but also is affected by many other variables.

MODERNIZATION AS A DIFFUSION PROCESS

Rotation, in summary, has led to the identification of a number of separate clusters of variables, each measuring distinctive aspects of the general patterns of modernization. Urbanism-Asian Trade; Education and Literacy; Mixture, Migration, and European Settlement; and Core Connectivity provide more detailed descriptions of the underlying uniformities brought out in the unrotated version, particularly with respect to the broad Development Dimension, which explained 63 per cent of the variance before rotation.

The results of rotation, in addition, strongly support the view of modernization as a process of spatial diffusion. A high degree of intercorrelation exists among the *factor scores* of the four rotated dimensions despite the fact

TABLE 23
ROTATED DIMENSION IV: CORE CONNECTIVITY

Identification	Loading	Brief Label (Lowest Scores)
DISTA	.83	Close to Nairobi
NBIFO	.82	High telephone connectivity to Nairobi
KPEXA	.37	Large percentage passing KPE
KANUS	.33	Early growth of KANU
ACASH	.30	Large African cash income

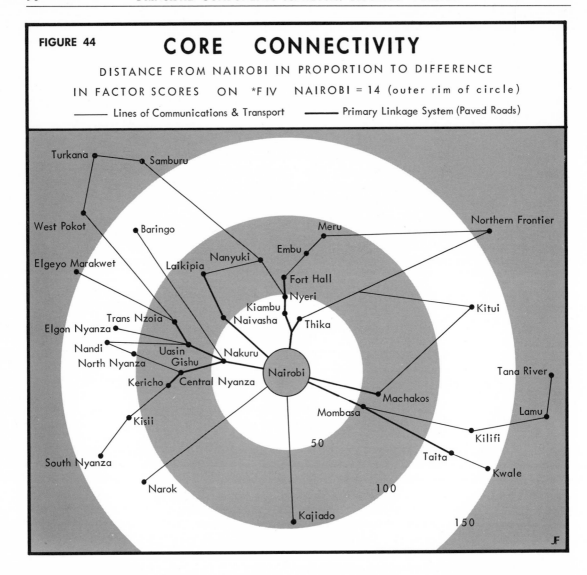

FIGURE 44

CORE CONNECTIVITY

DISTANCE FROM NAIROBI IN PROPORTION TO DIFFERENCE

IN FACTOR SCORES ON *F IV NAIROBI = 14 (outer rim of circle)

——— Lines of Communications & Transport ——— Primary Linkage System (Paved Roads)

that they are measuring different facets of the modernization process. For example, the Spearman Rank Correlation Coefficient between the scores of districts on Core Connectivity and *F1 is .95, with *F2 it is .93, and with *F3 it is .90. Similarly high coefficients exist between district scores on the other rotated dimensions.

It appears, therefore, that the spatial expressions of the four dimensions are highly associated. Put in another way, those districts ranking high on Core Connectivity also tend to rank high on Urbanism, Education, and the impact of European Settlement. The mix may vary when specific districts are taken into account, one ranking above average on the

Education Dimension but below on Urbanism. This type of variation emerges largely from the differences between the two modernization subsystems and does not prevent the over-all patterns from being remarkably highly correlated in geographic space.

Modernization, therefore, seems to have followed a regular spatial path. Nairobi, by ranking well above the other districts on all four dimensions, is clearly the major nucleus for this diffusion and the generator for the entire system. This view is supported strongly by the importance of Nairobi as the dominant node in both the European and African Subsystems. By simply using the factor scores for *F4, one can obtain a reliable predictor of the relative level of modernization in any given district.

Following Nairobi are a number of districts from both the Scheduled and Non-Scheduled Areas: Mombasa, Nakuru, Kiambu, Thika, Nyeri, Uasin Gishu, and Central Nyanza. The rankings of these districts on the dimensions vary slightly according to whether they are parts of the European or African Subsystems. Thus Kiambu ranks tenth on Mixture, Migration, and European Settlement but second on Education and Literacy, whereas for Uasin Gishu the corresponding ranks are five and eight.

The order of districts that follow is essentially the same as for the Development Dimension discussed previously. Again, there are slight variations in rank by dimension according to which subsystem a district is assigned, but these are not great enough to prevent a very high correlation when all districts are taken into account.

It appears then that the principal forces which have shaped the human geography of modernizing Kenya have produced very similar patterns of areal differentiation. This conclusion provides further evidence for the contention that modernization is basically a process of spatial diffusion and is highly systemic in that a whole cluster of events tends to occur as an area modernizes.

Furthermore, an examination of the spatial patterns produced by the rotated dimensions supports the view developed earlier in this study that the evolution of the transport network, particularly the Kenya-Uganda Railway and its branches, established the framework which guided the diffusion of modernization. The railways, to a very great extent, created the urban system in Kenya, provided the backbone for the growth and development of the White Highlands, stimulated the spread of Asian traders, hastened the development of African education in certain areas, and played a major role in the emergence of Nairobi as the focal point of social communications in Kenya.

THE ROTATED DIMENSIONS AND THE "SYSTEM OF MODERNITY"

The results of the rotated analysis provoke comparison with what Daniel Lerner terms the "System of Modernity"—the complex and highly interrelated group of processes which characterizes the evolution of a modern participant society. He postulates three major phases in this development: (1) urbanization, (2) literacy, and (3) media participation.[2]

Urbanization, according to Lerner, is "the transfer of population from scattered hinterlands to urban centers that stimulates the needs and provides the conditions needed for 'take-off' toward widespread participation. . . .increases in urbanization tend in every society to multiply national increases in literacy and media participation." After reaching a critical level, however, which Lerner estimates at approximately 25 per cent, "urbanization no longer automatically guarantees equivalent increases in consumption. The need then shifts to modernizing the conditions which govern consumption."

In the second phase, "literacy is both index and agent. To spread consumption of urban products beyond the city limits, literacy is an efficient instrument . . . [and] also the basic skill required for operation of a media system. Only the literate produce the media contents which mainly the literate consume. Hence, once societies are about 25% urbanized, the highest correlation of media consumption is with literacy."

Lerner's third phase is media participation. "Once people are equipped to handle the new experiences produced by mobility (via their move to the city), and to handle the new experiences conveyed by the media (via their literacy), they now seek the satisfactions which integrate these skills. They discover . . . the tingle of wondering 'what will happen next'— the tingle which sounds the knell of traditional society, of routinized lifeways in which everyone *knew* what would happen next because it had to follow what came before . . . . [R]ising media participation tends to raise participation in all sectors of the social system. In accelerating the spread of empathy, it also diffuses those other modern demands to which participant institutions have responded: in the consumer's economy via cash (and credit), in the public forum via opinion, in the representative polity via voting."

---

[2] Discussion of this topic and the quotes which follow are based upon *The Passing of Traditional Society,* Chapter II, particularly pp. 61–64. A further elaboration on this theme can be found in Daniel Lerner, "Communications Systems and Social Systems."

Although Kenya is still in the traditional category as outlined by Lerner (less than 10 per cent urbanized, under 20 per cent literate and dependent primarily upon oral communications rather than mass media), many of the systemic characteristics of modernization are evident. The fact that *F1 explained a larger portion of the total variance than any of the other rotated dimensions seems to support the view of urbanization as the initial spark plug for modernization. As a primary phase, it has developed further than the others in terms of its impact on Kenya and represents the most important component differentiating levels of modernization from district to district.

In addition, the high loadings for most communications variables on *F1 suggest that media participation expands concurrently with increasing urbanization. Similarly, political activity, particularly as measured by SOCIE and to a lesser extent by KANUS, are positively and closely associated with the Urbanism Dimension.

The greatest divergence from the general scheme is found for Education and Literacy. The major education variables load highest on a separate dimension and are not very closely associated with the Urbanism-Asian Trade Dimension. This does not mean that a single measure of urbanization and a single measure of education will not be highly correlated—TOWNP and LITER, for example, have a simple rank correlation of .69. The over-all Urbanism Dimension, however, taking into account a large number of associated variables within the system, is not related to the Education and Literacy Dimension, with its ancillary indices.[3]

If one sets aside those variables which load most highly on subsequent dimensions, most of which are those considered least relevant to the major patterns of modernization, the smallest loadings on *F1 are for COLED (.37), LITER (.36), and PRIMA (.21). Simi-

larly, the smallest loadings for *F2 include TOWNP (.10), PPLET (.21), ENGPA (.24), EUROP (.30), and ASIAN (.30). The very low loading for TOWNP—much lower than for ASIAN or TRADE (.40) and exceeding only that for MIXTU (−.08)—is particularly noteworthy.

What this appears to indicate is that the *urban system* in Kenya is not yet effectively integrated with the *education system*. Urbanization and educational development remain as two distinct phases or processes which, although diffusing along similar paths, still have not yet reached the point of complementarity that would thrust the country closer to modernity.

The implications of this lack of accordance for contemporary Kenya are important. Except in the quasi-urban hinterlands of Nairobi and Kisumu, there has not been the high degree of rural-urban interaction so essential to the growth of a nation. African educational development took place primarily within a separate modernization subsystem and was not therefore functionally linked to the growth of urbanization and the communications media which characterized the major European-dominated areas. Colonial attitudes toward the urban African and the domination of the towns by Europeans and Asians prevented the growth of a large permanent African urban population until recent years. Furthermore, these barriers prevented the expansion of African literacy from acting as an agent for the diffusion of urban attitudes and institutions into the rural areas. Indeed, one may argue with some success that the growth of literacy in the former African reserves has led to the infusion of many rural attitudes and outlooks into the urban areas of Kenya.

The association between education level and Development was also lower than expected in the unrotated analysis, where it was shown that districts scoring roughly the same on the Development Dimension could vary widely on levels of African education. This divergence, however, was greatest in the middle range of F1 (e.g., for such districts as Fort Hall and Laikipia) and decreased significantly toward the highest levels, suggesting that the two processes may increase their articulation as modernization progresses.

---

[3] It is extremely difficult to characterize the dimensions—which are orthogonal and therefore mathematically independent—with a nomenclature that is also *totally* "independent" in a conceptual sense, particularly in an explanatory study such as this. We have no verbal symbols which can define with numerical precision the equivalent of mathematical orthogonality.

IX

The Geography of Modernization in Kenya:
Some Broader Implications and Conclusions

THE GEOGRAPHY OF MODERNIZATION
AND INDEPENDENT KENYA

The contemporary spatial patterns of modernization in Kenya are largely the products of the attitudes and objectives of the former colonial power and the resident European minority. It will take many years before these patterns cease to reflect the functions and requirements of a colonial territory and become restructured to serve an independent African government attempting to construct a cohesive national community within its territorial boundaries.

European settlement and patterns of cultural contact were guided first by the political and humanitarian goals of Great Britain and later by European concepts of land use and land tenure. The existence of what to Western eyes appeared as unused land led to the implantation of a white island into the complex and fluid traditional milieu and to the generation of forces which started the processes of change for the African population.

The imprint of colonial penetration and the establishment of effective administrative control temporarily froze the pre-European cultural geography, and Kenya was compartmentalized into a series of European and African "reserves." The requirements of the colonizers, however, demanded that this new system of cells not be airtight. The construction of roads and railways, the growth of towns, the introduction of a money economy and taxation, the spread of education, and a number of other forces acted to draw the African out from his traditional social matrix into a new network of social communications much broader and more powerful in terms of the demands put upon him than any other he had encountered before.

The forces of transition were thus channeled through a superimposed system of circulation and administration which reflected the designs of the colonizing power. Attention was focused on the White Highlands and other areas where Europeans were concentrated, while the coast (outside of Mombasa) and similarly peripheral areas were largely ignored. At the same time, however, development in the White Highlands and urban centers had a "lift-pump" effect on the surrounding African reserves, leading to the emergence of two distinct but articulated subsystems which controlled the growth and diffusion of modernization throughout Kenya.

The impact of modernization was therefore highly uneven. Traditional social and economic organization, pre-European patterns of migration, and, perhaps most importantly, *geographic proximity and accessibility to the major nodes and flow lines within the new circulatory system* affected the degree to which various peoples of Kenya were exposed to and transformed by the processes of change. Some, like the Kikuyu, changed rapidly, while others remained almost totally bound by tradition. Modernization thus created a new kind of social gap that was in many ways greater than that which existed prior to European contact.

In some instances, this gap was pronounced *within* the same ethnic group. Mention has been made of the distinctions which have arisen between the Kiambu, Fort Hall, and Nyeri Kikuyu; the Central and South Nyanza Luo; and the Machakos and Kitui Kamba. In terms of the factor scores on the Development Dimension, for example, Kiambu differs by 48 points from Nyeri, which in turn scores almost 100 points higher than Fort Hall District. The differential among the Luo is over 230 and among the Kamba over 200. These differences have been reflected in the nature and size of the emerging African elite and its role in the over-all political framework of Kenya.[1]

---

[1] For example, of the Africans listed in *Who's Who in East Africa*, compiled by Gordon Wilson for Marco Surveys, Ltd. (Nairobi, 1964), 52 stated that they were born in Central Nyanza, only 16 in South Nyanza. The figures for Machakos and Kitui are 26 and 7, respectively.

The gap *between* ethnic groups has been accentuated further by the existence of the two modernization subsystems. Some areas not only score low on Development but have also remained out of the mainstream of African political, economic, and social change. The consequences of this division into African and European Subsystems are evident in the development of political parties in Kenya.

In Figure 45, the graph of F1 and F2 is used to plot the approximate votes and number of seats received by the two leading parties, KANU and KADU, in the 1963 Senate election.[2] The districts of Quadrant II—the leading sectors of the African Subsystem—were clearly the centers of KANU support, with a substantial proportion of the vote in Quadrant III also going to KANU. KADU, in contrast, received its greatest support from the districts of Quadrant IV, those which are underdeveloped and outside the African Subsystem. A substantial KADU vote was also cast in the relatively well developed former White Highland districts of Quadrant I.

This configuration buttresses the contention that KADU grew primarily as a reaction of the smaller, less modernized ethnic groups against the larger, more powerful ones. Moreover, it suggests that this reaction was heavily supported by the non-African communities that have dominated the areas within the European Subsystem. Europeans and Asians saw an opportunity to retain some political power by backing a party which appealed to those groups most isolated from the main currents of African nationalism, most likely to

hold favorable attitudes toward them, and probably most easy to influence.[3]

KADU was a negative or "anti" party from the start, particularistic, and traditionally oriented. It lacked a dynamic program for nation building and fostered a form of regionalism that could only be detrimental to the economy and political cohesion of the state. But with strong European and Asian backing, the party was able to win a substantial proportion of the parliamentary seats, particularly in the Senate.[4] It is felt that the dissolution of KADU in 1964 was a sign of maturity in the evolving polity and an indication of increasing interaction between the Kenyan equivalents of the "haves" and "have-nots."[5]

Changes in the internal structure of communications and administration also reflect the conflict of interests between the two modernization subsystems, particularly since independence has brought the African Subsystem into control of the reins of power. The control has enabled the new Kenya government to produce spatial manifestations of an African set of attitudes and objectives. One example of these changes was discussed earlier in relation to the plans for increasing postal facilities in the attempt to equalize service throughout Kenya. It is no surprise to learn that the over-served areas are nearly all part of the European Subsystem (the Scheduled Areas and the coastal districts), while the planned new facilities are to be located primarily within the African.

Another example can be seen in the reorganization of urban administration (Figure 46). Under the "reconstruction exercise" of 1963,

---

[2] Since the election was based on the new regional boundaries, an effort was made to apportion the voting according to the boundaries used in this study. For example, Elgon Nyanza was considered a KADU district although one of the two units into which it was split (Busia) voted KANU. The total vote, however, was in favor of KADU. Nyandarua District, composed of portions of Laikipia and Naivasha, was excluded entirely (it voted overwhelmingly for KANU), Embu (now two districts, both of which voted KANU) was considered as one district, and Laikipia and Nanyuki (now merged into one) were considered separately.

The Northern Frontier Districts were entirely excluded. One district (Isiolo) voted KANU, one (Marsabit) voted for the Northern Province United Association, while the others (Mandera, Garissa, Moyale, and Wajir) boycotted the election. Kitui, Machakos, and West Pokot elected Independent candidates, but the KANU-KADU votes were included in the total figures.

---

[3] For an excellent discussion of the parties, issues, and results of the 1963 election, see C. Sanger and J. Nottingham, "The Kenya General Election of 1963," *Journal of Modern African Studies* (1964), pp. 1–40.

[4] KADU, for example, won the two Masai districts of Kajiado and Narok, which had only 23,068 voters between them, while KANU captured such heavily populated areas as Fort Hall and Central Nyanza, with 115,932 and 165,155 voters respectively. With less than half the vote of KANU, KADU was able to capture nearly as many Senate seats. *Ibid.*, p. 35.

[5] The more recent split in KANU may also be a sign of increasing maturity, for it appears based on programmatic and ideological differences *within* the more modernized groups and is not simply an ethnic reaction. The major question today is whether KANU is strong enough to accept such opposition if it remains overt, constitutional, and in favor of maintaining the territorial integrity of Kenya.

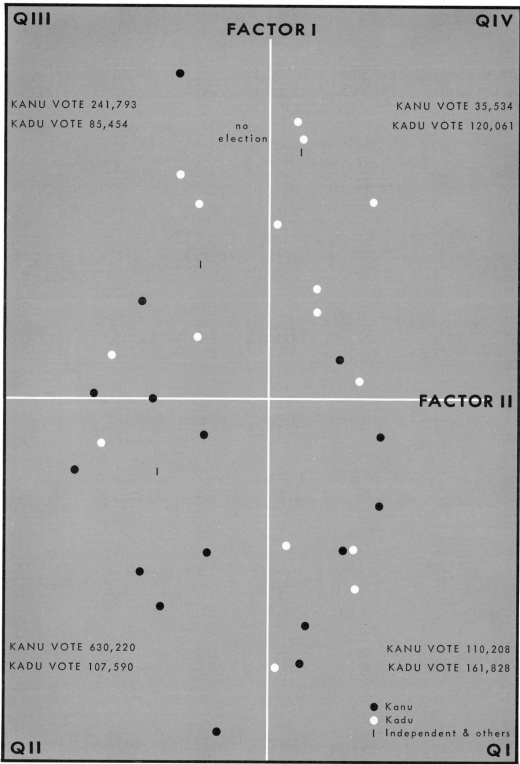

QIII   FACTOR I   QIV

KANU VOTE 241,793   KANU VOTE 35,534
KADU VOTE 85,454   KADU VOTE 120,061

no
election

FACTOR II

KANU VOTE 630,220   KANU VOTE 110,208
KADU VOTE 107,590   KADU VOTE 161,828

● Kanu
○ Kadu
I Independent & others

QII   QI

Dots Refer to Same Administrative Districts and Scaling as Figure 37

FIGURE 45. POLITICAL PARTIES AND MODERNIZATION SUBSYSTEMS

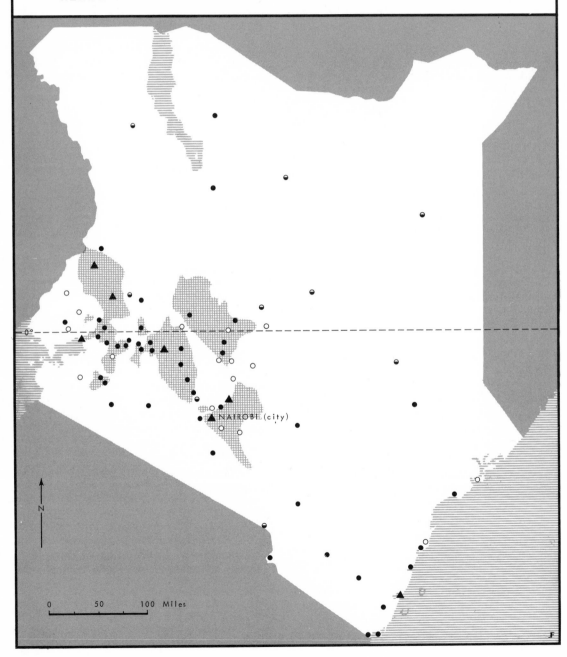

FIGURE 46

URBAN ADMINISTRATIVE ORGANIZATION (after 1963)

▲ MUNICIPALITIES
○ URBAN COUNCILS
◔ REMAINING TOWNSHIPS

● DE-GAZETTED TOWNSHIPS
▦ SCHEDULED AREAS

▲ NAIROBI (city)

N

0   50   100 Miles

many townships—predominantly those within the former White Highlands—were de-gazetted and lost most of their former functions. In addition, a new local government unit, the Urban Council, was established to enable certain centers to have a greater control over local matters. Most of these urban councils are located within the African Subsystem and represent a further attempt to reduce the areal inequalities created during the colonial era.

There is still further evidence of the spatial reorganization of Kenya growing out of the attempt by the African-controlled government to produce an infrastructure more suitable to its needs and functions: the high priority given to improving the major road links between Kenya and her neighbors (e.g., the Eldoret-Tororo and Athi River–Namanga roads); the rapid progress in bituminization of the Nairobi-Mombasa road despite the enormous expense and the realization that feeder roads in the major agricultural areas would produce greater monetary returns; the great emphasis in the Development Plan on extending television service to the coast; the creation of the Voice of Kenya and the Kenya News Agency to coordinate and control the diffusion of information; the establishment of National Schools and the increased emphasis on secondary education; the efforts to bring about a "back-to-the-land" movement to relieve the over-urbanization which has occurred, especially in Nairobi; the attempts to avoid further piling-up of industry in the Nairobi area by promoting development elsewhere in Kenya; and, probably most important of all, the vast program of agricultural resettlement and community development in the former White Highlands, upon which so much of the future stability and cohesiveness of the Kenya nation depends.

It is still too early to gauge the success of these efforts and plans, and it may be that the patterns established during the colonial period have developed enough inertia to prevent any rapid reorganization. There is no doubt that the change in leadership, and consequently in national objectives, will result in modifications in the space content of Kenya. Just how much change and how rapidly it will take place, however, is not yet known.

In Kenya, as in most African states, government participation in and direction of the modernization process has been increasing. Some argue that without such controlled modernization, preindependence inequalities would intensify and become more rigid, creating a potentially static condition of class and ethnic cleavages and conflict.[6] Consequently, the government is forced to assume a predominant role in development planning, not only for economic advancement but also for social and political organization and change.

This in turn has led to the pre-eminence of the political sector. Economic development plans, agricultural reorganization and resettlement programs, plans for educational expansion and community development—these have become largely political documents directed toward political goals. Whether the Mombasa Road will "pay off," or the resettlement of the White Highlands increase agricultural production, or a post office in western Luo country handle sufficient business to be economical is often not the most important question. Economic development is only one component of modernization. Kenya and the other new states, while stimulating economic growth, must build stable and cohesive national communities—even if this may occasionally require uneconomic procedures.[7]

The patterns of human geography which evolved under colonial control have, therefore, frequently proved to be dysfunctional to the goals of the independent government of Kenya. The need to reorganize and reshape the spatial system inherited from Great Britain is one of the key issues facing Kenya today. Indeed, it ranks among the foremost problems confronting the entire post-colonial world. The geographically uneven impact of modernization and the absence of or barriers to a coordinated effort to construct a cohesive, modern African community have resulted in great inequalities both within and among the

---

[6] David Apter, for example, notes that "unplanned development results in social inequalities, which can easily harden into more or less permanently organized classes, each with its own subculture, as has occurred in many parts of Latin America." *The Politics of Modernization* (1965), p. 13.

[7] One of the difficulties encountered by economic advisers in Africa is to recognize and evaluate the noneconomic factors which pervade development planning. What may appear to be economically unfeasible—a national airline for a small country or, more specifically, a rail link between Zambia and Tanzania—may be extremely important as symbols of national independence and unity.

various ethnic groups in Kenya and in a structure of social communications directed toward serving a minority, not fulfilling the contemporary requirements of the country as a whole.

This situation provides a fertile and exciting field for geographical research, for a new and very different set of decision makers has assumed control over the driving forces behind the spatial organization and differentiation of Kenya and its people. The wholesale restructuring and alteration of the patterns of human geography that evolved during the colonial period has been discussed throughout this study. Manifestations of the attempts to create a new spatial and behavioral system more suitable to the needs of independent Kenya have just been outlined. It is not unlikely that during the next decades there will take place a process of geographical change as revolutionary as that which transformed the archipelago of buffered agricultural islands in a pastoral sea into contemporary Kenya.

NATIONAL POLITICAL INTEGRATION IN KENYA: A GEOGRAPHIC GENERALIZATION

An implicit theme throughout this study has been the spatial evolution of the Kenya nation—the nature of the initial culture contact; the growth of the network of social communications; the development of two modernization subsystems; the emergence of Nairobi as a political core area; the diffusion of social, economic, and political change; the establishment of an African political community; the impact of independence. The topic has not been examined directly, for national allegiance and identification are primarily psychological manifestations investigable on a state-wide basis only through large-scale and extremely costly survey research into individual and group behavior.

Alternatively, the question of national political integration has been approached through an analysis of the geography of modernization. As mentioned earlier, the two processes are not the same, but examining the spatial patterns of modernization within a state provides valuable insight into the basic problems and progress of nation building. The highly uneven geographical impact of modernization in Kenya, for example, particularly when coupled with the wide range of barriers erected by the colonial government against ethnic interaction, produced a fragmentation

of the Kenya polity which stands today as a major challenge to national unity.

How well integrated are the various sections of Kenya? Can one identify patterns of spatial variation in national cohesiveness and express them accurately on a map? In this final section, an attempt has been made to draw together findings from the combination of historical, empirical, cartographic, and statistical approaches used in this study of the geography of modernization to form a composite picture of the patterns of national political development and integration in Kenya. The objective is not to provide a detailed summary of the study, but to derive some implications relevant to the problems of nation building.

The product of this synthesis is shown in Figure 47, which, although highly generalized and impressionistic, represents a first attempt to describe the dynamic framework of human geography in a developing country in terms of the most significant processes affecting it: the forces leading to the transition from traditional systems of social, economic, and political organization and behavior to more modern forms based on the cohesive nation-state. It is a preliminary and subjective representation of the Kenya nation within a spatial framework during the period immediately following independence in 1963.

The basis of the map is eclectic. In part, it is derived from the principal components analysis, particularly from the level of Development (F1) within the African Subsystem and the factor loadings and scores on the four rotated dimensions. In part, it also reflects the findings of Chapters IV and V dealing with the extent and intensity of the various facets of social mobilization and the patterns of circulation within the network of social communications. Much of the detail is an outgrowth of extensive interviewing in nearly all the districts of Kenya.[8]

---

[8] The author conducted interviews with administrative officials in 28 of the 36 districts dealt with in this study concerning the structure of communications, political participation, and the patterns of modernization within each district. The officials were asked, for example, which part of their district had the highest level of educational development, where most of the political leaders came from, where the economy was most highly developed, what the circulatory structure looked like, and what role they felt the district's population played in contemporary Kenya. The largely impressionistic results were compared with

The final product, however, is not a systematic distillation from all these sources but more an individual perception of the Kenya nation as it is expressed spatially. Such a geographical generalization may stimulate further thought on the challenging problems involved in measuring areal variations in political integration and suggest a framework for further elaboration and comparison.

Nairobi: The Core Area

Nairobi is clearly the most modernized part of Kenya and the hub of the nation—an easily identifiable core area. Karl Deutsch notes that "the density that makes a core area is one of traffic and communications rather than mere numbers of passive villagers densely settled on the soil."[9] The dominance of Nairobi in the network of communications and transport—as well as in the over-all social, economic, and political organization of Kenya—has been accented throughout this study. It is illustrated further in Table 24.

TABLE 24
DEGREE OF CONCENTRATION IN NAIROBI AND OTHER NATIONAL NUCLEI OF SELECTED MEASURES OF MODERNIZATION

Variable	Nairobi District(%)	All National Nuclei (%)
Total population	4	17
Urban population (over 5,000)	42	87
Postal traffic	47	80
Radios	46	80
Televisions	78	95
Railway passengers	15	60
English newspapers	60	83
Swahili newspapers	27	68
Telephones	55	88
Telephone traffic	30	63
African paid laborers	17	45
Total African wages	28	60
Post-secondary educated Africans	16	no data
Registered political societies	34	no data

Although containing only 4 per cent of the Kenya population, Nairobi has close to half or more of the total urban population, postal traffic, radios, television sets, English newspaper circulation, and telephones. About 17 per cent of the African labor force is employed in Nairobi, but more significantly they receive 28 per cent of all African wages. The capital is the headquarters for over a third of the registered political organizations and the origin or destination for a large proportion of the railway, road, and telephone traffic of Kenya.

Proximity to and close interaction with Nairobi have been shown to be areally associated with high levels of modernization, indicative of the importance of core connectivity in the over-all patterns of transition. In other words, the areas most closely interacting with Nairobi tend also to be the most urbanized; have the best developed trade, transport, and communication networks; and contain the wealthiest, most literate, and best educated African population in Kenya.

If sufficient comparable data were available, these relationships could prove extremely valuable in the identification and analysis of core areas elsewhere and for research into the relative impact of core connectivity in the developing as well as the developed countries. For example, can the key variables on the Core Connectivity Dimension (NBIFO, DISTA, PEMPL, ACASH, RADIO), weighted according to their factor loadings and modified to fit into a new location, be used as a predictor of geographical differences in modernization in other African countries? Can an index of concentration be developed in combination with a connectivity measure to determine the relative importance of core areas to their respective territories? Does the core area in a developing country play a different role than one in the more developed sections of the world? These are important questions for the political geographer to answer.[10]

available statistical data, election results, newspaper accounts, and personal observation. The only districts not included in the survey were the Northern Frontier, Turkana, Samburu, Tana River, Lamu, Kitui, Narok, and Meru, although some information was obtained about these areas from former district officials stationed in other sections of the country.

[9] "The Growth of Nations," p. 174.

[10] Political geographers have all too often been satisfied with an essentially subjective identification of core areas and a historical description of their role in the growth of a nation-state Stress has usually been placed upon the uniqueness of these areas, thus stifling significant comparative research. It is essential that more dynamic and analytical definitions be developed which take into account some of the general characteristics of core areas and provide precise yardsticks for cross-national examination.

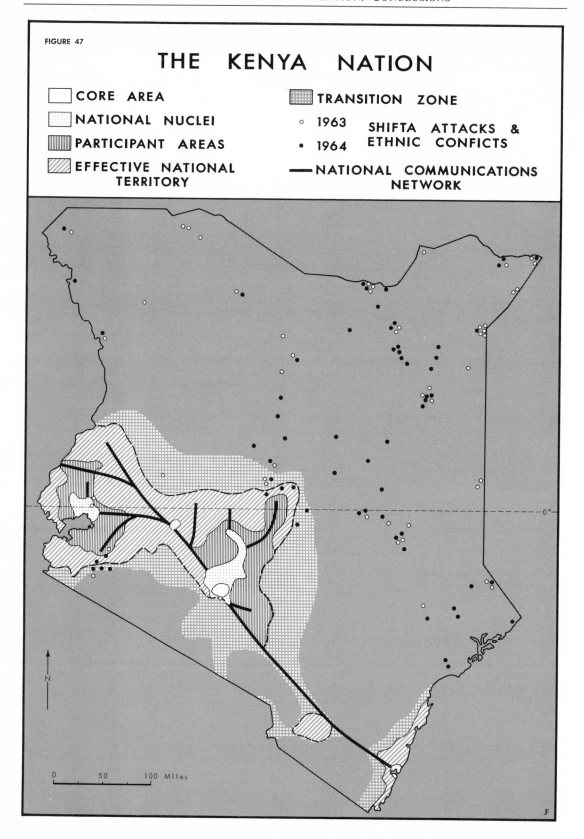

FIGURE 47

THE KENYA NATION

□ CORE AREA
▨ NATIONAL NUCLEI
▥ PARTICIPANT AREAS
▧ EFFECTIVE NATIONAL
    TERRITORY

▦ TRANSITION ZONE
○ 1963   SHIFTA ATTACKS &
● 1964   ETHNIC CONFICTS
— NATIONAL COMMUNICATIONS
    NETWORK

The National Nuclei

In a broader context, Deutsch has written the following:

> The shift to an economy and culture based on wider interchange takes place at different times and different rates of speed in different regions. The result is often the existence of more "advanced" regions side by side with more "underdeveloped" ones. The former are then often in a position to function as centers of cultural and economic attraction for some of the population of the latter, and thus become nuclei of further integration.[11]

These more "advanced" regions in Kenya are the national nuclei shown in Figure 47. They include Nairobi and most of its immediate hinterland; Kisumu and the quasi-urban areas surrounding it; and the towns of Nakuru and Mombasa. In addition to being the most highly modernized sections of the country, these areas contain the major focal points of political integration and the prime generators, transformers, interpreters, and distributors of the forces of change.

When the other leading areas, comprising about 13 per cent of the population, are added to Nairobi, many of the figures in Table 24 rise to more than 80 per cent. This is a rather startling proportion, powerful evidence of the high degree of areal concentration of modernization characteristic of most new states.[12]

This concentration is due largely to the key role played by the major urban centers in the initial phases of modernization and nation building. During this period, the urban centers virtually are the nation and contain the bulk of the modernized, national elite. But it should be noted that two largely rural areas have also been included within the national nuclei. One extends northward from Nairobi to encompass nearly all of Kiambu District and the major communications and transport corridor through Thika and Fort Hall to Nyeri. The other surrounds Kisumu, is elongated to the northwest through Maseno and Yala, and includes most of North and South Gem and Seme Locations in Central Nyanza and North and South Maragoli and Bunyore Locations in North Nyanza.

Occupied mainly by the Kikuyu, Luo, and Luhya (the leading groups in the African Subsystem), these areas have acted as the most important source regions for the modernized elite of Kenya. A large proportion of the political leadership was born or educated here and, with their major nodes of Nairobi and Kisumu, they became the locus of African nationalism and political party development. The two areas contain all six of the National Schools, several of which (Alliance High School at Kikuyu, Maseno Secondary School), along with other large schools located nearby (St. Mary's School at Yala, Kijabe High School, Nyeri Boys Secondary School), played critical roles in the evolution of Kenya politics—and politicians.

Although urban life in most of the larger towns in these two major national nuclei—Nairobi, Kisumu, Thika, Fort Hall, and Nyeri—is still dominated by the immigrant communities, many of the smaller centers have emerged as hives of African social, economic, and political activity which, to an observer, appears more sophisticated and modern than that in other settlements of similar size elsewhere in Kenya. These include Maseno and Yala in the west and Kiambu, Kikuyu, Limuru, Ruiru, Sagana, and Karatina in the east.[13]

Nakuru and Mombasa have not yet developed the high level of feedback with their surrounding areas that exists around Nairobi and Kisumu. This contrast is closely related to their situation within the European Subsystem and the barriers to social communications and integration associated with it. In the future, however, they are likely to assume greater importance in the integrative process and may perhaps best be termed incipient national nuclei.

---

[11] "The Growth of Nations," pp. 173–74.

[12] Discussing primarily industrial development, Edward Ullman has written: "Concentration within countries is the rule. This fact may signal the operation of a general localization principle in man's use of the earth: initial location advantages at a critical stage of change may become magnified in the course of development." In "Regional Development and the Geography of Concentration," *Papers and Proceedings of the Regional Science Association* (1958), p. 196. But will not the extremely high degree of concentration existing in Kenya today have to *decrease* with increasing development? This question deserves much more intensive research.

[13] There is a great need to test this and related observations more closely by conducting comparative research on the smaller urban settlements of Kenya to determine variations in role structure, communications behavior, and attitudinal change.

Mombasa emerged as the major port of northern East Africa during the early stages of transport growth, eclipsing its neighbors and sending them into a period of stagnation from which they never recovered. The coastal circulatory system was similarly weakened as Mombasa came to function more as the outlet for the interior than as a focus and generator of coastal development. Consequently, the impact of Mombasa on the surrounding Mijikenda peoples has been weakened by its role as satellite of the interior.

The coastal region, with over 600,000 people, presents one of the most critical problems of regional integration facing contemporary Kenya. There were threats of secession in the Coastal Strip at the time of independence and frequent expressions of sectional interests both before and since. The African government is keenly aware of the need to build closer ties between the coast and the interior, and the amalgamation of KANU and KADU may have been a step in this direction. But it is equally important that Mombasa, while increasing its contacts with the rest of Kenya, intensify its role as an integrative nucleus and generator of development *within* the coastal region.

The Taita people occupy a potentially pivotal role in the tying together of the coast and the interior. On the map of nodal flow of telephone communications (Figure 20) the Taita area stood out as the only isolated cell within the network, reflecting its location within a zone of relatively weak and competitive attraction between Nairobi and Mombasa. Although administratively part of the Coast Region (formerly Coast Province), the Taita have always had close ties with interior peoples. Taita District was the only one within the less developed sector of the European Subsystem (Quadrant IV in Figure 45) to vote for KANU in the 1963 elections and has participated, although usually marginally, in the mainstream of African politics since the 1920's. Increased development in the district, especially improved transport and communications to and within the Taita Hills, where the bulk of the population resides, may prove to be an important factor in reducing regional isolation throughout the coast by providing a more effective bridge to the interior.

Formerly known as the capital of the White Highlands, Nakuru, like Mombasa, has never acted symbolically or functionally as a major focal point of integration and identification for large numbers of Africans. Today, however, particularly with the settlement program in the Scheduled Areas, Nakuru has the potential to become one of the most important centers for national political integration in all of Kenya—and possibly for an East African Federation.

Whether Nakuru will fulfill its potential depends heavily upon the success of the settlement program. As the program progresses, it is likely that the association between Nakuru and white settlement will be reduced. Freed from its ethnic and racial associations and favored by its central and highly accessible location, Nakuru and the surrounding highland areas can become the setting for the admixture of peoples so vital to the growth of a nation. While much of the periphery of the Scheduled Areas has already been absorbed into the adjacent African Land Units in the administrative reorganization of 1963, it would seem imperative that the remainder of the old White Highlands be transformed into a testing ground for inter-ethnic cooperation and nation building—to become a truly *national* area and not another set of ethnic compartments.

The area extending westward from Nakuru toward Kericho and Kisumu, and including the towns of Njoro, Molo, Londiani, and Lumbwa, is likely to play a very important role in future developments. Kikuyu expansion into the area east of Nakuru has not been effectively challenged by other major groups, but in the area to the west pressures have begun to build against these aggressive and land-hungry migrants from central Kenya. As more of this section of the former White Highlands is opened to African farmers and traders, the strength and future progress of inter-ethnic cooperation may face its severest test.

Identification of the four national nuclei has been based upon the levels of modernization derived from the principal components analysis and the patterns of structure and flow within the circulatory system. Each of these areas, which score high on nearly every measure of modernization, acts as the node for large circulation regions which encompass the bulk of Kenya's population and provide the spatial framework for the movement of goods, people, and information. Only Nairobi, however, has expanded beyond these regional bounds to function as the core area for virtually all of Kenya—a relationship brought out most clearly in the Core Connectivity Dimension.

As yet, none of the other national nuclei has attained a comparable position. But it is important to note that the Kisumu nucleus has the potential for much further growth and could easily develop into a major sectionalist focus, particularly if the internal political stability of Kenya is threatened. Kisumu already has a large participant and modernized population within its broad hinterland in western Kenya. And if all of East Africa were taken into account, it would occupy a key central position between the two most modernized regions of the combined territories: the Kenya Highlands and the borderlands of Lake Victoria in Uganda, Kenya, and Tanzania. In addition, although the relations between the Nilotic Luo and the Bantu Luhya and Kisii have never been especially friendly or cooperative, each has close ethnic affinities across the borders of Kenya which may become more politically important in the future.

The growth of sectionalism in the Lake Victoria region would be a greater disintegrative force in Kenya than the isolation of the coast. For this reason, it becomes increasingly important that Nakuru—located between the two major population clusters and national nuclei focused on Nairobi and Kisumu—act as a knot in the network of social communications tying together the Kikuyu and related groups to the east and the Luo, Luhya, Kisii, and others in the West.[14]

---

[14] The assembly seat for Nakuru Town, where the Kikuyu are a majority, has been held until recently by Achieng Oneko, a Luo. But in the 1966 split in KANU, Mr. Oneko broke from the ruling party to join a new organization led by another Luo, Oginga Odinga, and in the ensuing special election lost his seat to a Kikuyu. These developments are indicative of the key role already being played by Nakuru in Kenya politics. It must be stressed that the new party, the Kenya People's Union (KPU), is not entirely Luo and that large numbers of Luo, particularly in South Nyanza, remain loyal to KANU. The party split, however, may have serious repercussions on national integration in Kenya if it develops into a direct Luo-Kikuyu confrontation or becomes purely regionally based.

The Participant Areas

The next level in the regional hierarchy of national political integration consists of the densely populated and largely rural areas closely connected with the Nairobi and Kisumu nuclei and those areas along the principal transportation arteries (shown as the national communications grid in Figure 47). Whereas the national nuclei direct and generate the processes of change and integration, these areas provide the most important political "market."[15] With a fairly well developed circulatory system and relatively high educational level, the participant areas have dominated African politics in both the pre- and post-independence periods.

Except for some of the towns along the national grid, this level of the hierarchy is basically equivalent to the districts clustered in the more developed quadrant of the African Subsystem. The largest section is located north and east of Nairobi, where villagization, land consolidation, early European contact, transport development, accessibility to the national core area, and many other factors have produced a well-articulated system of human interaction, an efficient economic foundation, and probably the most modernized rural Africans in Kenya. The only other large area where a rural-urban feedback has developed to any great extent is located in western Kenya and focused on Kisumu.

The national grid represents the skeletal network of major linkages connecting the national nuclei and other important urban centers. It forms the geographical backbone for the circulatory system of Kenya. The four nuclei are all connected by rail and, except for a stretch still to be completed between Nairobi and Mombasa, by paved highway. Nearly all the other sections of the grid are associated with paved roads or with roads expected to be paved under the current Development Plan, 1964–1970, and with existing and proposed railway lines. A large proportion of the most highly modernized population outside the national nuclei are located in close proximity to this grid, particularly in such towns as Eldoret, Kitale, Kakamega, Bungoma,

---

[15] Note that each level includes all the levels preceding it. For example, one of the national nuclei includes the core area, and the participant areas include the national nuclei.

Kericho, Kisii, Naivasha, Thomson's Falls, Gilgil, Machakos, Nanyuki, Embu, and Meru.

The Effective National Territory

The light-toned areas on the map represent the effective national territory—that portion of Kenya which contains virtually the entire mobilized and nationally conscious population and the bulk of the developed economy and national infrastructure, and which owes sufficient allegiance to the central government to accept peaceful change under its direction. It consists of the national nuclei, which subdivide its area into spheres of influence, and the participant areas, which are its leading sectors. Thus, the previous categories consist of various levels of functional differentiation of the effectively organized area: its core, major nodes and lines of circulation, and regions of most intensive development.

The major portion of the effective national territory lies within the dashed lines in Figure 47. The largest section consists of a bow-tie shaped region in the Kenya Highlands, with Nakuru at the knot between two broader sections. One extends from the foothills of Mount Elgon on the Uganda border southward to Kisii, Kericho, and sections of South Nyanza. The other stretches from Meru and Nanyuki north of Mount Kenya to the hills of Ukambani southeast of Nairobi. Important outliers exist along the coast and in Taita District. In addition, several administrative centers not shown on the map should probably be included (e.g., Kitui and its environs, Kajiado, Narok, Kabarnet).

Much of this area, particularly sections of the former White Highlands, has not been included in the previous category because of its association with the European Subsystem. Although relatively well developed and in close interaction with the participant areas, the existence of a wide range of economic, social, political, and psychological barriers prevented it from becoming the spatial locus for the mainstream of African politics in Kenya. This situation has begun to change rapidly, however, since independence, particularly with the progress of the settlement program and the dissolution of KADU. The differences between the two modernization subsystems are becoming less pronounced, and the geographical milieu of national politics is expanding.

The cross-hatched area beyond the broken gray lines in Figure 47 is a zone of transition containing a number of peoples (South Nyanza Luo, Kitui Kamba, Suk, Tugen, Njemps, Elgeyo, Marakwet, Samburu, Masai, and several coastal groups) who are among the least modernized and most tradition bound in Kenya, but who have participated at least marginally in recent political developments and are likely to increase their involvement in the future. The process of social mobilization has begun, but it has not yet been effective enough to draw these areas fully into the national picture.

Political ideology and allegiance are unclear and highly changeable in this transition zone. In 1963, a KADU candidate won an uncontested election in West Pokot (occupied primarily by the Suk) and then immediately crossed the floor to KANU. Representatives from Baringo and West Pokot bolted from KANU in 1966, only to ask for reacceptance several days later. These are typical occurrences in this politically unstable zone.

Areas Beyond Effective National Control

The shaded areas of the map are beyond effective national control and functionally not part of the Kenya nation in that the critical level of consensus that would permit centralized planning to be accepted and take effect has not yet been reached. As in the transition zone, political allegiance is unsettled and erratic. But, in addition, the level of participation in national politics is extremely low and, more importantly, the frequency of internal conflict is such that the impress of the central government appears weak and ineffective.

The fragility of government control in this area is clearly evident in the pattern of local conflict during the two years immediately following independence. Each small circle on Figure 47 represents a major armed raid or inter-ethnic confrontation stemming either from anti-government motives or traditional enmities.[16] In nearly all cases, at least one life was lost or major damage was done to property.

By far the bulk of these conflicts involved the *shifta*, armed Somali who have been ravag-

---

[16] Data for the map were obtained from reports of *shifta* activities and major inter-ethnic conflicts in the *East African Standard* during 1963 (open dots) and 1964 (closed dots).

ing most of northeastern Kenya since independence in an attempt to detach this portion of the country and unite it with Somalia. Although concentrated in the heavily Somali areas at first, the attacks have begun to spread further afield since 1963—to the northern coast in Lamu District, along the Tana River Valley, into parts of Kitui and Meru Districts, and even into portions of the Rift Valley right up to the margins of the effective national territory.[17]

A large portion of the area beyond effective national influence must therefore be considered a zone of competitive attraction. Here a rival and antagonistic focus of social mobilization exists, aimed at secession and thereby creating the most immediate threat to the *de jure* national integrity of contemporary Kenya.

The remaining areas, however, consisting of the northwestern section of Kenya (primarily Turkana District), much of Masailand, and portions of the almost empty *nyika* between the coastal plain and the highlands, are

significantly different. In these areas, there is no important source of competitive nationalism. The population remains internally focused and bound in tradition, unwilling to transfer more than the minimum amount of autonomy and allegiance to the central government. A peak of this indifference is reached in Turkana, as consistently at the bottom of all measures of modernization as Nairobi is at the top, where traditional conflict and cattle raiding across the border with Uganda has continued with little abatement since pre-colonial times.

In summary, the effectively organized territory of the Kenya nation has been shown to encompass only a rather small portion of the state-area, although it does contain most of the total population. Large sections of the country remain either indifferent or antagonistic to the goals of nation building, while an extensive transition zone continues to be ambivalent in its national outlook. Even within the effective national territory, there are several regional problems to be overcome, especially in maintaining close interaction and cooperation between the national nuclei.

These conclusions certainly do not spell the inevitable failure of nation building in Kenya. They merely point out some of the obstacles to be overcome in the process, which, it must be remembered, has only recently come under the direction of the actors themselves. Most of the existing problems are vestiges of colonial rule and will require time, capital, stability, and forceful African leadership to be solved.

---

[17] At one time, there was a possibility that the *shifta* would ally themselves with former Mau Mau fighters who remained in the forests north of Mount Kenya and would thus threaten part of the more densely populated and relatively well developed section of Kenya. Note the cluster of closed dots in Meru District. The threat has since passed, and most of the former Mau Mau have left the forest and expressed their allegiance to the central government. Nevertheless, this northern fringe of the effectively organized area continues to exist as a major internal strategic front for the Kenya government.

X

The Spatial Dimensions of Modernization: Considerations for Future Research

The concept of modernization, as a focus for the study of change in the contemporary world, has become a potent centripetal factor in social science research. Whether defined very broadly or restricted to one or another of its major components, the modernization process has attracted scholars from several disciplines who have discovered common or at least complementary objectives in their research activities. The subject is being viewed from many different perspectives, each contributing its own distinctive part to understanding the complex interplay of forces involved in the transition from traditional to modern ways of life.

The particular perspective used in this study has been spatial. An attempt has been made to discuss how the dynamic forces of change have expressed themselves in a pattern of areal variation in levels of modernization in Kenya and how these patterns may be interpreted with respect to their historical evolution and contemporary consequences. But a number of observations and conclusions have been made which have wider implications, both in relation to the interdisciplinary investigation of modernization in all developing areas and, in particular, to the examination of its more distinctly spatial dimensions. In this final chapter, the focus has been broadened beyond Kenya to discuss briefly these wider implications and to suggest a number of questions and themes for future research.

Throughout Africa, modernization has not been indigenously generated but has resulted from the *superimposition of a modern system of social, economic, and political organization and behavior over a mosaic of predominantly small-scale traditional societies.* The new system encompassed much larger areas and involved a greatly expanded world view. Although more highly differentiated as a whole, extreme specialization at the local level was characteristic since the framework of ex-change and interaction extended well beyond the usually parochial and self-sufficient traditional units. Territorial organization was functionally based and structured around a network of primary transport and communications linkages, which in turn hinged upon a system of modern urban nodes. Innovation and change were channeled through this formal framework rather than absorbed or accommodated in blanket fashion as was typical in traditional societies.

The old pattern of ethnically circumscribed cells, with flexible frontiers reflecting the dynamics of territorial occupation and control, was overlaid by a formal administrative system with rigid boundaries serving the purposes of a frequently distant, centralized authority. The urban, administrative and circulatory systems thus provided a new means of spatial integration, a superimposed structure within which the forces of change were introduced and diffused and around which the patterns of functional organization evolved.

The modern graft, however, became tightly interwoven with the traditional base in only a few areas, which grew into the major nuclei of modernization and integration for the masses of the population. Transition to modernity was most rapid in these areas, and the African population interacting most closely with them supplied the bulk of the indigenous social, economic, and political elite. The Nairobi area, for example, like the coastal regions in most West African countries, became the primary generator and distributor of the forces of change for all of Kenya. Connectivity with Nairobi, as measured by the fourth rotated dimension in the present study, is spatially associated with high levels of urbanism, well-developed transportation and communications, widespread African education and literacy, and nearly all other important measures of modernization.

As suggested earlier, this relationship supplies a framework for comparative analysis of the degree of spatial "dominance" both for various centers within the same country as well as for the leading centers in several African states. By using a combination of the highest loading variables on the Core Connectivity Dimension, weighted accordingly, a very revealing index could be developed for this purpose. Have Accra, Kampala, or Dakar, for example, dominated the areal impact of modernization in their respective countries to the extent that Nairobi has? Using this index, how do Lagos and Port Harcourt compare?

Also worthy of further investigation are the factors which contributed to the growth of these major nuclei. In many cases, it appears that locational advantages during the early stages of colonial contact, penetration, and development, when the basic infrastructure of urban-administrative centers and transport links was established, were critical to their growth. Also important, however, was the nature of traditional society in the areas involved. But it will be extremely difficult to weigh separately the degree to which the ease and rapidity of transition in certain societies led to the growth of major nuclei and the degree to which the establishment of a major center of development stimulated the rapid modernization of the surrounding peoples. Did the Nairobi or Kampala areas become the dominant nuclei for their respective territories because of inclinations inherent in traditional Kikuyu or Ganda society? Or was the rapid modernization of these groups due very largely to the implantation of the colonial center in their midst? Presumably, the answer lies in a blend of the two, but the question deserves more intensive study than it has been given.

Once firmly established, the major nuclei acted as magnets for further development throughout the colonial period, attracting the preponderant share of capital investment and attention from the colonizing power. The contrast between them and the more isolated areas thus became increasingly magnified.

The extent to which modernization became concentrated in these major nuclei is one of the most outstanding features of contemporary African states. In Kenya, 17% of the total population plays an overwhelmingly dominant role in the modern system, as revealed in Table 24. It would be most interesting to discover how heavily modernization has been concentrated in other African states and how the degree of concentration has affected the patterns of economic and political development.

The problems arising from the high concentration of development are clearly illustrated in the economic sphere. Simple economic growth, measured in terms of Gross National Product per capita, may be temporarily sustained in small pockets of development (as in Liberia, for example), but without a wider and more effective distribution of development, regional and social inequalities become intensified and the cohesiveness and stability necessary for continued and institutionalized growth may disappear. Economists have long recognized this important distributional component in economic development and its occasional incompatability with simple incremental growth, but there remains much that can be done by geographers and regional scientists within the context of their specifically spatial perspective.

The heavy accumulation in small areas is formidable evidence of the *restrictions to the spread of modernity* which have existed in Africa from the beginning of the colonial period. It is also perhaps inherent in the superimposed nature of the modern system, for development and change have not taken place in a coordinated and integrated fashion but have continued to pile up in certain areas while others remain virtually unaffected. Moreover, whereas the modern system may have had a degree of functional unity with respect to the objectives of the colonial power, its impact on the African population was highly localized and did not permit, in most cases, the growth of a cohesive territorial community.

In many parts of Africa, particularly in the areas of greatest European settlement, there emerged islands of development which were clearly dominated by immigrant communities and appeared to have only a limited direct impact on the indigenous population. Instead of acting as the nuclei for the assimilation of the masses into modern society, as similar areas had in the developed countries, powerful barriers to mobility between regions and classes arose to hinder further the growth of an integrated African society within the colonial framework.

These islands that developed inevitably did have "lift-pump" effect in mobilizing large sectors of the population, most commonly through labor migration and the growth of African cash crop agriculture, but this process usually took place not within the societal structure of the major islands themselves but within new nuclei located generally close by and within the traditional framework of ethnic cells. Thus, rather than creating an ethnically mixed national community, the impact of modernization was highly compartmentalized, and multiple systems of leadership and role differentiation developed within these ethnic compartments. Many, if not most, of the so-called "tribal" problems facing independent Africa today have arisen from this ethnically localized and non-integrated interplay between the superimposed and traditional systems.

One of the consequences of this process in Kenya was the growth of two clearly identifiable areal subsystems, each with its own leading sectors and distinctive mix of modernizing influences. This was not a simple economic dualism, with advanced and predominantly European and Asian areas standing in contrast to and isolation from backward, noncommercialized and wholly traditional African sectors, i.e., a "have and have-not" situation. Each subsystem had its own more and less developed areas, but because of the barriers to assimilation within the immigrant-dominated subsystem, its "lift-pump" effect was felt largely in the densely populated reserves fringing the eastern and western edges of the White Highlands, in the African Subsystem. Furthermore, the strength and persistence of these barriers stimulated the growth of an African nationalism strongly opposed to the politically dominant colonial minority, which had established its own form of nationalism within the European Subsystem (particularly if Nairobi is considered as the focal area of both).

Thus, two districts, such as Kiambu and Uasin Gishu or North Nyanza and Laikipia, which scored roughly the same on the unrotated summary dimension of Development, could and did play entirely different roles in the modernization of the African population. The growth of two modernization subsystems, closely interacting but significantly different in the types of forces operating and in their impact on the indigenous population, was one of the most striking areal reflections of the superimposed nature of modernization in Kenya.

It should be noted, however, that these subsystems were identified through the use of indicators which do not necessarily reflect behavior directly. Not only is it necessary to conduct comparative studies in other developing areas to ascertain whether or not similar breakdowns occur, but it is also important to examine in greater detail the *behavioral consequences* of this subsystem differentiation in Kenya. Can one identify, for example, significant differences in outlook and values between a Kiambu Kikuyu and one living in Uasin Gishu?

Geographers have usually neglected to examine areal variations in individual and group behavior which are not already thoroughly documented (e.g., voting behavior) or directly expressed on the landscape. In general, geographers have not had extensive experience with modern social survey techniques and the use of questionnaires. There is a need, however, to expand investigations into the spatial dimensions of human perception, attitudes, and behavior if geographers are to contribute to one of the most rapidly growing fields of social science research. As a simple illustration, it would be interesting to take either the map of the Development Dimension (Figure 41) or that of the Kenya nation (Figure 47) and examine the degree to which the areal patterns described correspond with actual differences in individual or small group behavior.

The spatial dimension, however, encompasses far more than the areal differentiation growing out of the uneven impact of modernization and the attempts at nation building. It also involves the *framework of spatial interaction,* which may be more relevant to the success of these efforts than the variations from place to place in levels of development.

Development concentration, for example, is not only characteristic of the new states of Africa or Asia but is a dominant feature of the more advanced countries as well.[1] The major differences lie not in the intensity of concentration but in the degree to which the major developed areas have become focal points in a wider web of relationship and interaction embracing virtually the entire population. Thus it becomes important to discover not

---

[1] See Ullman, "Regional Development and the Geography of Concentration."

only the way in which the areal system is differentiated but also the pattern and structure of interaction among its component parts.

This problem gives rise to a number of questions which have been dealt with only briefly in this study. For example, what are the patterns of intraterritorial trade? To what extent have various sections of the country become part of a functionally interdependent economic system? What are the patterns of connectivity and accessibility within the transport network? What proportion of the population is within reach of an all-weather road? What types of changes occur with the introduction of a new transport link? To what degree are the urban centers linked together? How centralized is the flow of messages, goods, and people? What are the major channels for the areal spread of information? How effective is government control in various parts of the state area, and what are the major mechanisms through which the government makes itself felt? Are there important centers of regionalism or sectionalism which threaten internal cohesion?

Illustrative of the more general research problems is the analysis of *the urban system.* Urban centers can be viewed as aggregative nodes within a broader network of social, economic, and political relationships—"peak points" within the spatial dimensions of modernization and change. Rather than emphasizing the unique site and situational characteristics of specific urban centers, an increasing number of geographers are beginning to concern themselves with more generic and theoretical themes, such as the growth of a functional hierarchy of central places, the patterns of interurban linkages and information flow, the impact of urbanization on spatial patterns of agricultural production, migration and political participation, and with other forms of processual relationship between urbanization and the human milieu within which it takes place.[2]

But further work is still needed, for example, along the lines of *The Towns of Ghana,* by Grove and Huszar.[3] This stimulating study examines the role of service centers in Ghana within the framework of Central Place Theory,[4] in a detailed analysis of the present urban system and government policy objectives. It not only describes the present pattern but offers concrete suggestions for future development that would sustain economic growth at the same time it fostered a more integrative distribution of goods and services throughout Ghana.

A number of techniques have been developed in both geography and the other social sciences which can be used effectively in the study of spatial interaction within the new states of Africa. Graph theory, for example, is useful in determining the levels of accessibility and connectivity for nodes within the transport and communications network[5] and for identifying the structure of nodal regions in an area.[6]

Transaction flow analysis provides another tool with great potential for analyzing the flow of information and the pattern of greater-than-expected interaction between areas.[7] It supplies a means for determining the salient linkages within a given system—connections between units which indicate that a high level of mutual awareness and relevance exists. This structure of salient transaction flows is the primary skeletal glue which holds the system together and provides the basis for successful territorial integration.

A large number of additional topics deserving further examination, by geographers as well as other social scientists, have been referred to throughout this study. These include the problems in ethnic mapping of noncentralized societies, the relationship between economic "satisfaction" and political participation, the role of the smaller towns in the modernization

---

[2] For a discussion of recent urban geographic research in Africa, see the Special Geography Issue of *African Urban Notes,* Vol. II, No. 3 (1967), edited by Edward W. Soja.

[3] David Grove and Laszlo Huszar, *The Towns of Ghana: The Role of Service Centers in Regional Planning* (Accra: Ghana Universities Press, 1964).

[4] An excellent introduction to this topic can be found in Brian J. L. Berry and Allen Pred, *Central Place Studies: A Bibliography of Theory and Applications.* Philadelphia: Regional Science Research Institute, Bibliography Series Number One (1961).

[5] See K. J. Kansky, *The Structure of Transportation Networks: Relationships Between Network Geometry and Regional Characteristics* (Chicago: Department of Geography Research Paper No. 84, 1963).

[6] Nystuen and Dacey, *op. cit.*

[7] See, e.g., Steven J. Brams, "Transaction Flows in the International System," *American Political Science Review* (1966), pp. 880–98.

process, the problems arising from immigrant domination of the urban system, the impact of distance and geographical location on the patterns of transition, the spatial readjustments growing out of independence, the growth of urbanism in areas which themselves contain no large towns, the problems of mapping variations in national unity and disunity, the comparison of intrastate vs. interstate dimensions of modernization, the systemic nature of the modernization process, and the comparative role of core areas throughout the developing world.

It is perhaps appropriate that this concluding chapter is filled with unanswered questions and suggestions for further research. The primary objectives of this study have been to analyze the geography of modernization in Kenya and to examine the implications of the spatial perspective for the interdisciplinary analysis of modernization in the developing areas. In a major sense it has been heavily exploratory in approach and methods, seeking not so much to test original hypotheses as to search for some identifiable patterns and processes which relate to existing theories and observations from the rapidly expanding literature on the problems of the new states. If the spatial perspective of the geographer has enabled new questions to be asked or opened fresh avenues for further investigation which could contribute to a greater understanding the modernization process, then this study will have proved successful.

APPENDIXES

APPENDIX A

SOURCE AND EXPLANATION OF VARIABLES

DEMOGRAPHIC CHARACTERISTICS:

1. PODEN (Population density)—Data on mean density per square mile from the 1962 Population Census were obtained from the *Statistical Abstract 1964*, published by the Government of Kenya, Economic and Statistics Division, Ministry of Finance and Economic Planning (1964), p. 8.

2. EUROP (European population)—Total numbers of Europeans in each district were obtained from *Kenya Population Census, 1962,* Advance Report of Volumes I and II, published by the Economics and Statistics Division, Ministry of Finance and Economic Planning (January, 1964), p. 5.

3. ASIAN (Asian population)—Source for the total number of Asians is the same as for the above.

4. MIXTU (Ethnic mixture)—Percentages were obtained by subtracting the proportion of the total population of each district made up by the two largest ethnic groups. The results range from Turkana (.3 percent), the most homogeneous, to Mombasa (67.3 percent), the most heterogeneous. Ethnic data are from the *Kenya Population census, 1962,* Advance Report of Volumes I and II.

5. TOWNP (Extent of urbanization)—An accurate relative picture of urbanization by district could not be obtained by using commonly accepted thresholds, such as towns of more than 5,000. Nineteen of the thirty-six districts do not have a town of this size, and census data are incomplete for towns with smaller populations. Therefore, the figures used are based on the population of the largest urban nucleus in each district and range from 350 for Elgeyo-Marakwet to 266,794 for Nairobi. Data source is *Kenya Population Census, 1962,* Volume I.

EDUCATION (African Only):

6. COLED (Post-secondary education)—This variable is based upon the number of Africans with thirteen or more years of education and provides a rough approximation of the distribution of the educated African elite. In some ways, this is also a measure of the historical evolution of education in Kenya—the greatest numbers being located in those districts where well-developed educational systems were established during the colonial era. Data were derived from the as yet unpublished material on education from the 1962 census, made available to the author by the Ministry of Finance and Economic Development.

7. LITER (Literacy)—This variable attempts to measure minimal adult literacy: the percentage of males over twenty years of age who have had some education. Data source is the same as for above.

8. PRIMA (Primary education)—This variable is based upon the percentage of the African male population between the ages of five and nine who have at least one year of education, plus the same figure for females. Figures for total primary school enrollment by district were not available. Data source is the same as for COLED. The figures reflect the distribution of existing educational facilities.

9. KPEXA (Education quality)—Percentage passing the Kenya Preliminary Examination for entry into secondary schools in 1962 was obtained from the Ministry of Education, Government of Kenya.

COMMUNICATIONS AND TRANSPORT:

10. TOPOS (Total postal traffic)—Average weekly figures for total number of items received and sent out by all postal facilities in each district in 1963. Data were made available by the Services Controller (Postal), Ministry of Works, Communications and Power.

11. PPLET (Per capita postal traffic)—Figures for this variable are based upon population divided by total postal traffic and actually represents the number of people per item handled. The range is from .32 per letter in Nairobi to more than 260 in Turkana. Data on population are from the 1962 census; postal data is the same as for TOPOS.

12. SWAPA (Swahili newspaper circulation)—Average weekly circulation figures (1963) for *Baraza* (one issue), *Taifa Leo* (six issues), and *Taifa Kenya* (one issue) were obtained from the circulation departments of the East African Standard and East African Newspapers publishing groups and divided into the total

119

district population to produce figures on the number of people for each paper sold during an average week. All circulation figures were authenticated by the Audit Bureau of Circulation.

13. ENGPA (English newspaper circulation)—This variable was developed similarly to SWAPA, but the papers used were the *Daily Nation* (six issues), the *East African Standard* (daily: six issues), the *East African Standard* (Sunday; one issue), and the *Sunday Nation* (one issue).

14. RADIO (Distribution of radio licenses)—The number of wireless licenses issued for 1964 provides the basis for this variable. Data were supplied by the Licensing Department, Kenya Government.

15. NOTEL (Distribution of telephones)—The East African Posts and Telecommunications Administration (EAP&TA) supplied information on the number of telephones in use in 1963.

16. TRAFF (Road traffic density)—Simple road density without the introduction of traffic information is a poor measure of the significance of road transport. Although there are some good traffic flow maps available from the Road Authority, it is impossible to transform these data accurately into district figures. Consequently, this variable has been based upon grants given by the central and local governments for road maintenance in each district, divided by the area of the district. Since the maintenance grants are allotted according to traffic density classes, it is felt that this measure is the best available for indicating the importance and development of road transport. It should be noted, however, that only the major trunk and secondary roads have been included. There remain some administrative roads and, particularly in the Scheduled Areas, a dense minor road network—but these are not well traveled.

CONNECTIVITY WITH THE CORE AREA (Nairobi):

17. DISTA (Road distance to Nairobi)—This variable is derived from the road mileage between Nairobi and the administrative headquarters of each district along the shortest major route.

18. NBIFO (Telephone connectivity with Nairobi)—This variable is based on the percentage of all calls made in each district that was directed to Nairobi. Data source is the nine-hour telephone traffic census (9 A.M. to 12

noon, three days a week) made in 1962 and supplied to the author by the EAP&TA.

ECONOMIC DEVELOPMENT:

19. TAXPP (Tax per capita)—Figures are based on the Graduated Personal Tax (in shillings) collected from Africans in 1962–63 divided by the total African population. The GPT is based upon estimated earnings and property. Because of the high value placed on cattle, many of the primarily pastoral districts (Narok, Kajiado, West Pokot) have high per capita taxes. Data source is the Ministry of Local Government.

20. TRADE (Value of trade license issued)—Figures are based on revenues received from all ethnic groups for the issuance of trade licenses for 1961–62 (in pounds). The price of licenses varies with the estimated size of stock—375 shillings for stock valued at over £300, 112.5 shillings for between £100–300, and 45 shillings for less than £100. Data source is the Inland Revenue Service, Nairobi.

21. PEMPL (Percentage of Africans employed)—This variable is based upon the percentage of Africans engaged in paid employment in 1961. Data source: Labor enumeration figures supplied by the Ministry of Finance and Economic Development.

22. AVSAL (Average African salaries)—Total emoluments (in pounds per annum) to Africans in 1961 divided by the total number employed was used to construct this variable. Data source is same as above.

23. ACASH (African cash income)—A combination of total emoluments plus total cash income from agriculture and livestock. The latter figures were derived from the district Annual Reports of the Ministry of Agriculture for 1962.

POLITICAL DEVELOPMENT:

24. SOCIE (Distribution of Political Associations)—This variable is based upon the number of political societies registered in 1963 by the Registrar's office, Kenya government.

25. KANUS (Growth of KANU)—A rough measure of the diffusion of political development, this variable is based on the number of days separating the official registration of KANU as a political party (November 5, 1960) and the establishment of a branch office in each district. Data source is the Registrar's Office.

ORIGINAL DATA MATRIX
PART I: DEMOGRAPHIC

	PODEN	EUROP	ASIAN	MIXTU	TOWNP
Nairobi	1387	28,128	86,922	64.0	266,794
Kiambu	557	2820	1174	4.5	2533
Thika	117	1014	2998	18.2	13,952
Fort Hall	491	150	802	.6	5389
Embu	183	171	764	3.8	5213
Nyeri	428	635	1448	1.6	7857
Meru	125	251	950	1.4	3308
Nanyuki	20	1174	1050	20.5	10,448
Naivasha	52	2825	1009	17.4	6452
Nakuru	97	3682	7346	36.0	38,181
Laikipia	26	691	650	25.5	5316
Uasin Gishu	61	1211	3804	45.3	19,605
Trans-Nzoia	81	1320	2136	39.4	9342
Baringo	32	47	69	1.8	782
Nandi	167	112	135	3.2	1962
Elgeyo-Marakwet	160	44	19	3.1	350
West Pokot	30	50	49	6.5	850
Kajiado	8	220	653	13.1	2078
Narok	15	55	169	6.4	1621
Machakos	95	605	1134	1.2	5510
Kitui	24	68	415	.9	2447
Elgon Nyanza	232	81	738	2.8	1589
North Nyanza	507	273	976	2.5	3939
Central Nyanza	268	768	10,101	2.9	23,526
South Nyanza	160	167	522	2.9	1449
Kisii	690	148	729	.8	4530
Kericho	183	1294	2910	18.6	7692
Taita	15	151	533	15.4	2533
Kwale	49	729	674	6.1	1008
Kilifi	51	1244	1074	6.9	5818
Mombasa	1694	5305	43,713	67.3	108,872
Tana River	3	24	23	11.0	889
Lamu	8	30	249	32.5	5828
Samburu	7	33	43	1.3	1387
Turkana	6	11	29	.3	2385
Northern Frontier	5	146	501	2.3	1768

ORIGINAL DATA MATRIX
PART II: EDUCATION

	COLED	LITER	PRIMA	KPEXA
Nairobi	586	56.8	54.3	35.2
Kiambu	251	54.4	50.5	49.4
Thika	47	49.4	45.6	ND
Fort Hall	210	45.0	50.5	50.8
Embu	61	34.7	41.0	39.7
Nyeri	184	54.3	67.0	58.8
Meru	154	28.5	32.0	44.8
Nanyuki	34	38.7	38.0	86.5
Naivasha	11	42.6	32.5	69.8
Nakuru	179	46.0	36.9	73.2
Laikipia	4	32.4	24.5	81.3
Uasin Gishu	29	32.8	58.0	44.3
Trans-Nzoia	50	41.8	27.2	49.7
Baringo	119	21.8	17.7	45.6
Nandi	144	31.8	50.8	36.6
Elgeyo-Marakwet	44	19.8	24.1	38.3
West Pokot	11	9.1	15.2	23.6
Kajiado	24	7.1	14.3	31.6
Narok	0	8.0	11.7	41.3
Machakos	196	30.5	26.1	45.5
Kitui	18	12.1	14.0	27.7
Elgon Nyanza	122	40.9	29.0	35.4
North Nyanza	207	36.1	39.1	51.6
Central Nyanza	124	28.6	36.0	42.3
South Nyanza	81	37.5	38.2	41.9
Kisii	332	40.5	34.6	32.6
Kericho	111	36.2	36.2	33.3
Taita	26	33.0	44.8	17.2
Kwale	91	17.4	17.6	26.0
Kilifi	19	13.6	11.8	19.5
Mombasa	121	40.1	40.6	32.6
Tana River	15	11.6	21.8	25.8
Lamu	4	19.4	13.7	ND
Samburu	ND	ND	ND	30.0
Turkana	ND	ND	ND	ND
Northern Frontier	ND	ND	ND	34.6

ND = No data

ORINGINAL DATA MATRIX
PART III: COMMUNICATIONS AND TRANSPORT

	SWAPA	ENGPA	TOPOS	PPLET	RADIO	NOTEL	TRAFF
Nairobi	7	2	995.3	.32	18,847	13,798	237.76
Kiambu	45	87	52.4	7.76	620	805	59.14
Thika	21	16	36.8	2.69	1051	450	45.54
Fort Hall	157	143	19.0	18.11	344	72	29.08
Embu	121	149	14.9	19.71	400	75	13.03
Nyeri	47	52	37.9	6.72	602	278	22.32
Meru	158	212	10.4	45.12	376	74	6.01
Nanyuki	27	22	19.0	3.02	471	351	13.98
Naivasha	32	16	24.8	2.97	477	328	31.84
Nakuru	19	14	137.3	1.73	2291	1552	30.42
Laikipia	78	66	18.8	3.72	424	219	8.11
Uasin Gishu	27	18	52.9	1.90	1364	548	35.01
Trans-Nzoia	24	23	32.6	3.02	917	370	29.21
Baringo	(7750)	(12,000)	2.2	58.76	9	10	1.37
Nandi	181	281	18.0	6.62	127	32	14.60
Elgeyo-Marakwet	(7250)	(11,250)	2.2	73.60	6	0	7.58
West Pokot	1513	(4500)	.5	119.66	3	0	1.13
Kajiado	161	192	4.8	14.20	129	17	2.26
Narok	1394	1468	3.4	32.66	52	25	1.69
Machakos	186	151	33.6	16.38	447	134	9.21
Kitui	332	615	6.4	44.42	162	0	1.29
Elgon Nyanza	170	620	12.1	28.70	360	31	12.76
North Nyanza	116	308	37.5	16.22	235	57	24.78
Central Nyanza	61	63	93.1	7.13	1863	609	13.44
South Nyanza	226	648	14.3	33.68	47	28	7.35
Kisii	222	434	16.2	32.09	345	52	20.01
Kericho	82	83	61.3	6.39	818	470	20.22
Taita	64	115	12.0	7.47	214	33	2.93
Kwale	184	119	5.5	28.96	56	28	8.49
Kilifi	87	109	17.1	14.48	308	148	6.53
Mombasa	6	4	298.0	.60	7150	4190	196.19
Tana River	(30,000)	2458	1.4	21.84	4	2	.48
Lamu	(9500)	638	2.1	11.18	85	21	1.49
Samburu	ND	2263	1.1	50.80	1	0	.13
Turkana	(20,000)	(25,000)	.6	261.49	2	0	.29
Northern Frontier	ND	(14,750)	1.4	43.77	14	5	.17

( ) = Rough estimates
ND = No data

ORIGINAL DATA MATRIX
PART IV: ECONOMIC

	TAXPP	TRADE	PEMPL	AVSAL	ACASH
Nairobi	18.68	49,746	40.22	125.68	9,953
Kiambu	1.53	3,366	8.63	69.27	2,985
Thika	1.96	3,921	41.28	56.07	2,193
Fort Hall	.88	2,432	1.90	100.99	1,152
Embu	1.59	2,002	2.14	89.68	1,595
Nyeri	1.38	4,205	4.02	96.98	1,375
Meru	1.30	2,554	1.43	90.07	1,850
Nanyuki	1.64	2,091	23.17	52.08	665
Naivasha	.41	2,061	34.00	37.98	901
Nakuru	1.53	9,302	26.06	52.19	3,072
Laikipia	1.04	1,907	18.91	41.95	545
Uasin Gishu	.96	4,637	31.81	44.79	1,361
Trans-Nzoia	.58	3,350	25.10	43.82	1,042
Baringo	.34	359	2.61	66.99	293
Nandi	.82	324	1.64	91.09	376
Elgeyo-Marakwet	.57	666	0.53	93.81	217
West Pokot	1.19	292	1.58	64.81	159
Kajiado	1.71	726	4.04	118.92	549
Narok	1.29	626	0.93	97.01	233
Machakos	.64	3,279	2.87	80.89	1,976
Kitui	1.44	1,585	0.85	95.91	789
Elgon Nyanza	1.00	2,022	0.83	119.02	930
North Nyanza	.61	2,612	1.12	109.26	956
Central Nyanza	.66	7,347	2.81	87.14	1,747
South Nyanza	.69	1,737	0.47	96.17	506
Kisii	.35	2,152	1.71	87.55	1,363
Kericho	.82	5,161	14.62	54.41	3,291
Taita	1.30	1,206	9.04	66.48	612
Kwale	.99	1,205	3.66	61.76	637
Kilifi	1.27	2,300	3.53	66.36	1,030
Mombasa	9.65	30,515	29.18	125.51	4,096
Tana River	1.77	466	1.07	130.26	109
Lamu	.99	870	2.20	97.19	77
Samburu	1.99	299	1.02	78.81	147
Turkana	.27	337	0.57	104.64	165
Northern Frontier	.20	400	0.63	109.04	103

ORIGINAL DATA MATRIX

	POLITICAL		CONNECTIVITY WITH NAIROBI	
	SOCIE	KANUS	DISTA	NBIFO
Nairobi	1221	1	—	—
Kiambu	182	209	10	12.38
Thika	109	254	27	25.93
Fort Hall	29	232	56	35.94
Embu	30	287	87	13.91
Nyeri	74	204	97	14.61
Meru	32	251	177	13.27
Nanyuki	40	758	122	11.65
Naivasha	26	218	54	21.63
Nakuru	201	167	97	11.15
Laikipia	23	266	108	11.21
Uasin Gishu	91	261	195	10.73
Trans-Nzoia	56	581	238	10.13
Baringo	2	951	184	7.60
Nandi	16	504	225	1.54
Elgeyo-Marakwet	2	1680	223	0
West Pokot	3	718	258	0
Kajiado	17	546	53	36.92
Narok	4	698	100	16.67
Machakos	70	255	40	41.43
Kitui	48	187	102	0
Elgon Nyznaz	44	194	265	2.20
North Nyanza	148	332	244	4.42
Central Nyanza	322	380	212	20.29
South Nyanza	62	399	247	0
Kisii	78	475	219	4.17
Kericho	77	547	178	5.63
Taita	20	357	230	2.59
Kwale	19	763	327	0
Kilifi	43	716	343	1.20
Mombasa	493	217	307	29.03
Tana River	6	1380	453	0
Lamu	9	1675	523	0
Samburu	4	848	186	0
Turkana	1	1316	456	0
Northern Frontier	7	1385	337	16.05

MATRIX OF RANKED DATA

		PODEN	EUROP	ASIAN	MIXTU	TOWNP	COLED	LITER	PRIMA	KPEXA
1.	Nairobi	02	01	01	02	01	01	01	03	22
2.	Kiambu	04	05	10	19	21	03	02	05	09
3.	Thika	16	11	06	10	06	20	04	07	(10)
4.	Fort Hall	06	23	17	35	15	04	06	06	07
5.	Embu	11	20	18	20	17	18	16	09	18
6.	Nyeri	07	15	09	29	09	07	03	01	05
7.	Meru	15	18	16	30	20	09	23	19	13
8.	Nanyuki	28	10	13	08	07	22	12	13	01
9.	Naivasha	21	04	14	11	11	29	07	18	04
10.	Nakuru	17	03	04	05	03	08	05	14	03
11.	Laikipia	26	14	23	07	16	31	19	23	02
12.	Uasin Gishu	20	09	05	03	05	23	18	02	14
13.	Trans-Nzoia	19	06	08	04	08	19	08	21	08
14.	Baringo	24	30	31	28	35	14	24	26	08
15.	Nandi	12	25	29	21	26	10	20	04	20
16.	Elgeyo-Marakwet	14	31	36	22	36	21	25	24	19
17.	West Pokot	25	29	32	16	34	30	31	28	33
18.	Kajiado	31	19	22	13	25	25	33	29	27
19.	Narok	29	28	28	17	28	33	32	33	17
20.	Machakos	18	16	11	32	14	06	21	22	12
21.	Kitui	27	27	26	33	23	27	29	30	29
22.	Elgon Nyanza	09	26	19	25	29	12	09	20	21
23.	North Nyanza	05	17	15	26	19	05	15	11	06
24.	Central Nyanza	08	12	03	23	04	11	22	16	15
25.	South Nyanza	13	21	25	24	30	17	13	12	16
26.	Kisii	03	24	30	34	18	02	10	17	25
27.	Kericho	07	07	07	09	10	15	14	15	24
28.	Taita	30	22	24	12	22	24	17	08	35
29.	Kwale	29	13	21	18	32	16	27	27	30
30.	Kilifi	22	08	12	15	13	26	28	32	34
31.	Mombasa	01	02	02	01	02	13	11	10	26
32.	Tana River	36	34	35	14	33	28	30	25	32
33.	Lamu	32	33	27	16	12	32	26	31	(36)
34.	Samburu	33	32	33	31	31	(35)	(35)	(35)	28
35.	Turkana	34	36	34	36	24	(36)	(36)	(36)	(31)
36.	Northern Frontier	35	35	30	27	37	(34)	(34)	(34)	23

		PPLET	TOPOS	SWAPA	ENGPA	RADIO	TAXPP	TRADE	PEMPL	AVSAL
1.	Nairobi	01	01	02	01	01	01	01	02	02
2.	Kiambu	15	07	09	13	09	10	09	12	23
3.	Thika	05	10	04	04	06	04	08	01	29
4.	Fort Hall	21	14	18	17	19	23	14	22	09
5.	Embu	22	20	17	18	15	08	20	21	18
6.	Nyeri	12	08	10	09	10	12	07	14	12
7.	Meru	31	24	19	21	16	13	13	26	17
8.	Nanyuki	08	15	07	07	12	07	17	08	32
9.	Naivasha	06	13	08	05	11	32	18	03	36
10.	Nakuru	03	03	03	03	03	09	03	06	31
11.	Laikipia	09	16	13	11	14	18	21	09	35
12.	Uasin Gishu	04	06	06	06	05	22	06	04	33
13.	Trans-Nzoia	07	12	05	08	07	30	10	07	34
14.	Baringo	33	29	(31)	(34)	31	34	32	19	24
15.	Nandi	11	17	22	22	25	24	34	24	16
16.	Elgeyo-Marakwet	34	30	(30)	(33)	32	31	28	35	15
17.	West Pokot	35	36	29	(32)	34	17	36	25	27
18.	Kajiado	17	27	20	20	24	06	27	13	05

( ) = Estimated Ranks

MATRIX OF RANKED DATA (*Continued*)

	PPLET	TOPOS	SWAPA	ENGPA	RADIO	TAXPP	TRADE	PEMPL	AVSAL
19. Narok	27	28	28	29	28	15	29	30	11
20. Machakos	20	11	24	19	13	28	11	17	21
21. Kitui	30	25	27	25	23	11	23	31	14
22. Elgon Nyanza	24	22	21	26	17	19	19	32	04
23. North Nyanza	19	09	16	23	21	29	12	27	06
24. Central Nyanza	13	04	11	10	04	27	04	18	20
25. South Nyanza	28	21	26	27	29	26	22	36	13
26. Kisii	26	19	25	24	18	33	16	23	19
27. Kericho	10	05	14	12	08	25	05	10	30
28. Taita	14	23	12	15	22	14	24	11	25
29. Kwale	25	26	23	16	27	21	25	15	28
30. Kilifi	18	18	15	14	20	16	15	16	26
31. Mombasa	02	02	01	02	02	02	02	05	03
32. Tana River	23	33	(35)	31	33	05	30	28	01
33. Lamu	16	31	(34)	28	26	20	26	20	10
34. Samburu	32	34	(33)	30	36	03	35	29	22
35. Turkana	36	35	(36)	(36)	35	35	33	34	08
36. Northern Frontier	29	32	(32)	(35)	30	36	31	33	07

	ACASH	TRAFF	NOTEL	DISTA	SOCIE	KANUS	NBIFO
1. Nairobi	01	01	01	01	01	01	01
2. Kiambu	05	03	04	02	05	06	14
3. Thika	06	04	08	03	07	11	06
4. Fort Hall	14	09	18	07	21	09	04
5. Embu	10	17	16	08	20	15	12
6. Nyeri	11	11	12	09	11	05	11
7. Meru	08	25	17	15	19	10	13
8. Nanyuki	21	15	10	14	18	28	15
9. Naivasha	19	06	11	06	22	08	07
10. Nakuru	04	07	03	10	04	02	17
11. Laikipia	25	21	13	13	23	14	16
12. Uasin Gishu	13	05	06	19	08	13	18
13. Trans-Nzoia	15	08	09	25	14	24	19
14. Baringo	28	30	29	17	35	31	20
15. Nandi	27	14	22	23	27	21	26
16. Elgeyo-Marakwet	30	22	32	22	34	36	(30)
17. West Pokot	32	32	34	28	33	27	(31)
18. Kajiado	24	27	28	05	26	22	03
19. Narok	29	28	26	11	32	25	09
20. Machakos	07	19	15	04	12	12	02
21. Kitui	20	31	33	12	15	03	(28)
22. Elgon Nyanza	18	18	23	29	16	04	25
23. North Nyanza	17	10	19	26	06	16	22
24. Central Nyanza	09	16	05	20	03	18	08
25. South Nyanza	26	23	25	27	13	19	(29)
26. Kisii	12	13	20	21	09	20	23
27. Kericho	03	12	07	16	10	23	21
28. Taita	23	26	21	24	24	17	24
29. Kwale	22	20	24	31	25	29	(34)
30. Kilifi	16	24	14	33	17	26	27
31. Mombasa	02	02	02	30	02	07	05
32. Tana River	34	33	31	34	30	33	(35)
33. Lamu	36	29	27	36	28	35	(26)
34. Samburu	33	36	35	18	31	30	(33)
35. Turkana	31	34	36	35	36	32	(32)
36. Northern Frontier	35	35	30	32	29	34	10

( ) = Estimated ranks

APPENDIX B
FULL RESULTS OF PRINCIPAL
COMPONENTS ANALYSIS (BEFORE ROTATION)

MATRIX OF FACTOR LOADINGS

Variable	Factor 1	Factor 2	Factor 3	Factor 4
PODEN	.68	.62	−.14	−.19
EUROP	.91	−.22	.01	−.08
ASIAN	.95	−.04	−.10	−.05
MIXTU	.47	−.74	−.22	−.04
TOWNP	.85	−.22	−.10	−.04
COLED	.63	.65	−.07	−.12
LITER	.84	.24	.07	−.12
PRIMA	.77	.27	−.03	−.04
KPEXA	.56	.17	.67	−.01
TOPOS	.95	.08	−.03	−.12
PPLET	.85	−.39	−.09	−.03
SWAPA	.95	−.20	.01	.01
ENGPA	.93	−.30	.00	04
RADIO	.97	−.07	−.03	−.01
NOTEL	.97	−.11	−.01	−.09
TRAFF	.92	.11	.02	−.16
DISTA	.55	.15	.48	.58
NBIFO	.65	.13	.27	.45
TAXPP	.29	−.26	−.41	.70
TRADE	.93	.10	−.14	−.09
PEMPL	.79	−.51	09	.04
AVSAL	−.28	.50	−.57	.33
ACASH	.90	.23	−.10	.04
SOCIE	.87	.20	−.25	−.09
KANUS	.74	.32	−.03	.32

FACTOR SCORES

Factor 1		Factor 2		Factor 3 (5.8%)		Factor 4	
1. Nairobi	33.6	1. Laikipia	55.6	1. Mombasa	28.7	1. Trans-Nzoia	48.8
2. Mombasa	93.2	2. Nanyuki	55.2	2. Tana River	13.6	2. Kisii	43.2
3. Nakuru	94.4	3. Lamu	52.3	3. Nairobi	12.5	3. Kericho	41.5
4. Thika	129.2	4. Kilifi	48.3	4. Lamu	11.4	4. North Nyanza	40.4
5. Kiambu	148.4	5. Uasin Gishu	47.7	5. Kilifi	5.9	5. Kwale	38.2
6. Uasin Gishu	162.9	6. Trans-Nzoia	47.6	6. Elgon Nyanza	4.6	6. Uasin Gishu	36.7
7. Nyeri	178.9	7. Naivasha	44.7	7. Taita	−3.2	7. South Nyanza	36.2
8. Central Nyanza	198.8	8. Taita	43.0	8. Kitui	−5.2	8. Kilifi	35.5
9. Kericho	205.0	9. Kwale	35.3	9. North Nyanza	−6.8	9. Elgeyo-Marakwet	35.3
10. Naivasha	209.8	10. Kajiado	35.0	10. Kericho	−7.4	10. Central Nyanza	34.8
11. Trans-Nzoia	209.8	11. Thika	32.9	11. Kwale	−7.8	11. Lamu	33.3
12. Nanyuki	242.0	12. Nakuru	30.3	12. South Nyanza	−8.5	12. Nandi	32.8
13. Fort Hall	273.5	13. Tana River	30.0	13. Central Nyanza	−9.0	13. Turkana	31.7
14. Machakos	276.8	14. West Pokot	29.8	14. Kisii	−9.4	14. Baringo	28.6
15. North Nyanza	298.5	15. Samburu	28.6	15. Turkana	−10.0	15. Naivasha	25.8
16. Laikipia	305.9	16. Kericho	25.6	16. Kajiado	−10.1	16. Elgon Nyanza	25.0
17. Embu	307.1	17. Mombasa	22.3	17. W. Pokot	−11.2	17. Northern Frontier	24.1
18. Meru	341.3	18. Narok	21.4	18. Nandi	−12.4	18. W. Pokot	23.8
19. Kisii	343.3	19. Northern Frontier	14.3	19. Samburu	−13.5	19. Nakuru	22.4
20. Kilifi	358.0	20. Turkana	9.4	20. Embu	−13.5	20. Taita	20.7
21. Taita	378.6	21. Nairobi	4.8	21. Uasin Gishu	−13.7	21. Nanyuki	20.0

FACTOR SCORES (Continued)

Factor 1		Factor 2		Factor 3 (5.8%)		Factor 4	
22. Elgon Nyanza	381.0	22. Central Nyanza	1.0	22. Nyeri	−15.2	22. Mombasa	19.3
23. Nandi	399.2	23. Embu	−0.7	23. Meru	−15.5	23. Laikipia	19.1
24. Kajiado	422.4	24. Kitui	−2.3	24. Nakuru	−16.3	24. Kiambu	17.3
25. South Nyanza	429.8	25. Baringo	−2.4	25. Kiambu	−18.0	25. Machakos	15.3
26. Kwale	443.6	26. Nandi	−3.5	26. Northern Frontier	−18.5	26. Fort Hall	13.8
27. Kitui	467.6	27. Elgeyo-Marakwet	−8.5	27. Thika	−19.7	27. Tana River	13.8
28. Narok	504.7	28. Kiambu	−14.0	28. Elgeyo-Marakwet	−20.8	28. Nyeri	13.8
29. Baringo	523.6	29. Machakos	−16.4	29. Trans-Nzoia	−22.9	29. Meru	10.4
30. Lamu	524.7	30. Meru	−18.0	30. Narok	−23.1	30. Thika	8.4
31. Elgeyo-Marakwet	549.6	31. South Nyanza	−20.5	31. Fort Hall	−26.0	31. Embu	6.6
32. West Pokot	576.6	32. Nyeri	−20.5	32. Nanyuki	−28.3	32. Samburu	4.5
33. Northern Frontier	582.2	33. Elgon Nyanza	−29.8	33. Machakos	−30.2	33. Kitui	1.3
34. Tana River	582.6	34. North Nyanza	−33.3	34. Laikipia	−37.6	34. Nairobi	1.0
35. Samburu	599.2	35. Kisii	−35.8	35. Baringo	−41.1	35. Narok	−1.1
36. Turkana	643.6	36. Fort Hall	−42.0	36. Naivasha	−46.9	36. Kajiado	−14.8

APPENDIX C
ADMINISTRATIVE ORGANIZATION: 1966

Owing to pressures from KADU and support from the European and Asian communities, the administrative system of Kenya was reorganized at the time of independence. Eight new regions were created to replace the old provinces, many district boundaries were modified, and several new districts were formed. Figure 48 displays the set of administrative boundaries currently in effect in Kenya. For further information on the establishment of this new administrative system, see the *Report of the Regional Boundaries Commission,* London (1962), Cmd. 1899.

KEY TO THE DISTRICTS SHOWN ON THE MAP

1. Bungoma	15. Nandi	28. Meru
2. Busia	16. Kericho	29. Embu
3. Kakamega	17. Nakuru	30. Kitui
4. Central Nyanza	18. Narok	31. Machakos
5. South Nyanza	19. Kajiado	32. Mandera
6. Kisii	20. Nyandarua	33. Wajir
7. Turkana	21. Nyeri	34. Garissa
8. Samburu	22. Kirinyaga	35. Tana River
9. West Pokot	23. Fort Hall	36. Lamu
10. Trans-Nzoia	24. Kiambu	37. Taita
11. Elgeyo-Marakwet	25. Thika	38. Kilifi
12. Baringo	26. Marsabit	39. Kwale
13. Laikipia	27. Isiolo	40. Mombasa
14. Uasin Gishu		41. Nairobi Area

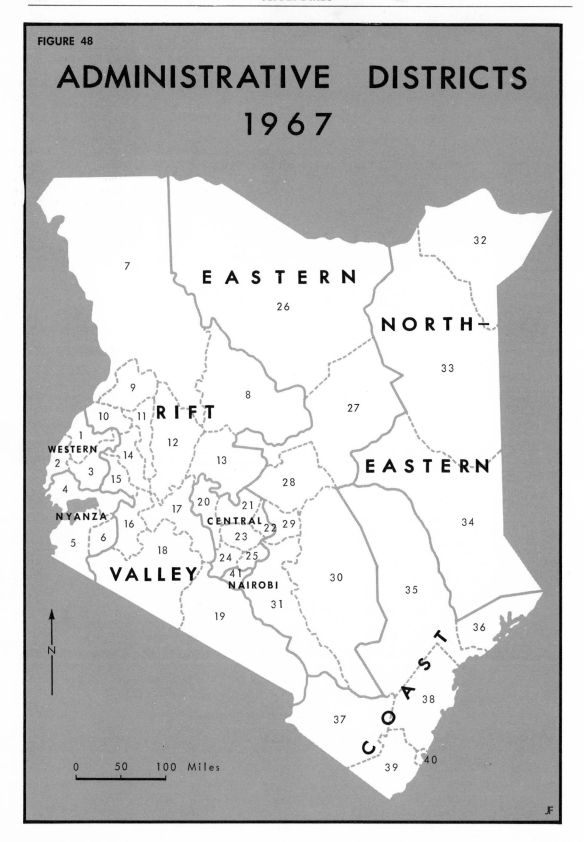

FIGURE 48

ADMINISTRATIVE DISTRICTS 1967

BIBLIOGRAPHY

Books and Articles

Ackerman, E. A. "Where is a Research Frontier?" *Annals of the Association of American Geographers,* LIII (1963), 429–40.

Almond, G. A., and J. S. Coleman (eds.). *The Politics of the Developing Areas.* Princeton, 1960.

———, and S. Verba (eds.). *The Civic Culture: Political Attitudes and Democracy in Five Nations.* Princeton, 1963.

Apter, David. *The Politics of Modernization.* Chicago, 1965.

Baker, S. J. K. "The Population Geography of East Africa," *East African Geographical Review,* No. 1 (1964), 1–6.

———. "The East African Environment," in Oliver and Mathew (eds.), *History of East Africa,* I (1963), 1–22.

Barwell, C. W. "A Note on Some Changes in the Economy of the Kipsigis Tribe," *Journal of African Administration,* VIII (1956), 95–101.

Belshaw, D. G. R. "Agricultural Settlement Schemes in the Kenya Highlands," *East African Geographical Review,* No. 2 (1964), 30–36.

Bennett, George. "Settlers and Politics in Kenya, up to 1945," in Harlow and Chilver (eds.), *History of East Africa,* II (1965), 265–332.

———. *Kenya: A Political History.* London: Oxford University Press, 1963.

———. "The Development of Political Organizations in Kenya," *Political Studies,* II (1957), 113–30.

———, and C. G. Rosberg. *The Kenyatta Election: Kenya 1960–1961.* London, 1961.

Berry, B. J. L. "Basic Patterns of Economic Development," in N. Ginsburg (ed.), *Atlas of Economic Development,* Chicago (1961), 110–19.

———. "An Inductive Approach to the Regionalization of Economic Development," in Ginsburg (ed.), *Essays on Geography and Economic Development,* Chicago (1960), 78–107.

Brasnett, J. "The Karasuk Problem," *Uganda Journal,* XXII (1958), 113–22.

Burke, F. G. "Political Evolution in Kenya," in S. Diamond and F. G. Burke (eds.), *The Transformation of East Africa: Studies in Political Anthropology,* (1966), 184–239.

Carey Jones, N. S. "The Decolonization of the 'White Highlands' of Kenya," *Geographical Journal,* CXXXI (1965), 186–201.

Carothers, J. C. *The Psychology of Mau Mau.* Nairobi, 1954.

Castagno, A. A. "The Somali-Kenya Controversy," *Journal of Modern African Studies,* II (1964), 165–88.

Cattell, R., H. Breul, and H. P. Hartman. "An Attempt at More Refined Definition on the Cultural Dimensions of Syntality in Modern Nations," *American Sociological Review,* XVII (1951), 66–72.

Clayton, E. S. *Agrarian Development in Peasant Economies: Some Lessons From Kenya.* London, 1964.

Cole, Sonia. *The Prehistory of East Africa.* Hammondsworth, 1964.

Coleman J. S. (ed.). *Education and Political Development,* Princeton, 1965.

Coupland, R. *East Africa and Its Invaders, From Earliest Times to the Death of Seyyid Said in 1856.* London, 1938.

———. *The Exploitation of East Africa, 1856–1890.* London, 1939.

Cutright, Phillips. "National Political Development: Measurement and Analasis," *American Sociological Review,* XXVIII (1963), 253–64.

Dakeyne, R. B. "The Pattern of Settlement in Central Nyanza," *Australian Geographer,* VIII (1962), 183–91.

Delf, George, *Asians in East Africa.* London, 1963.

Deutsch, K. W. "Social Mobilization and Political Development," *American Political Science Review,* LV (1961), 493–514.

———. "Shifts in the Balance of Communication Flows: A Problem of Measurement in International Relations," *Public Opinion Quarterly,* XX (1956), 152–55.

———. *Nationalism and Social Communication.* Cambridge, Mass., and New York, 1953.

———. "The Growth of Nations: Some Recurrent Patterns of Political and Social Integration," *World Politics,* IV (1953), 168–95.

———, and Foltz, W. (eds.). *Nation Building.* New York, 1963.

Eliot, C. *The East Africa Protectorate,* London, 1905.

Emerson, Rupert. *From Empire to Nation,* Cambridge, Mass., 1960.

Etherington, D. M. "Land Settlement in Kenya: Policy and Practice," *East African Economic Review,* X (1963), 22–34.

Fair, T. J. D. "A Regional Approach to Economic Development in Kenya," *South African Geographical Journal,* XLV (1963), 55–77.

Fearn, H. *An African Economy. A Study of the Economic Development of the Nyanza Province of Kenya, 1903-1953.* London, 1961.

Ford, V. C. R. *The Trade of Lake Victoria.* East African Institute of Social Research, East African Studies No. 3. Kampala, 1955.

Forrester, M. W. *Kenya Today: Social Prerequisites for Economic Development.* 's Gravenhage, 1962.

Golds, J. M. "African Urbanization in Kenya," *Journal of African Administration,* XIII (1961), 24–28.

Goldthorpe, J. E. *Outlines of East African Society.* Kampala, 1958.

———, and F. B. Wilson. *Tribal Maps of East Africa and Zanzibar.* East African Institute of Social Research, East African Studies No. 13. Kampala, 1960.

Gould, Peter R. "A Note on Research into the Diffusion of Development," *Journal of Modern African Studies,* II (1964), 123–25.

Gregory, J. W. *The Great Rift Valley.* London, 1896.

Gulliver, Pamela, and P. H. Gulliver. *The Central Nilo-Hamites.* Ethnographic Survey of Africa. London, 1963.

Hachten, William A. "The Press in a One-Party State: Kenya Since Independence," *Journalism Quarterly,* XLII (1965), 262–66.

Haggett, P. *Locational Analysis in Human Geography.* New York, 1966.

Harlow, V., and E. M. Chilver (eds.). *History of East Africa.* Vol. II. Oxford, 1965.

Harman, Harry H. *Modern Factor Analysis.* Chicago, 1960.

Hazlewood, A. *Rail and Road in East Africa.* Oxford, 1964.

Hickman, G. M., and W. H. G. Dickens. *The Lands and Peoples of East Africa.* London, 1960.

Hill, M. F. *Permanent Way.* Vol. I: *The Story of the Kenya and Uganda Railway.* Nairobi, 1950.

———. *The White Settler's Role in Kenya," Foreign Affairs,* XXXVIII (1960), 638–45.

Hobley, C. W. *Kenya: From Chartered Company to Crown Colony.* London, 1929.

Hollingsworth, L. W. *The Asians of East Africa.* New York, 1960.

Homan, F. D. "Consolidation, Enclosure and Registration of Title in Kenya," *Journal of Local Administration Overseas,* I (1962), 11–12.

Hoyle, B. S. "Recent Changes in the Pattern of East African Railways," *Tijdschrift voor Economische en Sociale Geografie,* LIV (1963), 237–42.

Hughes, Anthony. *East Africa: The Search for Unity.* Baltimore, 1960.

Hunter, Guy. *Education for a Developing Region: A Study in East Africa.* London, 1963.

Huntingford, G. W. B. "The Peopling of the Interior of East Africa by its Modern Inhabitants," in Oliver and Mathew (eds.), *History of East Africa,* I (1963), 58–93.

———. *The Nandi of Kenya: Tribal Control in a Pastoral Society.* London, 1953.

———. *The Southern Nilo-Hamites.* Ethnographic Survey of Africa. London, 1953.

Huxley, Elspeth. *The New Earth.* New York, 1960.

———. *White Man's Country.* 2 Vols. London, 1953.

———, and M. Perham. *Race and Politics in Kenya.* London, 1944.

Ingham, Kenneth. *History of East Africa.* London, 1962.

International Bank for Reconstruction and Development. *The Economic Development of Kenya.* Baltimore, 1963.

James, L. "The Kenya Masai: A Nomadic People Under Modern Administration," *Africa,* XII (1939), 49–73.

Kaiser, Henry F. "The Varimax Criterion for Analytical Rotation in Factor Analysis," *Psychometrika,* XXIII (1958), 187–200.

Kendall, M. G. *A Course in Multivariate Analysis.* London, 1961.

Kilson, M. L. "Land and Politics in Kenya: An Analysis of African Politics in a Plural Scoiety," *Western Political Quarterly,* X (1957), 559–81.

Lambert, H. E. *Kikuyu Social and Political Institutions.* London, 1956.

Lawley, D. N., and A. E. Maxwell. *Factor Analysis as a Statistical Method.* London, 1963.

Lerner, Daniel. *The Passing of Traditional Society: Modernizing the Middle East.* Glencoe, Ill., 1958.

———. "Communications Systems and Social Systems: A Statistical Exploration in History and Policy," *Behavioral Science,* II (1957), 266–75.

Lewis, I. M. *Peoples of the Horn of Africa.* Ethnographic Survey of Africa. London, 1955.

Low, D. A. "British East Africa: The Establishment of British Rule, 1895–1912," in Harlow and Chilver (eds.), *History of East Africa,* II (1965), 1–56.

———. "The Northern Interior, 1840–1884," in Oliver and Mathew (eds.), *History of East Africa,* I (1963), 297–351.

Mair, L. P. *Primitive Government.* London, 1962.

Marco Surveys. *Who's Who in East Africa,* 1963/ 64. Nairobi, 1964.

_____. *Elgon Nyanza.* Survey conducted for the Agency for International Development. Nairobi, 1962.

Masefield, G. B. "A Comparison Between Settlement in Villages and Isolated Homesteads," *Journal of African Administration,* VII (1955), 64–68.

Matheson, Alastair. "Kenya's Trunk Roads," *Road International,* XIV (1963), 50–52.

Megee, Mary. "Economic Factors and Economic Regionalization in the United States," *Geografiska Annaler,* XLVIIB (1965), 125–37.

Middleton, J. "Kenya: Changes in African Life, 1912–1945," in Harlow and Chilver (eds.), *History of East Africa,* II (1965), 333–94.

_____. *The Kikuyu and Kamba of Kenya.* Ethnographic Survey of Africa. London, 1965.

Morgan, W. T. W. "The 'White Highlands' of Kenya," *Geographical Journal,* CXXIX (1963), 140–55.

Noble, D. S. "The Coastal Dhow Trade of Kenya," *Geographical Journal,* CXXIX (1963), 498–501.

Nye, J. S. *Pan-Africanism and East African Integration.* Cambridge, Mass., 1965.

Nystuen, John D., and Michael F. Dacey. "A Graph Theory Interpretation of Nodal Regions," *Papers and Proceedings of the Regional Science Association,* VII (1961), 29–42.

O'Connor, A. M. "New Railway Construction and the Pattern of Economic Development in East Africa," *Transactions of the Institute of British Geographers.* XXXVI (1965), 21–30.

Ogot, B. A. "British Administration in the Central Nyanza District of Kenya," *Journal of African History,* IV (1963), 249–74.

Ojany, F. F. "The Physique of Kenya: A Contribution to Landscape Analysis," *Annals of the Association of American Geographers.* LVI (1966), 183–96.

Oliver, Roland. "Discernible Developments in the Interior, c.1500–1840," in Oliver and Mathew (eds.), *History of East Africa,* I (1963), 169–211..

_____. *The Missionary Factor in East Africa.* London, 1952.

_____, and G. Mathew. *History of East Africa.* Vol. I. Oxford, 1963.

Pedraza, G. J. W. "Land Consolidation in the Kikuyu Areas of Kenya," *Journal of African Administration,* VIII (1956), 82–87.

Peristiany, J. G. *The Social Organization of the Kipsigis.* London, 1939.

Pollack, N. C. "Industrial Development in East Africa," *Economic Geography.* XXXVI (1960), 344–54.

_____. "Agrarian Revolution in Kikuyuland," *South African Geographical Journal,* XLI (1959), 53–58.

Prescott, J. R. V. "The Geographical Basis of Kenya's Political Problems," *Australian Outlook,* XVI (1962), 270–82.

Prins, A. H. J. *The Swahili-Speaking Peoples of Zanzibar and the East African Coast.* Ethnographic Survey of Africa. London, 1961.

_____. *The Coastal Tribes of the Northeastern Bantu.* Ethnographic Survey of Africa. London, 1952.

Pritchard, J. M. *A Geography of East Africa.* London, 1962.

Pye, Lucian, *Politics, Personality, and Nation Building: Burma's Search for Identity.* New Haven: Yale University Press, 1962.

_____ (ed.). *Communications and Political Development.* Princeton, 1963.

Richards, A. I. (ed.). *East African Chiefs.* London, 1959.

Rosberg, C. G., and J. Nottingham. *The Myth of Mau Mau: Nationalism in Kenya.* New York, 1966.

Rotberg, R. I. "The Rise of African Nationalism: The Case of East and Central Africa," *World Politics,* XV (1962), 75–90.

Rummell, R. J., H. Guetzkow, H. Sawyer, and R. Tanter. *Dimensionality of Nations.* Evanston, forthcoming.

Russell, E. W. (ed.). *The Natural Resources of East Africa.* Nairobi, 1962.

Russett, Bruce. "Delineating International Regions," in J. S. Singer (ed.), *Quantitative International Politics: Insights and Evidence* (1967).

_____, H. Alker, K. W. Deutsch, and H. Lasswell. *World Handbook of Political and Social Indicators.* New Haven, 1964.

Sanger, C., and J. Nottingham. "The Kenya General Election of 1963," *Journal of Modern African Studies,* II (1964), 1–40.

Schnore, Leo. "The Statistical Measurement of Urbanization and Economic Development," *Land Economics,* XXXVII (1961), 229–45.

Service, Elman. *Primitive Social Organization: An Evolutionary Perspective.* New York, 1962.

Sorrenson, M. P. K. "Land Policy in Kenya, 1895–1945," Appendix I to Harlow and Chilver (eds.), *History of East Africa,* II (1965), 672–89.

Southall, A. W. "Population Movements in East Africa," in K. M. Barbour and R. M. Prothero (eds.), *Essays in African Population,* London (1961), 157–92.

Sutton, F. X. "Education and the Making of Modern Nations," in Coleman (ed.), *Education and Political Development* (1965), 51–74.

Taaffe, E. J., R. L. Morrill, and P. R. Gould. "Transport Expansion in Underdeveloped Countries," *Geographical Review,* LIII (1963), 503–29.

Tandberg, O. G. "The Indo-Pakistanis Importance for the Urbanization of Kenya," *Pakistan Geographical Review,* XVII (1962), 17–24.

Taylor, D. R. F. "New Tea Growing Areas in Kenya," *Geography,* L (1965), 373–75.

_____. "Changing Land Tenure and Settlement

Patterns in the Fort Hall District of Kenya," *Land Economics*, XL (1964), 234–37.

Thompson, John H., S. C. Sufrin, P. R. Gould, and M. A. Buck. "Toward a Geography of Economic Health: The Case of New York State," *Annals of the Association of American Geographers* LII (1962), 1–20.

Thomson, J. *Through Masai Land.* London, 1885.

Trimmingham, J. S. *Islam in East Africa.* London, 1964.

Ullman, E. "Regional Development and the Geography of Concentration," *Papers and Proceedings of the Regional Science Association,* IV (1958), 179–98.

Van Dongen, I. S. "Mombasa in the Land and Sea Exchanges of East Africa," *Erdkunde,* XVII (1963), 16–38.

——— . *The British East African Transport Complex.* Chicago, 1954.

Wagner, Gunter. *The Bantu of North Kavirondo.* Vol. I, London, 1949; Vol. II, London, 1956.

Walmsley, R. M. *Nairobi: The Geography of a New City.* Kampala, 1957.

Whitely, W. H. "The Changing Position of Swahili in East Africa," *Africa,* XXVI (1956), 343–53.

Wood, Susan. *Kenya: The Tensions of Progress.* 2nd ed. London, 1962.

Wrigley, C. C. "Kenya: The Patterns of Economic Life, 1902–1945," in Harlow and Chilver (eds.), *History of East Africa,* II (1965), 209–64.

Government Publications

Colony and Protectorate of Kenya. *African Land Development in Kenya, 1946–1962.* Nairobi, 1962.

——— . *Atlas of Kenya.* Drawn and compiled by the Survey of Kenya. Nairobi, 1959, 1962.

——— . *Historical Survey of the Origins and Growth of Mau Mau* (Corfield Report). Nairobi, 1960.

——— . *Report of the Committee to Carry Out an Economic Survey of South Nyanza and Kericho Districts—With a View to Advising Whether the Economic Potential Would Justify Railway Development.* Nairobi, 1957.

——— . *The Agrarian Problem in Kenya.* Note by

Sir Philip Mitchell, Governor of Kenya. Nairobi, 1947.

——— . *The Liguru and the Land* (N. Humphrey). Nairobi, 1947.

——— . *Report on the Transport in Sotik-Kericho District.* Nairobi, 1947.

——— . *The Kikuyu Lands* (N. Humphrey). Nairobi, 1945.

——— . *Blue Book* for the East Africa Protectorate and Kenya Colony. Nairobi, 1905–46.

East African High Commission, Statistical Department. *African Population of Kenya Colony and Protectorate: Geographical and Tribal Studies.* East African Population Census, 1948. Nairobi, 1950.

Government of Kenya. *Annual Reports.* Department of Agriculture, Department of Settlement, Kenya Road Authority, Ministry of Education. Nairobi.

——— . *Development Plan, 1964–1970.* London, 1964.

——— . *Education Committee Report* (Simeon H. Ominde, chairman), Part I. Nairobi, 1964.

——— . *Government Observation on the Report of the Lutta Commission of Inquiry into the Financial Position and Administration of the Kenya Broadcasting Company.* Nairobi, 1964.

——— . *Kenya Population Census, 1962.* Advance Report of Vols, I and II and Vol. I. Nairobi, 1964.

——— . *Statistical Abstract.* Nairobi, 1963–65.

Government of the United Kingdom. *Kenya Coastal Strip.* Joint Statement by the Secretary of State for the Colonies and the Chief Minister of Zanzibar. London, 1963. (Cmd 1971)

——— . *Kenya: Report of the Northern Frontier District Commission.* London, 1962. (Cmd 1900)

——— . *Kenya: Report of the Regional Boundaries Commission.* London, 1962. (Cmd. 1899)

——— . *Report of the East Africa Royal Commission, 1953–55.* London, 1955. (Cmd. 9475)

——— . *Kenya Land Commission: Evidence and Memoranda.* London, 1934. (Col. 116)

——— . *Report of the Kenya Land Commission* (Carter Report). London, 1934. (Cmd. 4556)

——— . *Indians in Kenya.* London, 1923. (Cmd. 1922)

INDEX

Aberdares: 6, 13, 25

ACASH: defined, 120; 75, 78, 82, 93, 95, 97, 107

Accra: 115

Achievement orientation: among the Kikuyu, 24–26

African Broadcasting Service: 44

African Education and Literacy Dimension (*F2): factor loadings, 92; general interpretation, 95; intercorrelations with other rotated dimensions, 98; and system of modernity, 100; 97, 99

African Land Development Bank: 59

African Land Units: *see* Native Reserves

African Nationalism: quasi-urban areas as centers of, 51; and Modernization Subsystems, 82–83, 88; and political parties, 102; *see also* Political development

African Subsystem: and separate development, 49–51; labor migration and ethnic mixture, 53–56; interaction with European Subsystem, 53–56, 82–88, 92–97; Kikuyu in, 54; cash crop agriculture, 56, 59; and Dimension II, 82–83; and Development Dimension, 82–88; and rotated dimensions, 92–97; and Nairobi, 98–99; and diffusion of modernization, 99–100, 116

Afrikaners: *see* Boers

Aga Khan: 41

Air transport: 32n

Alliance High School: 51

Arabs: coastal trading population, 8, 13, 15, 21, 27; trading posts, 48; percent urbanized, 49

Arusha: 46n, 81

ASIAN: defined, 119; 74, 78, 92, 93, 94, 100

Asians: along coast, 15; settlement, 21, 23, 25; political role of, 31; newspapers, 41, 42; radio, 44; in towns, 48, 49; in White Highlands, 53, 59; trade licenses issued, 60; in Central Nyanza, 67, 79; role of Asian trader in modernization, 93–95, 97; *see also* ASIAN

Athi-Galana: 6–7

Athi River: 49, 105

AVSAL: defined, 120; 74, 77, 82, 88, 91

Bantu: migrations, 8–10; languages, 8; Tanganyika Bantu, 10

Bantu Kavirondo: *see* Luhya

Baraza: newspaper circulation, 41, 42

Baraza ("meeting"): 44n

Baringo district: number of political organizations, 67; spread of KANU, 67; Modernization Subsystems, 88; political ambivalence in, 112

Behavioral research: on behavioral change and modernization, 4–5, 116; needed on economic satisfaction and political participation, 32, 80, 85, 117

Boers: 17, 19

Boundaries: colonial, 4; administrative, 23; ethnic, 11–13; and buffer zones, 11–13, 19–21, 53; of White Highlands, 17–21; Kenya-Tanzania, 80–81; of Masai Reserve, 81; of districts used in study, 71; in 1966, 129–30

British East Africa Broadcasting Corp.: 44

Broderick Falls: railway traffic, 36

Buganda: 2, 16

Bugusu: 13; *see* Luhya

Bungoma: and railway, 29, 36; planned radio relay station, 44; national communications grid, 111

Bunyore: level of modernization vs. other Luhya, 55; and national nuclei, 109

Busia: 102n

Butere: railway branch, 29, 36, 59; railway traffic, 34, 36

Caravan trade: routes, 15, 16, 27–28; and urban pattern, 48

Cash crop agriculture: among Kisii and Meru, 32, 80, 85; African, 53, 56–60; in Scheduled Areas, 56, 59; income from, 56, 59; and political participation, 80, 85; *see also* ACASH

Censuses: Population Census of, 1962, 49, 53, 55, 119; 1934 Agricultural Census 1934, 53; 1948 Population Census, 55

Central Nyanza district: compared with South Nyanza district, 24, 55, 80n, 81, 85, 101; Maseno division, 51; Luhya in, 55; African education, 62; 1963 election, 66, 102; number of political organizations, 67; spread of KANU, 67; Development Dimension, 78–81 *passim*; migration from 81n; Modernization Subsystems, 83, 85, 87–88; diffusion of modernization, 99; national nuclei, 109

Central Place Theory: 117

Central Province: road traffic, 34; railway line, 36; newspapers, 42; coffee, 59; land consolidation, 59; 1963 elections, 66

Coast: physical geography, 6, 8; trade and external contacts, 13, 15, 27, 32n; relative decline and isolation of, 24, 29, 46–47, 81–82, 85, 101; road traffic, 34; postal services, 36; radio and TV service, 46, 105; early mission schools, 60; stronghold of KADU, 67; Development Dimension, 78, 81–82; Modernization Subsystems, 83, 85, 87, 101; and Mombasa, 109; effective national territory, 112, 113

Coastal Strip: 16, 21, 110

100, 109–11; villagization, 51, 53; in White Highlands, 53; and ethnic mixture, 53; and paid employment, 56; urban system, 92, 100, 117; and urbanism, 92–93, 99; and Asians, 92–95; and system of modernity, 99–100; urban administration, 102–103; importance of small towns, 109, 110; *see also* TOWNP

Vanga: 15, 27

Varimax rotation: 72

Vihiga division: part of quasi-urban area, 51

Villagization: impact on urbanization, 51, 53; and land consolidation, 59

Vipingo: 39

Voi: railway line, 29; roads, 31; proposed radio relay station, 44; and spatial structure of telephone communications, 46–47; sisal estates, 88

Voice of Kenya: 44

Voluntary associations: difficulty collecting data on, 65–66; number of registered political organizations, 67; *see also* KANU, KADU, SOCIE

Wajir: telegraph, 39, 46; treatment in principal components analysis, 69; 1963 elections, 102n

Wanga (Hanga): centralized authority system, 13

West Pokot district: number of political organizations, 67; spread of KANU, 67; Modernization Subsystems, 88; 1963 elections, 102n, 112; political ambivalence in, 112

White Highlands: growth of, 17–21; 23–24, 29; size and population in 1933, 21; Kikuyu in, 24–26, 53–56 *passim*; postal facilities, 36; telephones, 40; urbanization, 51, 53; labor migration and ethnic mixture, 53–56 *passim*; 1962 population, 53; cash crop agriculture, 56, 59; and Nakuru, 78; *see also* Scheduled areas, European subsystem

Winam division: as part of Kisumu urban region, 51

Witu: 39

Wiyathi: 41

Yala: railway traffic, 36; postal services, 37, 39; St. Mary's School, 51, 109; national nuclei, 109

Young Kavirondo Association: 51

Zanzibar: sultanate of Zanzibar, 15, 16; first telegraph line, 27n; post office, 36; *see also* Tanzania